T0311479

The Challenges of Public Procurement Reforms

Public procurement affects a substantial share of world trade flows, amounting to 1000 billion euros per year. In the EU, the public purchase of works, goods and services has been estimated to account on average for 16 percent of GDP. The novelty of this book is that it focuses on the new European Union Directives approved in 2014 by the EU Parliament.

The book consists of original contributions related to four specific themes of interest to the procurers' day-to-day role in modern public purchasing organizations – both economists and lawyers – allowing for relevant exchanges of views and "real time" interaction. The four sections which characterize the book are Life-cycle Costing in Public Procurement; Calculating Costs and Savings of Public Procurement; Corruption and Probity in Public Procurement and Public Procurement and International Trade Agreements: CETA, TTIP and beyond. These themes have been chosen for their current relevance in relation to the new European Public Procurement Directives and beyond. The original format features, as is the case with the first three volumes, an introductory exchange between leading academics and practitioners, from differing disciplines. It offers a series of sequential interactions between economists, lawyers and technical experts who supplement one another, so as to enrich the liveliness of the debate and improve the mutual understanding between the various professions.

This essential guide will be of interest to policymakers, academics, students and researchers, as well as practitioners working in the field of EU public procurement.

Annalisa Castelli is Associate Professor of Public Economics at the University of Cassino and Southern Lazio, Italy.

Gustavo Piga is Professor of Economics at the University of Rome Tor Vergata, Italy.

Stéphane Saussier is Professor of Economics at Sorbonne Business School, France.

Tünde Tátrai is Professor of Economics at the Corvinus University of Budapest, Hungary.

Routledge Studies in Public Economics and Finance

The Challenges of Public Procurement Reforms
Edited by Annalisa Castelli, Gustavo Piga, Stéphane Saussier and Tünde Tátrai

For more information about this series, please visit:
www.routledge.com/Routledge-Studies-in-Public-Economics-and-Finance/
book-series/LICPUBECONFIN

The Challenges of Public Procurement Reforms

**Edited by
Annalisa Castelli, Gustavo Piga,
Stéphane Saussier and Tünde Tátrai**

LONDON AND NEW YORK

First published 2021
by Routledge
2 Park Square, Milton Park, Abingdon, Oxon OX14 4RN

and by Routledge
52 Vanderbilt Avenue, New York, NY 10017

Routledge is an imprint of the Taylor & Francis Group, an informa business

British Library Cataloguing-in-Publication Data
A catalogue record for this book is available from the British Library

Library of Congress Cataloging-in-Publication Data
Names: Interdisciplinary Symposium on Public Procurement
(4th : 2018 : Paris, France) | Castelli, Annalisa, editor.
Title: The challenges of public procurement reforms /
edited by Annalisa Castelli [and three others].
Description: Abingdon, Oxon; New York, NY: Routledge, 2020. |
Series: Routledge studies in public economics and finance |
"4th Interdisciplinary Symposium on Public Procurement
[held in Paris in 2018]"– Introduction. |
Includes bibliographical references and index.
Identifiers: LCCN 2020014523 (print) | LCCN 2020014524 (ebook)
Subjects: LCSH: Government purchasing–Law and legislation–European
Union countries–Congresses. | Government purchasing–Economic aspects–European
Union countries–Congresses. | Law reform–European Union countries–Congresses.
Classification: LCC KJE5632.A8 I58 2018 (print) |
LCC KJE5632.A8 (ebook) | DDC 352.5/323672114–dc23
LC record available at https://lccn.loc.gov/2020014523
LC ebook record available at https://lccn.loc.gov/2020014524

ISBN: 978-0-367-90267-4 (hbk)
ISBN: 978-1-003-02347-0 (ebk)

Typeset in Times New Roman
by Newgen Publishing UK

Contents

Figures

Tables

Contributors

André Åslundh is a senior consultant at Adect AB.

Christopher H. Bovis is Professor of Business Law at the Business School of the University of Hull.

Annalisa Castelli is Associate Professor of Public Economics at the Department of Economics and Law, University of Cassino and Southern Lazio.

Lucian Cernat is Chief Trade Economist at the European Commission.

Marion Chabrost is an economist at Compass Lexecon.

Francesco Decarolis is Associate Professor at Boston University.

Dacian C. Dragos is Professor of Administrative Law at Babes-Bolyai University Cluj Napoca Romania.

Mihály Fazekas is Assistant Professor at Central European University.

Andreas H. Glas is Associate Professor at Bundeswehr University Munich.

Jean Heilman Grier is Trade Principal at Djaghe, LLC.

Zornitsa Kutlina-Dimitrova is a senior economist at the European Commission.

Bogdana Neamtu is Associate Professor of Administrative Sciences at Babes-Bolyai University Cluj Napoca Romania.

Gustavo Piga is Professor of Economics at the Department of Economics and Finance, University of Rome Tor Vergata.

Áurea Adell Querol is Senior Consultant at Ecoinstitut SCCL.

Josep Esquerrà i Roig is a senior consultant at Ecoinstitut SCCL.

Stéphane Saussier is Professor of Economics at Sorbonne Business School.

Fabrizio Sbicca is a manager at Autorità Nazionale Anticorruzione.

Bettina Schaefer is a senior consultant at Ecoinstitut SCCL.

Giancarlo Spagnolo is Professor of Economics at Rome Tor Vergata, SITE-Stockholm School of Economics, EIEF, CEPR.

Tünde Tátrai is Professor of Economics at the Corvinus University of Budapest.

Jan Telgen is Professor of Public Procurement at the University of Twente

Niels Uenk is a researcher and consultant at Utrecht University and University of Twente.

Madelon Wind is a researcher and consultant at the University of Twente

Christopher R. Yukins is Lynn David Research Professor in Government Procurement Law and Co-Director, Government Procurement Law Program at The George Washington University Law School.

Preface

After the 2013 "The Applied Law and Economics of Public Procurement" (edited by Gustavo Piga and Steen Treumer), which published the debates and papers of the First Interdisciplinary Public Procurement Symposium held in Rome; the 2015 "Public Procurement Policy" (edited by Gustavo Piga and Tünde Tátrai), which published the debates and papers of the Second Symposium held in Budapest; and the 2017 "Law and Economics of Public Procurement Reforms" (edited by Gustavo Piga and Tünde Tátrai), which published the debates and papers of the Third Symposiun held in Belgrade, we are delighted to see in print our fourth book arising from the Fourth Symposium, held in Paris, on Routledge's "Economics of Legal Relationships" series.

As is customary for this series, this book combines juridical and technical expertise so as to find a common terrain and language to debate the specific issues that a Public Administration in need of advancing and modernising in its purchasing operations has to face. The format of the book features, for each section, an introductory exchange between two reputed scholars of different disciplines, made of a series of sequential interactions between an economist and a lawyer who write and follow up on one another. Our aim, which we hope we have achieved, is to enrich the liveliness of the debate and improve the mutual understanding between the two disciplines. Two further chapters, possibly from experts from different disciplines again, conclude each section.

There are four parts to this book: life-cycle costing in public procurement; calculating costs and savings of public procurement; corruption and probity in public procurement; public procurement and international trade agreements: CETA, TTIP and beyond.

We do hope that this book, as in the past, will attract the interest of policymakers and practitioners working in the field of public procurement as well as academics. As scientists, public procurement remains our passion and we continue to believe that investing in skills and professionalism in this delicate field of action of Public Administration is the critical reform capable of positively impacting on the productivity of firms and on the social outcomes for citizens across the world.

Annalisa Castelli is Associate Professor at the University of Cassino and Southern Lazio, Italy.

Gustavo Piga is Professor of Economics at the University of Rome Tor Vergata, Italy.

Stéphane Saussier is Professor of Economics at Sorbonne Business School, France.

Tünde Tátrai is Professor of Economics at the Corvinus University of Budapest, Hungary.

The Academic partners of the Fourth Interdisciplinary Public Procurement Symposium were the Sorbonne University and the Faculty of Economics of the University of Rome Tor Vergata.

Foreword

The OECD's work on Public Procurement: Reshaping the global agenda

Paulo Magina

The 4th Interdisciplinary Symposium on Public Procurement is the right occasion to take stock of the OECD work on this relevant topic and highlight some of the major achievements and common challenges faced by OECD and non-OECD countries when it comes to improving public procurement systems.

The OECD has been working in public procurement related topics for over ten years now, first mainly by focusing on the integrity dimensions and, since 2013/2014, expanding it to cover the entirety of the procurement cycle and the strategic dimensions that come along with its sheer economic and social power. On average, per year, public procurement represents 12 per cent of GDP in OECD countries, one third of Government expenditures, of which over 60 per cent are spent at the sub-national level. In the European Union it is 16 per cent of GDP, and much more in developing economies, reaching 30 per cent in some cases.

The new OECD strategic approach to public procurement was initiated with the process that culminated with the adoption by the OECD Council of the 2015 Recommendation on Public Procurement, envisaged to reflect the transformation of procurement from a mere administrative function into a strategic tool. Its 12 integrated and intertwined principles plus the toolbox that followed, with checklists for each principle and a collection of over 100 case studies, including links to relevant work by many other organisations and partners, substantiates this progression with a wealth of information and evidence gathering. This is also aligned with the OECD characteristics, providing data and evidence for better policymaking.

This occasion is a rare opportunity to take stock of the amount of important things that were accomplished over the past five years, share the OECD vision on public procurement and present the emerging themes. Since adopting the recommendation, the OECD Public Procurement team has worked with many member and non-member countries, many international organisations, multilateral development banks, academia, the private sector and civil society to elevate public procurement to the place where it belongs. The OECD conducted large reviews of public procurement systems in the US, South Korea, Chile, Mexico, Colombia, but also in Malta, Peru, Kazakhstan,

Morocco, Tunisia and Algeria, for example, providing each of them with tailored advice, policy recommendations and concrete tools for effective improvement.

The OECD also worked with a hands-on approach, as in the case with Greece, Lithuania, Slovakia and Bulgaria just to name a few EU members. In these EC sponsored projects, the OECD helped the countries in overcoming structural issues, solving ex ante conditionality and developing coherent strategies, namely on professionalisation, training and e-procurement, providing practical support for a sustainable and permanent change in the countries' procurement systems.

Currently, the OECD is finalising important projects with Finland and Germany, to allow for a better understanding on how public procurement can contribute to the ongoing global discussion on productivity. For this purpose, it is analysing the impact of the work carried out by central purchasing bodies in the economy, with the aim of developing a framework of indicators that will be available for application in OECD countries and beyond. This work will also allow shedding light onto the relevance of public procurement for the sustainability of well-being, and what concrete indicators can be used to understand the impact of public procurement in each of the four capitals of the future well-being framework: natural, human, economic and social.

At the same time, the OECD brought evidence about the way countries are using public procurement in different ways and for broader policy objectives, the so-called strategic procurement. Recognising the influence that public procurement can have on societies, governments around the globe are taking a fresh look at how it can be leveraged. Procurement can address a diverse range of policy goals, including strengthening integrity in the public sector, promoting innovation and supporting sustainable and inclusive growth.

This worked started in 2014 with a compendium on integrity practices for the G20 and OECD countries, followed by a benchmark on green procurement in 2015. In 2017, the OECD launched the report on procurement for innovation and this year it will launch the report "SME's in Public Procurement: Practices and Strategies for Shared Benefits", about how 37 of the most advanced economies are using public procurement to support SME development and promote growth and innovation.

This is the first stocktaking of practices and strategies highlighting trends and policy options to facilitate SME access to public market opportunities. It also provides insights into how to support SME performance in public contracts. The report takes stock of the approaches used in various country contexts to integrating SME considerations into their public procurement systems. A political consensus exists on the need to facilitate SME access to government contracts. However, there is an ongoing debate on how to translate this into practice and notably on whether governments need to provide targeted support to address SME-specific challenges using different, and sometimes competing, policy objectives. The report further highlights the many challenges procurers and policymakers face in data collection and analysis for an evidence-based debate. Good evidence and data remains a priority.

Finally, it is important to highlight our main project related to assessment tools and indicators, the update of the Methodology for Assessing Procurement Systems (MAPS). A collaborative process coordinated by the OECD since 2015, brings together over 30 Stakeholders, including the majority of the multilateral development banks (MDBs), several countries and international organisations, aiming at aligning this methodology with international standards, including the OECD Recommendation, the EU Directives, the UNCITRAL model law, the procurement frameworks of the MDBs and open contracting standards. It also takes into account the Sustainable Development Goals.

The MAPS is a very ambitious project that finally allowed the international community to create a universal, harmonised and mutually reliable tool for assessing procurement systems of countries of all income levels or development status. On top of the methodology, the group developed extensive information, templates and guidance for its application. Between 2016 and 2017, the MAPS was tested in Norway, Chile and Senegal and after this validation period, the Stakeholders and OECD countries endorsed the methodology precisely in 2018. Currently, between 20 and 30 assessments are being carried out around the world by different partners in different regions, including Africa, Latin America and Asia. Some are planned for Europe as well, including in EU Member States and the Balkans. Additionally, the Chinese Government Procurement Assessment Tool – GPAT – currently under development, is based almost entirely on the MAPS framework and indicators.

This work and its ramifications resonate very well with the symposium's topics: A first day on sustainability and efficiency and a second day on integrity, competition and access, which, in fact, encapsulate many of the most relevant challenges of public procurement these days.

Some of the topics that will be the object of discussion here were already the object of the OECD's work. In fact, the OECD has been collecting evidence on how countries are dealing with the measurement of efficiency in their systems, namely savings, through a pilot study on several dimensions of Key Performance Indicators in 2015/2016 but the evidence was not sufficient to establish a framework that could be used by member countries. At the same time, this question is constantly part of requests from countries, as policymakers seek help in setting up reliable indicators to measure the performance. Life Cycle Costing (LCC) is also a dimension that is gaining a lot of interest and traction. Some work is already being done in helping countries to implement LCC considerations in their procurement projects, mainly by providing adequate capacity building. The OECD has been including LCC considerations in training manuals and devoting more time to it, but much more needs to be done, in terms of both guidance, practical tools and capacity building. The same applies to raising awareness on integrity, which is always a topic of great interest. The selected papers and the discussions throughout the symposium allow us to deepen our thinking around these very relevant matters.

As part of the OECD policymaking methodology, after a few years of adoption of its instruments, recommendations and standards, it is mandatory to evaluate the progress made in their implementation and adoption as policy instruments by member countries, as these are principles and practices member countries should follow. As the OECD Public Procurement Recommendation entered its fourth year, a survey was launched in the summer of 2018 to complement information, and over 30 OECD members replied to the call.

For this reason, ahead of formally presenting the report next year, this is a very good occasion to share three main findings, linking them to the daily challenges faced as policymakers, academics or practitioners.

The first finding:

The strategic alignment between the principles of the Recommendation and the objectives pursued by OECD countries is reflected in reforms of public procurement systems

To this end, the view on public procurement has been rapidly changing from administrative minutiae to a strategic governance tool. Reform of public procurement laws and regulations in the OECD countries reflected integrally the principles of the 2015 OECD Recommendation. Yet, countries have given more weight to certain principles – such as facilitating access, enhancing integrity, increasing transparency, improving efficiency and developing e-procurement – in their review process. In particular, EU member countries transposed the 2014 EU directives on public procurement (which gave a strong impetus to increased digitalisation throughout the procurement cycle), reinforced integrity measures and strengthened use of public procurement to pursue complementary policy objectives. These trends further expanded outside of Europe with increased accountability in public procurement through increasing transparency, open data considerations and enhancing integrity dimensions. At the same time, governments aim at achieving socio-economic development through public procurement. To this end, they especially dedicate efforts to facilitate the SMEs' access to public procurement processes, as mentioned earlier.

The second finding:

Beyond legislative reforms, efficiency enablers are gaining attention in procurement systems, notably via the expansion of the role of Central Purchasing Bodies in OECD countries

Central purchasing bodies (CPBs) are key players in strategic aggregation of demands, by increasingly assuming the role of managing collaborative procurement instruments such as framework agreements and dynamic purchasing systems, and making them available for increasingly broader networks of buyers. Compared to 2014, now almost all CPBs are implementing these instruments and other derivative forms of collective purchasing (like joint procurement, e-market places, etc.). However, beyond acting as an aggregator of needs, countries also recognise CPBs as hubs of expertise providing increased legal, technical, economic and contractual support.

And finally, the third finding:

Discussions in OECD countries are now not only on e-Procurement systems or uptake but rather on the expansion of its scope and integration into e-Government and digitalisation strategies, which impacts other areas like transparency

Governments increasingly avail themselves of the efficiency benefits of e-procurement systems. In particular, they are becoming more transactional – through increasing use of electronic submission of bids, electronic invoicing or data integration. The information is published in a less fragmented manner today. Countries are implementing and developing e-procurement solutions that centralise public procurement information and streamline the process also outside of Europe, integrating it with other governmental databases. Additionally, many EU countries have also updated their e-procurement systems in order to conform to the mandatory e-tendering, in line with the EU directives. Nevertheless, systematic assessment of the performance of public procurement systems is not sufficiently carried out; only about half of the countries have established a performance measurement system and even less do so against a defined set of targets. While stakeholder engagement, particularly with suppliers, takes place in a systematic way to improve the system, quantitative evidence could be further exploited. Open data standards are becoming more and more part of the specifications and contribute to integrating public procurement information into a wider debate and audience, increasing its visibility. However, at the same time there is a general concern about the degree of transparency: what does an adequate level of transparency mean? For which purpose is it intended? This is creating healthy tensions and ongoing debates between different communities, especially procurement, competition and anti-corruption, which will lead to important breakthroughs in the years to come.

The topics of the Symposium remain, therefore, completely aligned with the current discussions in the public procurement communities.

Paulo Magina
Head of the Public Procurement Unit,
Public Governance Directorate, OECD
Paris, May 2020

Part I

Life-cycle costing in public procurement

The new European Directive on Public Procurement opened the door to the use of award criteria designed to keep into account innovation, environmental and social issues in the process of determining the assignment of public contracts, also with the introduction of "life-cycle costing" (LCC) as mentioned in Article 67 and clearly defined in Article 68.

This explicit provision by law enhanced an interesting debate on the appropriateness of the integration of LCC parameters into public policies that still have the "most economically advantageous tender" as the leading light to ensure the best value for money.

Life-cycle costing moves beyond the simple purchasing price, including many other important costs distributed along the entire life of the procured good or service.

The implementation of this approach naturally raises several questions to be answered and challenges to be solved. Moreover, capacity building, especially designed tools, digital platforms and expertise, are needed to apply LCC in a proper way.

This first chapter of the book thus focuses on the desirability of this LCC approach within the realm of those available for the public expenditure processes of evaluation and selection of suppliers and also on its effective role as a sustainable public procurement tool.

The two debaters, Stéphane Saussier and Christopher H. Bovis, put on the table their main pros and cons on Articles 67 and 68 of the EU Directive, discussing the several different perspectives and highlighting the importance and difficulty of the development of a common and harmonized methodology among Member States.

The two contributions that follow are instead intended to focus the analysis with different analytical perspectives. Dragos and Neamtu review the broader concept of "life-cycle thinking" (LCT) both in private businesses and in the public sector, reasoning on its incorporation into legal definitions. On the other side Adell Querol, Schaefer and Esquerrà i Roig look at the same topic considering LCC as an economic tool which may or may not support green public procurement and that, to lead to a complementarity between the two and to avoid LCC being a competing rather than a complementary tool, a mixed approach should be followed.

1 Life-cycle costing in public procurement
Colloquium

Stéphane Saussier and Christopher H. Bovis

Opening remarks – *Stéphane Saussier*

How to organize the award of public procurement contracts efficiently is a major preoccupation for economists. Should we focus on price only? Should we introduce other criteria? Should we risk introducing discretionary power for public procurers? The new European Directive on public procurement clearly open the room for more criteria linked to innovation and environmental and social issues. It also suggests that the best offer may be selected on the basis of life-cycle costing.

Moving beyond price criteria

Life-cycle costing (LCC) can be defined as an economic assessment considering all agreed projected significant and relevant cost flows over a period of analysis expressed in monetary value.

The European Directive 2014/24/EU on Public Procurement gives credit to LCC. In Article 67, specifying contract award criteria, it is stated that:

> The most economically advantageous tender from the point of view of the contracting authority shall be identified on the basis of the price or cost, using a cost-effectiveness approach, such as life-cycle costing [...]. It may include the best price-quality ratio, which shall be assessed on the basis of criteria, including qualitative, environmental and/or social aspects, linked to the subject-matter of the public contract in question.

The same Directive in Article 68 gives a precise definition of LCC:

> Life Cycle Costing shall to the extent relevant cover parts or all the following costs over the life cycle of a product, service or works:
>
> (a) costs, borne by the contracting authority or other users, such as:
> - costs relating to acquisition,
> - costs of use, such as consumption of energy and other resources,

- maintenance costs,
- end of life costs, such as collection and recycling costs.

(b) costs imputed to environmental externalities linked to the product, service or works during its life cycle, provided their monetary value can be determined and verified; such costs may include the cost of emissions of greenhouse gases and of other pollutant emissions and other climate change mitigation costs.

Both direct costs and indirect costs shall be included in the LCC calculation. In the context of sustainable public procurement (SPP), the use of LCC is essential to move beyond considering only the purchase price of a good or service. Green and socially preferable assets may carry considerably higher purchasing price tags than their less sustainable substitutes. The idea is that the purchase price does not reflect the financial and non-financial gains that are offered by environmentally and socially preferable assets as they accrue during the operations and use phases of the asset life cycle.

At what cost?

It has long been recognized by economists that price should not be the only criteria to award contracts (Bajari et al., 2009). However, economists also highlight the risks associated with giving more discretionary power to public procurers.

The economic literature suggests that buyers deliberately choose to engage in award procedures that are opening up room for their discretionary power for efficiency reasons. The primary reason for introducing discretion (for example through negotiation) is that award procedures based on price auctions lead to inefficient outcomes if the good or service to be procured is technically complex and/or barely contractible (Goldberg, 1977; Bajari and Tadelis, 2001; Bajari et al., 2009). Negotiation either facilitates the dialogue between the parties, thereby reducing contractual incompleteness (Tadelis, 2011; Bajari et al., 2014), or eases the implementation of relational contracts (Calzolari and Spagnolo, 2009). In such cases, auctions without any negotiation prove to be inefficient due to the inability of the buyer to specify the contract. Several empirical studies confirmed that negotiation can be attractive when ex ante information from contractors is needed to make the contractual design as complete as possible (Decarolis, 2014; Coviello et al., 2018).

However, the economic literature also suggests that public procurers' discretion may be detrimentally used to favor a bidder during the award phase (Moore and Staropoli, 2018) in order to follow private agenda or due to corruption. This is probably in order to limit public procurer's discretion that Article 68 of the European Directive specifies that

Where contracting authorities assess the costs using a life-cycle costing approach, they shall indicate in the procurement documents the data to be provided by the tenderers and the method which the contracting authority will use to determine the life-cycle costs on the basis of those data.

(a) it is based on objectively verifiable and non-discriminatory criteria. In particular, where it has not been established for repeated or continuous application, it shall not unduly favour or disadvantage certain economic operators;
(b) it is accessible to all interested parties;
(c) the data required can be provided with reasonable effort by normally diligent economic operators, including economic operators from third countries party to the GPA or other international agreements by which the Union is bound.

Although the Directive provides for a definition of LCC (together with a list of cost items to be included in the calculation), no clear explanation on how this calculation can be performed is given. Many points need to be clarified before an extensive application of the LCC by public procurers can take place, including how externalities can be monetized. Some costs might be difficult to anticipate, like renegotiations that might occur during the execution stage of the contract.

Where do we stand?

Because there is no clear methodology and no easy way to use LCC without any risk of being challenged and accused of distorting award procedures, it appears that it is rarely used by public procurers. The results of a survey carried out on a sample of 119 public administrations from different countries (Nucci et al., 2016), clearly show that if green public procurement practices are commonly applied by public administrations, this is not the case of LCC, which still remains very limited due to some barriers such as

- lack of information on costs
- lack of reliable data sources for the evaluation of external and internal costs
- lack of competence and knowledge to accurately assess and verify information submitted by bidders in response to criteria (Nucci et al., 2016).

Opening remarks – *Christopher H. Bovis*

Is life-cycle costing a quantitative rather than a qualitative award criterion?

The new public procurement directives significantly alter the process of tender awarding, through assigning a relevant importance to life-cycle costing.

A new contract award criterion has been introduced in Article 67, "… the most economically advantageous tender from the point of view of the contracting authority shall be identified on the basis of the price or cost, using a cost-effectiveness approach, such as life-cycle costing ...”

Life cycle means all consecutive and/or interlinked stages – including research and development to be carried out, production, trading and its conditions, transport, use and maintenance – throughout the existence of a product or a works or the provision of a service, from raw material acquisition or generation of resources to disposal, clearance and end of service or utilization.

Life-cycle costing is a tool to evaluate the costs of a good or service, taking into account not just price (the upfront cost, usually incorporating production costs) but all costs which will accrue with operation and maintenance and finally disposal. When externalities are included, life-cycle costing becomes "an environmentally relevant methodology."

Life-cycle costing is portrayed as a key instrument in fostering innovation and achieving the goals of sustainable development laid down in the Europe 2020 Strategy.

The origins of life-cycle costing

The reason behind life-cycle costing is to make hidden costs and externalities visible during the procurement process and particularly the tender evaluation stage. Hidden costs are costs that affect the contracting party. Externalities are costs that affect a party who did not choose to incur them. The objective is to internalize an externality, so that costs will affect mainly parties who actually chose to incur them.

An externality is often related to environmentally related costs, which are fairly predictable. However, other external costs pose difficulties in their determination, such as sourcing commodities from conflict areas; disposal of toxic materials without recycling; negative impact on health/productivity. Therefore, in practice, life-cycle costing often focuses on selected external cost types (like environmental emissions) and on hidden costs which affect the contracting party, but which are regularly overlooked (costs of use, maintenance costs, end of life costs, taxes).

The concepts of life-cycle costing

According to the Procurement Directives, life-cycle costing can therefore be used in all three awarding options: (i) price or cost only, (ii) quality only, (iii) combination price/quality.

Price/cost-only awards are often used in ordinary and standardized procurement processes. This reflects the attributes of *the lowest price as award criterion*. When the lowest price has been selected as the award criterion, contracting authorities must not refer to any other qualitative consideration when deliberating the award of a contract. The lowest price is a sole quantitative benchmark that intends to differentiate the offers made by tenderers.

However, contracting authorities can reject a tender, if they regard the price attached to it as abnormally low. The lowest price appears to offer good conditions for life-cycle costing, on condition that there must be a methodology that requires product/service categorization.

The Procurement Directives list certain cost types, which life-cycle costing shall cover partially or entirely:

a) hidden costs, which are costs, borne by the contracting authority or other users, such as costs relating to acquisition, costs of use, such as consumption of energy and other resources, maintenance costs, end of life costs, such as collection and recycling costs;

b) externalities, which are costs imputed to environmental externalities linked to the product, service or works during its life cycle, provided their value can be determined and verified.

Calculation methods

The new public procurement directives do not provide a one-size-fits-all methodology, but hints toward the possibility of one, or several, harmonized methodologies in the future, Article 68 (III): Whenever a common method for the calculation of life-cycle costing has been made mandatory by a legislative act of the Union, that common method shall be applied for the assessment of life-cycle costs.

The public procurement directives stipulate that the definition of the life cycle of a product or a service must break down its costs into the different phases from acquisition to end of life. The life-cycle costing could include the costs accrued in all phases or only in some of them. The costs covered in any life-cycle costing method will depend on the level of commitment of, and the amount of information available to, those developing those methods of calculation.

Costs are also distinguished depending on the bearer, which could be the contracting authority or other users. The reason for the distinction appears that it would be possible to refer to environmental externalities only if their monetary value can be determined and verified. This approach renders difficult any reference to socio-economic and employment criteria in life-cycle costing.

Life-cycle costing is subject to a duty of transparency. The contracting authority shall indicate in the procurement documents both the data to be provided by tenderers and the method that will be used to determine the life-cycle costing. This method must have three cumulative requirements:

(a) it must be based on objectively verifiable and non-discriminatory criteria;

(b) it is accessible to all interested parties; and

(c) the data required can be provided with reasonable effort by normally diligent economic operators, including operators from third countries.

When a common method has been made mandatory, it shall be applied by all Member States and their contracting authorities. However, to avoid the uncontrolled propagation of life-cycle costing methods, if a common method is adopted and available to contracting authorities, reference must be made to methods developed in EU legislation or on the basis of EU legislation.

Life-cycle costing presupposes a monetization method which can be applied on the basis of data to be provided to the contracting authority. If price remains the award criterion, all externalities have to be incorporated and monetized as elements of the price. Developing life-cycle costing methodologies at the EU level would help their adoption by contracting authorities.

Discourse themes

Can a common methodology on life-cycle costing be adopted and shared by all Member States?

Is life-cycle costing attracted to the lowest price rather than to the best price–quality ratio?

Is life-cycle costing a quantitative rather than a qualitative award criterion?

Response to Christopher H. Bovis – *Stéphane Saussier*

Let me be a little bit provocative by answering some of the final questions/ remarks made by Christopher H. Bovis in his introductory remarks. He concluded by writing:

"Developing life-cycle costing methodologies at the EU level would help their adoption by contracting authorities." But realistically he also asked the question: "Can a common methodology on life-cycle costing be adopted and shared by all member states?" As well as two other questions that are "Is life-cycle costing attracted to the lowest price than to the best price-quality ratio?" and "Is life-cycle costing a quantitative rather than a qualitative award criterion?"

Concerning the possibility to develop LCC methodologies, I believe this is a crucial issue. The initial idea of LCC is not bad: often, the price is the dominant factor when choosing to buy a product service or process. However, initial costs only tell a fraction of the reality about the total cost of ownership of an asset. An assessment of the cost should include direct and indirect expenses, as well as some intangible costs that may be assigned a dollar value.

But, as I wrote in my opening remarks, because there is no clear methodology and no easy way to use LCC without any risk of being challenged and accused of distorting award procedures, it appears that it is rarely used by public procurers. However, I am not very confident, especially on the possibility of seeing a common methodology adopted and shared by all Member States. This is because this methodology is very demanding in terms of data, in order to measure adequately the whole cost of a product/service procured, especially social and environmental externalities, in a verifiable way. Usually, the public procurer lacks information on costs and reliable data sources for the evaluation of external and internal costs. In addition, there is also a lack of competence and knowledge by the public party to accurately assess and verify information submitted by bidders in response to criteria and to follow, during contract execution, the indicators.

I believe that those who are pushing for LCC try to replace qualitative award criteria (e.g. social clauses, environmental goals) that have their drawbacks in the public procurement process (see Saussier and Tirole (2015) for a discussion on this issue) for a more quantitative one. By replacing subjective criteria with more objective ones, we would expect an increase in competition and value for money and a move to more sustainable procurement decisions. However, as always, the devil is in the detail ...

In addition, the LCC should be ideally compared to the total benefits generated by the product/infrastructure/service that is procured to determine the viability or assess the value of a purchase, which can be done through a cost–benefit analysis. For complex products or infrastructures, the quality might differ from one offer to another, with different LCC and different benefits associated that render even more difficult an objective LCC methodology.

Response to Stéphane Saussier – *Christopher H. Bovis*

Discretion has been inherent in public procurement acquis from the inception of the regulatory framework. However, discretion has a major side effect: the non-visible boundaries in its application, which fuels a fear on the part of contracting authorities of potential breaches in public procurement rules.

Discretion of Member States in applying public procurement law emanates form the fact that its incorporation into the respective domestic legal orders is based on the integration vehicle of harmonization. Harmonization does not stop at the discretion of national systems to implement the prescribed acquis, but it also expands upon a whole new concept of decentralization, where public procurement law is entrusted in its compliance and enforcement upon the Member States. Decentralization of public procurement runs parallel to the similar effects in EU anti-trust application and enforcement.

There are two main categories where discretion of Member States in applying public procurement law may emerge. First, there is procedural discretion, particularly in the choice of award procedures and the ability to establish autonomous remedies for redress and access to justice in public procurement contracts. Second, discretion in substantive terms in applying public procurement rules exists in the fields of selection and qualification of economic operators, exclusion of candidates, and the choice and features of contract award criteria, mainly the most economically advantageous tender.

The life-cycle costing as the newly introduced award criterion of the public procurement directives epitomizes discretion as the underlying principle in the application of the directives.

Discretion of Member States in applying public procurement law is surrogate to the principle of proportionality. However, the principle of discretion reveals flexibility in the application of public procurement acquis by Member States. Flexibility in public procurement law is the conceptual link between the principle of discretion and the principle of proportionality. Flexibility has been developed and deployed by the jurisprudence of the Court of Justice of the European Union (CJEU) and is reflected in the fact that EU public procurement is enacted and implemented in domestic legal systems by reference to harmonization, but procurement rules are inherently flexible to accommodate compliance and legal interoperability with EU principles and policies. The doctrine of flexibility allows the principle of proportionality to be employed in the application of public procurement rules by national legal systems.

Throughout the evolution of public procurement acquis, the procedural phase in the procurement process culminated through the application of objectively determined criteria that demonstrate the logic behind the behavior of contracting authorities. There are two criteria on which the contracting authorities must base the award of public contracts: (a) the most economically advantageous tender, or (b) the lowest price.

When the award is made to the tender most economically advantageous from the point of view of the contracting authority, various criteria linked to the subject matter of the public contract in question, for example, quality, price, technical merit, aesthetic and functional characteristics, environmental characteristics, running costs, cost-effectiveness, after-sales service and technical assistance, delivery date and delivery period or period of completion, can be taken into consideration. The above listed criteria, which constitute the parameters of the most economically advantageous offer, are not exhaustive.

For the purposes of defining what does constitute a most economically advantageous offer, the contracting authority must specify in the contract notice or in the contract documents or, in the case of a competitive dialogue, in the descriptive document, the relative weighting which it gives to each of the criteria chosen to determine the most economically advantageous tender. Those weightings can be expressed by providing for a range with an appropriate maximum spread. Where, in the opinion of the contracting authority, weighting is not possible for demonstrable reasons, the contracting authority must indicate in the contract notice or contract documents or, in the case of a competitive dialogue, in the descriptive document, the criteria in descending order of importance.

The meaning of the most economically advantageous offer includes a series of factors chosen by the contracting authority, including price, delivery or completion date, running costs, cost-effectiveness, profitability, technical merit, product or work quality, aesthetic and functional characteristics, after-sales service and technical assistance, commitments with regard to spare parts and components and maintenance costs, and security of supplies.

The most economically advantageous offer as an award criterion has provided the opportunity to balance the economic considerations of public procurement with policy choices. Although in numerous instances, the importance of the economic approach to the regulation of public sector contracts has been maintained, it has also recognized the relative discretion of contracting authorities to utilize non-economic considerations as award criteria.

Life-cycle costing is a facet of the most economically advantageous offer as an award criterion. As such, it is subject to a duty of transparency, both in procedural and substantive terms. Currently, the discretion of contracting authorities and their Member States in applying life-cycle costing as an award criterion is absolute. There is no common methodology as a benchmark of calculating the determinants of life-cycle costing.

One of the main determinants which will shift the balance of discretion from absolute to relative in the application of award criteria by contracting authorities is the monetization of the life of a product or service that is destined for the public sector procurement process. When such monetization determinants are agreed as part of a common methodology across the EU, the confidence of the contracting authorities in utilizing life-cycle costing will increase.

Life-cycle costing could be a facet of the best price–quality ratio as a qualitative award criterion. Interestingly, the monetization basis of life-cycle costing will reveal its qualitative dimension in the award of public contracts.

Conclusions – *Stéphane Saussier*

I fully agree with the analysis of Professor Bovis on the fact that:

- for LCC to be fully effective, we would need efforts to converge, at the European level, on a common life-cycle costing methodology. This is a necessary condition.
- A common methodology would generate more confidence in the objectivity of the award procedures and used criteria, by reducing the discretion of public contracting authorities.

However, I see many difficulties in achieving such convergence toward a common simple methodology. Some of them are connected with the value of time, the time frame that should be retained for the LCC, the public purchasers' competences, the fact that LCC is data demanding, the cost of using such methodology and so on. The devil is in the details, and many details must be addressed before converging toward an accepted common methodology.

In addition, I believe that LCC is mainly a way to balance, more explicitly and more rigorously, the economic considerations of public procurement with policy choices, and, as an economist, I doubt the utility of such enlarged objectives for public procurement. Do we not have other instruments to reach policy objectives (which are very important) assigned to public procurement?

For example, taxation?

Finally, I am wondering if such a common objective LCC methodology is not a utopia that could be related to the complete versus incomplete contract debate in economics. If this is the case, looking for a reasonable approximation of the whole costs of public procurement would already be an improvement. However, it should be coupled with more accountability of public authorities as well as more transparency, because discretion will still remain important. But this would be a great achievement.

Conclusions – *Christopher H. Bovis*

Acceptance of life-cycle costing as an award criterion for public contracts denotes a departure from the lowest offer. This has two implications: first, the offer from economic operators which is assessed by reference to life-cycle costing could comprise qualitative factors, such as the environmental and socio-economic features; second, in order to assess an offer which assumingly is based upon life-cycle costing against other offers, which are either also based upon life-cycle costing or do not take life cycle as a feature in their costing, a common methodology is imperative.

Saussier and Tirole are instrumental in provoking discourse relevant to quantitative versus qualitative criteria in the award of public contracts. The side effects of lowest offer as an award criterion have been well demonstrated. The advantages of quantitative criteria for public contracts based on price are also universally acknowledged for enhancing openness and transparency principles.

What has been developed as the MEAT (most economically advantageous tender) criterion for the award of public contracts, with its current metastasis in BPQR (best price–quality ratio) reflects on a dilution of quantitative criteria and an injection of discretion on the part of contracting authorities to assess a tender offer based on promissory assumptions of economic benefit to it, provided these assumptions are contractually relevant to the subject matter of the engagement. And here is a gap which few have noticed thus far: MEAT and BPQR did not require a methodology, let alone a common methodology in assessing offers which assume their economic advantage to the recipient of the offer. In fact, the *acquis* confer quite a margin of discretion to contracting authorities in creating the list of factors, which, in their view, could describe the most economically advantageous benchmark in the respective offers for the delivery of the public contract.

Life-cycle costing presupposes a methodology for the monetization of cost components that will synthesize the benchmark for comparing respective offers from economic operators. Such methodology would require data that are accepted and adhered to by contracting authorities. And this is the challenge for European institutions: to move away from a discretionary framework under MEAT and BPQR to a confined and methodologically common platform in assessing costs over the lifespan of a product or a service.

References

Bajari, P. and Tadelis, S. (2001) "Incentives versus Transaction Costs: A Theory of Procurement Contracts," *RAND Journal of Economics* 32, no. 3, pp. 387–407.

Bajari, P., Houghton, S., and Tadelis, S. (2014) "Bidding for Incomplete Contracts: An Empirical Analysis of Adaptation Costs," *American Economic Review* 104, no. 4, pp. 1288–1319.

Bajari, P., McMillan, R., and Tadelis, S. (2009) "Auctions Versus Negotiations in Procurement: An Empirical Analysis," *Journal of Law, Economics, and Organization* 25, no. 2, pp. 372–399.

Calzolari, G. and Spagnolo, G. (2009) "Relational Contracts and Competitive Screening," Working Paper No. 7434.

Coviello, D., Guglielmo, A., and Spagnolo, G. (2018) "The Effect of Discretion on Procurement Performance," *Management Science* 64, no. 2, pp. 715–738.

Decarolis, F. (2014) "Awarding Price, Contract Performance, and Bids Screening: Evidence from Procurement Auctions," *American Economic Journal: Applied Economics* 6, no. 1, pp. 108–132.

Goldberg, V. P. (1977) "Competitive Bidding and the Production of Precontract Information," *Bell Journal of Economics* 8, no. 1, pp. 250–261.

Moore, J. and Staropoli, C. (2018) "Horizontal and Vertical Agreements in PPPs," in *The Economics of Public Private Partnerships*, ed. S. Saussier, and J. D. Brux, Switzerland: Springer.

Nucci, B., Iraldo, F., and Giacomo, M. R. (2016) "The Relevance of Life Cycle Costing in Green Public Procurement," *Economics and Policy of Energy and the Environment* 1, pp. 91–109.

Saussier, S. and Tirole, J. (2015) "Strengthening the Efficiency of Public Procurement," *Notes du conseil d'analyse économique* 3, no. 22, pp. 1–12.

Tadelis, S. (2011) "Public Procurement Design: Lessons from the Private Sector," *International Journal of Industrial Organization*, 30, no. 3, pp. 297–302.

2 Life-cycle thinking in EU public procurement

Moving beyond a simple 'buzz word'

Dacian C. Dragos and Bogdana Neamtu

Life-cycle thinking from concept to legal relevance

Worldwide, the quest for sustainability is getting more and more urgent, as the Earth and human society are faced with very daunting environmental problems. One particular strategy for reaching a more sustainable future is to work towards changing our consumption and production patterns. Life-cycle thinking (LCT) is closely intertwined with sustainable production and consumption, by considering all stages in the life of products where a reduction of negative impacts could be achieved. While this approach is widely recognized in the sustainability literature, its incorporation into more legal studies is challenging.

Increasingly, environmental policies and laws in the European Union refer to 'life-cycle thinking' as an important guidance for policy. The concept of life-cycle thinking however has no formal definition in EU law, making its application and relevance open to interpretation. A recent study on this subject argues that life-cycle thinking contributes positively to the development of environmental law, but that it may be applied in ways that limit its potential (Dalhammar, 2015). Other scholars (e.g. Hughes, 2017) think that recent developments in EU law, such as the drafting and adoption of the Circular Economy Package, will transform LCT into a legal concept. But even the scholars who strongly believe in the promise of LCT acknowledge that 'this will not be easy as compliance with the law requires specific requirements, a means of measuring conformity with those requirements, and appropriate conformity assessment measures' (Hughes, 2017, p. 15).

This study looks into how LCT applies to European public procurement and explores whether or not life-cycle methodologies are used in practice. Its ambition is to explore the challenges of transforming a management approach into a legal one and how these obstacles can be surpassed in order to make full use of LCT in sustainable public procurement.

Inclusion of life-cycle thinking into a broader sustainability framework

The literature on life-cycle thinking and life-cycle approaches is extremely diverse and constantly growing; it employs a myriad of partially overlapping concepts described in terms of tools, strategies, techniques and methodologies. Fava (2012) proposes a sustainability framework in order to understand, on the one hand, how life-cycle thinking is connected to the broader goal of sustainability and on the other hand, how various tools are used to operationalize the principles of life-cycle thinking into practice. Figure 2.1 below graphically presents his sustainability framework. At the top of the pyramid, there is sustainability as the ultimate goal, followed by life-cycle management systems and sustainable production and consumption. As described in the next sub-section, sustainable production and consumption represents a core and overarching objective of sustainable development. Life-cycle management is used in order to improve the sustainability performance of businesses and other organizations and to operationalize life-cycle thinking (Life Cycle Initiative, not dated). It is a management approach that translates the tools and methodologies envisioned under life-cycle thinking into practice. It is a product management system that helps businesses to minimize the environmental and social impacts associated with their products during their entire life cycle. Relevant and reliable datasets support life-cycle management, being placed at the bottom of the pyramid (UNEP, 2012a, p. 15).

Sustainable consumption and production (hereafter SCP) represents a key concept within the sustainability framework. Modern society imposes an enormous impact on the Earth. Global resource demand and environmental pressure have been drastically increasing as both population and per capita consumption are also on the rise (UNEP, 2011, p. 12). As early as 1972, the UN Conference on Human Environment alluded to the unsustainable trends

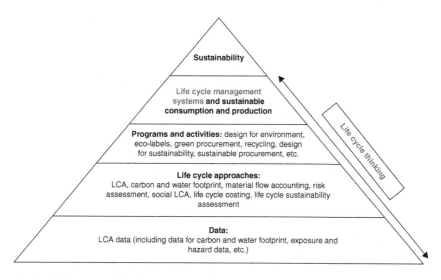

Figure 2.1 Sustainability framework.

in our society due to man's capability to transform his surroundings (UNEP, 2012a, p. 12). Both in 1992 during the first Rio summit, and then 20 years later, it was emphasized that these trends have to do with unsustainable patterns of production and consumption, which exceed the Earth's available resources and carrying capacity (UNCED, 1992). The 10-Year Framework of Programmes for SCP adopted at the Rio+20 summit in 2012 recognizes SCP as a core and overarching objective of sustainable development (Akenji and Bengtsson, 2014). Also, SCP was adopted as one of the Sustainable Development Goals (SDGs) in 2015 (United Nations, 2015).

There has been considerable work over the past 15 years or so on how consumption and production can be made more sustainable (Sabapathy, 2007, p. 7). Concepts predating sustainable production and consumption include 'eco-efficiency', 'cleaner production', and 'Factor-4 production'. SCP as such was coined and further clarified by businesses, governments and NGOs at the 1992 Rio de Janeiro Earth Summit and the 2002 World Summit on Sustainable Development (WSSD) in Johannesburg (Sabapathy, 2007, p. 7).

SCP is understood as

> the use of services and related products, which respond to basic needs and bring a better quality of life while minimizing the use of natural resources and toxic materials as well as the emissions of waste and pollutants over the life cycle of the service or product so as not to jeopardize the needs of future generations.
>
> (Symposium on Sustainable Consumption, 1994)

SCP thus provides a comprehensive framing for issues surrounding the use of resources – not only focusing on improvement of resource efficiency and minimizing its use but also addressing well-being and basic needs (Koide and Akenji, 2017, p. 6). In a similar vein, SCP aims to

> promote social and economic development within the carrying capacity of ecosystems by addressing and, where appropriate, delinking economic growth and environmental degradation through improving efficiency and sustainability in the use of resources and production processes and reducing resource degradation, pollution and waste.
>
> (United Nations, 2002, p. 7)

These definitions emphasize that SCP needs to be viewed as a holistic approach that has at its core a life-cycle perspective (Sonnemann et al., 2018), which implies a fundamental revision of the values and systems that drive current business models as well as individual attitudes and behaviors; it also emphasizes the need to de-link economic growth from resource consumption and from environmental degradation. The latter is also emphasized by the concept of the green economy, defined by UNEP (2010) as one that results in improved human well-being and social equity while reducing environmental risks and ecological scarcities.

Businesses, governments and other groups have developed a variety of techniques and approaches to encourage more SCP (Sabapathy, 2007, p. 11). This is in response to UNEP's warning (UNEP, 2012b) that the shift to SCP will not be achieved unless we have effective policies, social and techno-logical innovation, public and private investment, and the engagement of governments, business, consumers, educators and the media. Some of the techniques used to achieve SCP include: technology, innovation and design; resource productivity and efficiency; life-cycle assessment; closed loop production; sustainable procurement; and customer engagement (Sabapathy, 2007, pp. 11–14). Moreover, Akenji and Bengtsson (2014, p. 518) argue that an effective framing for SCP requires three things, namely: understanding the context under which SCP takes place; understanding patterns of production and consumption in society; and using a life-cycle perspective, prioritizing areas where production and consumption have the highest impact on society and the environment (food and agriculture, transport and mobility, housing and construction and manufactured goods). Sabapathy (2007, p. 4) refers to these conditions that are necessary for achieving SCP as drivers and enablers, which work together with the techniques described above.

Life-cycle thinking – the concept

Life-cycle thinking needs to be viewed as 'a systemic framework that takes a holistic view of the production and consumption of a product or service and assesses its impacts on the environment through the entire life cycle'. It is important to note also that 'LCT goes beyond focusing on a specific site or product' (Quantis, not dated). LCT can be employed by both private and public sectors due to the fact that 'life-cycle information is nowadays considered crucial to guide policy decisions and business strategies in many contexts' (Rete Italiana LCA, not dated).

LCT starts with acknowledging that products contribute to various envir-onmental as well as social impacts over their lifetime. Therefore, it seeks to identify environmental and or social improvement opportunities at all stages across the products' life cycle, from raw material extraction and conversion, through product manufacture, product distribution, use and fate at the end-of-life stage (Koroneos et al., 2013, p. 1). By looking at all stages, we make sure that 'improvements made to one part of the system in one country or in one step of the life cycle do not have negative consequences for other parts of the system which may outweigh the advantages' (Klöpffer, 2003, p. 158). In other words, 'LCT is essential for understanding and preventing uninten-tional burden shifting, whether between different kinds of impacts, different supply chain stages, or different stakeholders that might occur as a result of our management decisions' (Pelletier, 2015, p. 7515). Moreover, UNEP

(2012a, pp. 36–37) describes this process as balancing trade-offs and identifies five general categories of trade-offs: trade-offs between stages of the product value chain; trade-offs between environmental impact categories; trade-offs between the three sustainability pillars; trade-offs between societies/regions; and generational trade-offs.

What sets LCT apart from simple tools which employ a life-cycle approach is its overarching and integrative character. Life-cycle assessment (LCA), which will be discussed in a subsequent section, also explores impacts of products or services throughout their life cycle. However, it is too narrow in scope (only looks at environmental impacts) and it is applied at a micro-level (product).

LCT reflects a shift in how companies implement environmental protection initiatives. Traditionally, enterprises have been focused on environmental improvements to the production processes on-site, within their own perimeter fence (Danish Environmental Protection Agency, 2003, p. 1; Koroneos et al., 2013, p. 2; UNEP, 2012a). This represents a first necessary step in environmental protection; however, it is not sufficient for reaching sustainable development. A second step includes environmental management, which means ongoing improvements (Danish Environmental Protection Agency, 2003, p. 9). A third step refers to the creation of cleaner products, by including a life-cycle approach. In this way, LCT contributes to SCP. However, it goes beyond mere environmental impacts, and also looks at the socio-economic performance of a good throughout its life cycle. The overall aim is to facilitate links between the economic, social and environmental dimensions within an organization or throughout its entire value chain (Koroneos et al., 2013, p. 1). LCT goes therefore beyond SCP and strives to advance the goals of sustainable development.

But LCT is not just about the business sector. LCT applies to the daily decisions made at home and/or the workplace; decisions about creating sustainable services and how to develop modern communities (Koroneos et al., 2013, p. 3). It can be incorporated by all stakeholders – citizens, businesses and governments – into their daily decision-making (UNEP/SETAC, 2004, pp. 11–18). LCT has the capacity to inform these processes by putting reliable information about environmental, social and economic impacts into people's hands at the time of their decision-making (UNEP, 2012a, p. 13). In brief, LCT promotes: (a) awareness with regard to how specific decisions, even minor ones regarding daily operations, influence larger systems; (b) integration of medium and long-term perspectives as well as all types of impact into decision-making; (c) improving entire systems, not single parts of systems; (d) informed decisions, based on data (Koroneos et al., 2013, pp. 2–3).

LCT in the business sector

Businesses are currently moving towards employing LCT into operations management because it makes business sense. We are witnessing a shift towards a true triple-bottom-line approach, which means that businesses no longer think only about reducing the negative environmental impact of their products; they are rather considering both how products can lead to an environmental improvement but also how to incorporate social and economic impacts into their assessments (UNEP, 2012a, p. 21).

The Danish Environmental Protection Agency (2003, p. 14) and James (2005, pp. 5–6) distinguish between internal and external driving forces for implementing LCT in the business sector. Internal drivers, according to the Danish Environmental Protection Agency, include: the responsibility of management to minimize the environmental impacts from products and processes, the need for improved product quality, the desire for a better image, an opportunity to reduce costs, employees' interest and involvement, and new technological innovations (Danish Environmental Protection Agency, 2003, pp. 14–15). External drivers, according to the same study, include: laws and regulations, which can be extremely demanding; advantages in market competition; public demands; frontrunner position compared to the competitors; demands from business associations and networks; and collaboration among suppliers regarding environmental innovations (Danish Environmental Protection Agency, 2003, pp. 15–16).

Another study (Nygren and Antikainen, 2010, p. 13) proposes a different categorization of drivers and distinguishes among three categories: process-oriented, image-oriented and compliance-oriented ones. Interestingly enough, compliance-oriented drivers are described by the authors of the report as businesses looking towards the future; while right now life-cycle approaches are mostly voluntary, businesses are aware of the fact that very soon mandatory requirements from government bodies will become the rule rather than the exception.

LCT can be incorporated by enterprises at different stages in the production process (UNEP, 2012a, pp. 21–22): at the very beginning of the production cycle when products are just being developed (via design for environment); during production (via environmental and social life-cycle assessment, carbon and water footprint, supplier codes of conduct); marketing (via use of eco-labels, social and environmental certification); use (via informing users on energy and water use); disposal (via design for disassembly); and management (via sustainability reporting). Enterprises are different, have different capabilities, and depending on the context in which they operate some of the drivers described may be more powerful than others. This means that usually enterprises will start incorporating LCT in one or more areas, depending on the urgency they feel and potential benefits. The ultimate goal however, is to have more enterprises fully address the triple bottom line of sustainability.

LCT in the public sector

Traditionally, the role of governments regarding environmental protection was to set up production standards and emission caps within which businesses need to operate. A step forward was for governments to adopt and implement policies based on the idea of leading by example – incorporating sustainability considerations into their own internal operations. Public procurement is one of the fields in which, due to the sheer volume of public spending (8–30 percent of national GDP), public authorities have a real opportunity to stimulate production of green products and create demand for these products. But the role of the public sector is not limited to leading by example; it is now called upon to make strategic decisions resulting in the creation of an adequate framework for the transition to a green economy (UNEP, 2012a, p. 25).

Public procurement is perhaps the sector where LCT has known, over the last decades, the biggest applicability. Life-cycle approaches are not new to public procurement. The concept of life-cycle costing (LCC) in the product acquisition process originated in the United States, specifically by the Department of Defense in the 1960s. LCC is used as a systematic approach to ascertain total life-cycle cost of equipment. Due to the peculiarities of defense markets, where acquisition costs do not have a significant share in total costs, LCC in this area is used as the rule and not as an exception (Verma, 2015). Besides defense procurement, this approach of buying green and social has matured since the 1990s, to the extent that sustainable public procurement strategies at the sub-national, national and supra-national level have been implemented in both developed and developing countries. Sustainable public procurement means that governments purchase products and services that are 'environmentally preferable' and support regional and global markets for 'preferable' products and services (UNEP/SETAC, 2004, p. 13). A subsequent section of this chapter will address more in-depth the topic of sustainable procurement in the EU. Here, we just want to mention that public procurement is perhaps one of the fields where significant tensions occur between supporting/ favoring 'preferable' environmental and social products or services and other public objectives such as free completion and non-discrimination within the context of the internal market.

But LCT goes well beyond public procurement. UNEP/SETAC (2004, p. 13) identify at least five instances where governments can use LCT. First, government authorities at all levels when adopting policies should incorporate a life-cycle perspective in assessing the wide range of environmental and social impacts of these upcoming policies. LCT can thus inform government programs and help prioritize them (UNEP, 2012a, p. 26). As described under the sustainability framework by Fava, reliable data are at the foundation of life-cycle management and of different life-cycle approaches. While the industry is in most cases well equipped to document the impacts produced by a certain product, the gathering of data pertaining to broader social indicators and environmental and biodiversity indicators can be better done or facilitated by governments (UNEP, 2012a, p. 26). Other more specific actions that can be taken especially by local governments are related to life-cycle costing policies. Governments can thus promote pricing products and services to accurately reflect the cost of environmental degradation, health and social impacts

(OECD, 2011, pp. 1–3). Also, they can promote take-back policies which are the foundation for a recycling economy (UNEP/SETAC, 2004, p. 13). Finally, they can make sure that the impact of governmental operations on the environment is reduced (UNEP/SETAC, 2004, p. 13).

Limitations to LCT

Though LCT and its methodologies hold great promises for sustainability, there are nonetheless limitations associated with them. Most authors (UNEP, 2012a; James, 2005; Nygren and Antikainen, 2010, p. 14) argue that costs and resources and data availability are perhaps the most significant obstacles to be surpassed. The resources (costs) and time that need to be invested in collecting data, performing calculations and preparing reports are significant. The data collection stage is the most time consuming and can involve collecting data from numerous sources including reference books, previous life-cycle studies, government reports, databases, equipment loggers and laboratory reports. The availability and accessibility of the abovementioned data sets is another factor that needs to be considered along with the quality of the data. Some of these limitations can be overcome with the use of life-cycle software that has built-in databases, though quality of data still needs to be monitored (James, 2005). Other limitations include a lack of business drivers (Nygren and Antikainen, 2010, p. 14) as well as a lack of awareness and understanding, a lack of harmonization among methods, etc. (UNEP, 2012a, p. 47).

LCT tools

In this section we examine more in-depth three tools that operationalize into practice LCT and life-cycle management. These are life-cycle assessment, life-cycle costing and labels. They are examined here from a general point of view, with the purpose of linking them to LCT and more broadly to the sustainability framework. These tools can be used by a variety of stakeholders in different ways. The stakeholders' role, vis-à-vis these tools, needs to be understood in the context of the specific responsibilities and capabilities of each type of stakeholder. In the next section they will be analyzed in the context of European public procurement law and practice.

Life-cycle assessment

A system analysis is a tool that allows a product to be analyzed through its entire life cycle, from raw material extraction and production, via the material's use, to waste handling and recycling. Authors usually associate this approach with an industrial system from cradle to grave (Curran, 2016, p. 359) or even cradle to cradle (Muralikrishna and Manickam, 2017, p. 57). The most common tool for system analysis is LCA methodology (Stavropoulos et al., 2016, p. 626; Nygren and Antikainen, 2010, p. 9). LCA is 'a tool which undertakes a holistic review of a whole product or service system in order to identify or quantify the energy and material inputs, evaluate the related environmental outputs, and further appraise the corresponding impacts on the environment' (Filimonau, 2016, p. 12). It is recognized as a means to improve the environmental performance of products and to identify opportunities for mitigation of negative environmental impacts (Filimonau, 2016, p. 12).

The first studies that are now recognized as partial or proto LCAs date from the late 1960s and early 1970s. The scope of these studies was initially limited to energy analyses but was later broadened to encompass resource requirements, emissions loadings and generated waste (Hocking, 1991). The period 1970 to 1990 is described in the literature as the decades for the conception of LCA with widely diverging approaches, terminologies and results (Guinée et al., 2011, pp. 90–91). The 1990–2000 decade represents a period of convergence and standardization. Several international organizations became involved with LCA. SETAC focused on development and harmonization of methods while ISO adopted the formal task of standardization of methods and procedures (Guinée et al., 2011, p. 91). Starting with 2000, we have again divergence with regard to LCA. However, this decade can be described as focused on elaboration and is marked by the development of life-cycle costing and social life-cycle assessment (Guinée et al., 2011, p. 92). The future of LCA will most likely be marked by broadening its scope in order to cover all types of impacts and not only environmental ones and also in order to focus not only on product-related questions but rather on sector-related or even economy-wide ones (Guinée et al., 2011, pp. 93–94). In addition to broadening its scope, LCA will most likely deepen its assessment to include not just technological relations but also physical and economical ones (Guinée et al., 2011, p. 94). The LCA of the future is often referred to in the literature as LCSA (Life Cycle Sustainability Assessment) (Ekener et al., 2018; Keller et al., 2015).

An LCA is usually made in three steps with an additional interpretation step (Lee and Inaba, 2004, p. 3). These steps/stages are in accordance with the terminology and framework proposed by ISO 14040 (ISO 2006a) and ISO 14044 (ISO 2006b). The first stage, goal and scope definition, should clarify aspects such as the intended purpose of the study, the audience for which the results are intended, and the product that will be studied (James, 2005, p. 3). The scope of the LCA includes specification of the functional unit and system boundaries (James, 2005, p. 3). The functional unit is the measure of performance that the system delivers. In the Life Cycle Inventory Analysis (LCIA), inputs and outputs for a product are determined and quantified within the system boundaries (Nygren and Antikainen, 2010, p. 9). The third stage, impact assessment, is aimed at understanding and evaluating the magnitude and significance of the potential environmental impacts for a product system throughout the life cycle of the product (Nygren and Antikainen, 2010, p. 9). The impact assessment is performed in consecutive steps including classification, characterization, normalization and weighting. The LCIA phase also provides information for the life-cycle interpretation phase, where the final environmental interpretation is made.

LCA is only concerned with environmental impacts. It also looks at these impacts in a comprehensive manner, without identifying or quantifying their monetary value/cost.

LCA in the public sector and in procurement

LCA is mostly a tool to be utilized by businesses for the assessment of the environmental impact of their individual products. More recently it has been expanded as to incorporate the assessment of the impact of the entire business operation, at corporate level as opposed to product level (Filimonau, 2016). It is recognized as a powerful tool for impact assessment, corporate decision-making and policy design (Filimonau, 2016, p. 13).

In Europe, but also worldwide, LCA became part of policy documents and legislation towards the middle of the 1990s. At that time the focus was on packaging legislation, with mixed outcomes in terms of the success of this approach (Arnold, 1995). In the next decade, LCA became interlinked at the European level with Integrated Product Policy (European Commission, 2003). The European Commission encouraged the creation of the European Platform on Life Cycle Assessment, with the goal 'to promote the availability, exchange, and use of quality-assured life-cycle data, methods, and studies for reliable decision support in (EU) public policy and in business' (Guinée et al., 2011, p. 92).

LCA or simplified versions which incorporate LCA principles/technique can be found in limited instances in the public sector. When public authorities use it, the goal is similar to the private sector – decision-making and policy design. Both central and sub-national governments are faced within the framework of specific public policies with various alternatives that have different environmental impacts. Choosing among several policy alternatives can be done by using LCA. When public authorities procure certain goods where multiple technologies are available, LCA can be used to decide what to procure. Such examples could include a public library deciding whether to buy electronic books/devices or paper-based ones, or a municipality which could choose to manage its waste via incinerators or landfills, or a school district deciding whether or not to buy organic food for students' lunches. However, we should not forget that data is at the foundation of all LCT methodologies. The public sector, in most cases, will not have access to the data that producers have about the upstream and downstream impacts of a certain product or technology. In their case, policy design will be mostly based on LCA thinking/ principles, rather than proper LCAs as those conducted by producers.

Our conclusion is that, with respect to LCA, the public sector is rather an LCA enabler than a 'doer'. Its most powerful tools as enabler include: in fields where governments are singular buyers (defense) or when using procurement for innovation, public authorities could request that solutions offered by producers be based on detailed LCA; incorporate LCA thinking into policy designs or procurement where alternative solutions/technologies are available; facilitate collection of data about broader social and environmental impacts (those which businesses would have a more difficult time measuring); facilitate creation of standardized databases on environmental impacts of products and open/free access to these standardized databases for SMEs.

Life-cycle costing

An economic evaluation can be performed in many different ways and can include many different aspects of the economy. The aim of life-cycle costing is to include all costs during the entire life cycle of the product. This will result in a more accurate description of the entire cost for a product or process than just an analysis of the purchase price (Stripple, 2013, p. 23). LCC analysis is especially useful when project alternatives that fulfill the same perform-ance requirements, but differ with respect to initial costs and operating costs, have to be compared in order to select the one that maximizes net savings (Fuller, 2016).

In an LCC it is important to define the types of costs that are included and how they are presented (Schau et al., 2011, p. 2280). There are both internal costs – ordinary costs (material costs, labor costs, energy costs), which are paid by the different parts in a business transaction, and external ones – not nor-mally paid by the parties in a business deal, but by external parties (examples of such costs are costs for pollution damage and health costs). The bearers of external costs can be either particular individuals or society at large. External costs are in many cases difficult to quantify both physically and in monetary terms. Sometimes, the external costs can be of a non-monetary type. This makes external costs difficult to work with and uncertainties can be substan-tial. However, external costs may be very important and relevant (Stripple, 2013, p. 26), especially from the perspective of the public sector, whose role is to look out for the public interest. This will be further discussed in a subse-quent section, when referring to environmental and social externalities.

LCC in public procurement

LCC is a tool that has been used in certain areas of public procurement, for example defense procurement, for several decades. The reasons why LCC has been used in this field is because acquisition cost is not so significant when compared to other costs incurred during the operation and disposal of military equipment. This logic of total cost of ownership is currently being transplanted to other areas of public procurement without significant hurdles. The difficulty encountered, however, with LCC is when public governments want to include costs that do not have a clear monetary value. Such costs are related to environmental and social negative externalities associated with goods, services and works at different moments in their life cycle. Businesses have a less complicated view on LCC because for a business most costs will have a clear monetary value. When performing LCC, businesses will not include the cost of externalities, unless this is required through regulation or rewarded through certification or a label.

Public authorities pursuing sustainable procurement may want to include environmental and social costs. Examples of environmental costs would include various emissions into the atmosphere, water and soil (pollution), loss of biodiversity, climate change, etc. Social negative externalities could include health care problems for various groups in population, disruption of communities for indigenous populations, exclusion of certain groups from various opportunities, unfair price of labor, etc. Depending on where in the life cycle of a product one might want to identify and quantify environmental and social negative externalities, situations could become pretty extreme. We can imagine works projects where a specific type of wood used for floors might contribute to habitat loss in the Amazonian forest. The question in this case is, whether LCC is really the most suitable tool to address habitat loss in remote areas compared to where procurement takes place and if yes, can negative impacts really be monetized? How could a public authority assess how much deforestation costs? What types of units would be used to measure deforestation?

The most uncomplicated environmental aspects to monetize are those where there is a market for trading externalities. Clean Vehicle Directive, the only methodology available for calculating environmental LCC, draws upon the fact that for certain emissions there are markets and these markets allow governments to put a specific price on certain emissions. This ability to put a price on certain emissions is critical because, otherwise, the estimated cost of procurement will not stand the test in a court of law.

Our argument is not that environmental and social negative externalities during the life cycle of a good are not important. Our argument is that LCC can only work with costs that have a clear monetary value. For example, where governments want to encourage fair trade for the products they buy, they can do so through labels and certification systems. This removes the pressure from governments to engage with complicated pricing schemes for externalities that are difficult to monetize.

Eco-labels

Environmental product information schemes, including eco-labels, represent an important communication tool that aims at providing practitioners in various fields (public procurement included), as well as private consumers, with information on the environmental characteristics of products and services (Rubik et al., 2005, p. 29). Eco-labels are considered self-regulatory information instruments (for an extensive discussion on labels, see Neamtu and Dragos, 2015; Gunningham and Grabosky, 1998). Eco-labeling schemes work by providing information to consumers in order to reduce information asymmetry with regard to specific products or products' attributes. Various authors describe how product information is, in most cases, asymmetrically allocated between buyers and sellers (Karl and Orwat, 1999, pp. 214–217).

Labels have been around since the late 1970s – the first label, the Blue Angel, was introduced in 1978 by the German ministry for the Interior. Since then there has been a multiplication of these labeling schemes, of varying scope, size, nature and effectiveness (Crespi and Marette, 2005; Cohen and Vandenbergh, 2012); currently eco-labeling schemes exist in large numbers and many forms at the national, European and international level. Many of the EU Member States have introduced national eco-labeling programs (Bratt et al., 2011, p. 1631). Worldwide, according to Ecolabel Index, there are 463 environmental labels in 199 countries and 25 industry sectors (Ecolabel Index, not dated). The increasing number of labels is a challenge for consumers as they are faced with a variety of logos, with different levels of reliability and independence (UNOPS, 2009, p. 5). This is why the issue of coordination and harmonization has been on the agenda for years, both globally, administered by the Global Eco-labelling Network (GEN), and within the EU for voluntary programs (Bratt et al., 2011, p. 1631).

The European Commission launched in 1992 the EU Ecolabel (Council Regulation 880/92/EEC) in order to avoid the proliferation of environmental labeling schemes and to encourage higher environmental performance in all sectors for which environmental impact is a factor in consumer choice. The way in which the scheme works is currently stipulated by Regulation 66/2010/EU. The EU Ecolabel is part of the sustainable consumption and production policy of the Community, which aims at reducing the negative impact of consumption and production on the environment, health, climate and natural resources. The scheme is intended to promote those products that have a high level of environmental performance through the use of the EU Ecolabel (Recital 5, Regulation 66/2010). There is a wide range of products and services that can apply for the label and this range continues to grow year on year. However, 'only the most environmental products/services are allowed to bear the label and in order to get it, a strict criterion must be adhered to' (EUbusiness, not dated).

Labels in public sector and public procurement

Eco-labels are one of the voluntary tools considered by the EU for advancing the implementation of sustainable public procurement. Especially in the soft-law documents emanating in recent years from the Commission (European Commission, 2008, 2011a, 2011b), the use of eco-labels has been addressed/encouraged. Contracting authorities have been offered practical examples regarding how to correctly use eco-labels at different stages of the public procurement process.

In the 2014/24/EU Directive, a label is defined as any document, certification, or attestation that confirms that the works, products, services, processes or procedures in question meet certain requirements (Art 1(2) (23) of Directive 2014/24/EU). And label requirements refer to the requirements to be met by the works, products, services, processes or procedures in question in order to obtain the label in question (Art 1(2) (24) of Directive 2014/24/EU).

Generally speaking, procurement practitioners can use eco-labels to: translate the environmental criteria of the labels into technical specifications (only in cases when the market is mature and there are enough producers holding such labels); verify compliance with technical specifications; benchmark offers at the award stage (when the market is not mature enough, at the award stage it is possible to assign extra points for meeting additional environmental criteria that are preferred but are not compulsory elements of the bid); and use single issue and performance labels for a progressive approach (UNOPS, 2009, p. 13).

Life-cycle thinking in the context of the modernization of EU procurement

Traditionally, public procurement had to only be economically efficient, with little regard for other objectives than the purely economic ones. In the early stages it was the Court of Justice of the EU, rather than the Commission, that interpreted the Procurement Directives in force at the time as allowing under certain conditions the use of environmental and social criteria. However, in recent years it has been acknowledged that public procurement legislation is to be used to correct market and system failures. Thus, demand for certain technologies, products or services are encouraged via public procurement in order to stimulate the market. The ultimate goal of the reform was to strike some sort of a balance between old (traditional) and new (strategic) objectives in European public procurement.

The move towards life-cycle thinking in public procurement at the EU level emerged relatively late, around 2000, when green public procurement was included as a policy in a number of documents such as the EU Sustainable Development Strategy (2001–2011), the 6th Environmental Action Programme (2002–2012), the Lisbon strategy and Europe 2020 (for an extensive analysis on this, see Dragos and Neamtu, 2013, 2015). From 'secondary considerations' in the 2004 Public Procurement Directives (Arrowsmith and Kunzlik, 2009; Arnould, 2004; Caranta and Trybus, 2010), the need to include social and environmental considerations in public tendering procedures has led over time to the coining of new terms, much more powerful and all-encompassing, such as 'horizontal policies' (Arrowsmith and Kunzlik, 2009), 'sustainable procurement' (Caranta, 2014, pp. 165–167) or even 'strategic procurement' (Edler and Georghiou, 2007, p. 953).

The modernization package was predated by mandatory provisions for buying green: The 2008 Energy Star Regulation (obligation on central contracting authorities to buy energy-efficient IT office equipment – Regulation 106/2008/EC of the European Parliament and the Council of 15 January 2008 on a Community energy-efficiency labeling program for office equipment); the 2009 Clean Vehicles Directive (obligation on all contracting authorities to buy environmentally friendly vehicles – Directive 2009/33/EC of the European Parliament and the Council of 23 April 2009 on the promotion of clean and energy-efficient road transport vehicles); and the 2010 Energy Performance of Buildings Directive (obligation for new buildings owned or occupied by public authorities to be nearly zero energy by the end of 2018 – Directive 2010/31/EU of the European Parliament and of the Council of 19 May 2010 on the energy performance of buildings).

With the adoption of the new 2014 Directives on public procurement and concessions (Directive 2014/24/EU; Directive 2014/25/EU; and Directive 2014/23/EU; Schebesta, 2014, p. 129), the sustainability paradigm almost took over the realm of public procurement (at least at a declaratory level), and it was marketed as a major 'selling point' of the new legislation (Schebesta, 2014, p. 129). The three Directives introduced a number of novel provisions relating to the procurement of innovative and sustainable solutions, among which the use of LCC and labels.

In the above-described context, life-cycle costing was viewed as a novelty, one of the most fundamental modernization challenges and one of the specific tools to be used in order to advance the goals of sustainable public procurement. Life-cycle costing was already a possibility under the old generation of procurement Directives, as evidenced by the inclusion of this approach in the Clean Vehicles Directive (2009/33/EC) (Semple, not dated). LCC is also a so-called horizontal provision with great application potential (Semple, not dated).

Article 68 of Directive 2014/24/EU is dedicated entirely to this new concept, representing a useful clarification, thus encouraging contracting authorities to move away from evaluating the lowest delivery cost/price towards consideration of the whole-life/long-term cost of the works, supplies or services procured (Sigma, 2016, pp. 22–23). In our opinion this is still not enough to make a real impact on the way procurement is conducted in the EU.

Life-cycle thinking in Directive 2014/24/EU

Stages of procurement process where LCT can be found

Life-cycle thinking was introduced by the 2014/24/EU Directive as part of a wider endeavor to make sustainable procurement a strategic objective of public procurement. It is not called as such, but it can be found in different parts of the procurement process as an overarching concept. We can only speculate why LCT is not used in the text of the new Procurement Directives. Our opinion is that LCT as an overarching and integrated framework is for the most part associated with a management and non-legal perspective. Public Procurement Directives prefer to refer to the life cycle of products, services and works and, more specifically and narrowly, to specific tools associated with LCT.

Thus, LCT finds its expression in the different stages of the procurement process: in the stage of market consultations, in technical criteria related to the life cycle of the products or services, in life-cycle costing as part of the cost as award criteria, in the possibility to use labels, and in the performance requirements. Also, the 2014/24/EU Directive leaves room for sector-specific regulations to impose mandatory criteria relating to sustainability, including the use of LCT.

The role of sector-specific regulation

One way of dealing with LCT in public procurement is through sector-specific regulation of products, works or services. In this way, life-cycle costing becomes mandatory for the private market and thus can be used by the public markets as well.

Recital 95 of the 2014/24/EU Directive takes stock of the existing regulations and envisages a sector-driven development of new legal norms:

> The Union legislature has already set mandatory procurement requirements for obtaining specific goals in the sectors of road transport vehicles (Directive 2009/33/EC of the European Parliament and the Council (16)) and office equipment (Regulation (EC) No 106/2008 of the European Parliament and the Council (17)). In addition, the definition of common methodologies for life cycle costing has significantly advanced.
>
> It therefore appears appropriate to continue on that path, leaving it to sector-specific legislation to set mandatory objectives and targets in function of the particular policies and conditions prevailing in the relevant sector and to promote the development and use of European *approaches to life-cycle costing* as a further underpinning for the use of public procurement in support of sustainable growth.

Market consultation and procurement design

A first instance where LCT is evident is when public procurers consult the market in order to design the procedure and estimate the value of the procurement. An approach based on LCT would mean that the value is estimated taking into account the cost of the product, service or work based on a life-cycle costing calculation, where possible. Also, the identification of labels and the criteria they endorse is a good starting point in order to design the technical specifications.

At the preparatory stage, the objective is to assess the estimated cost of the product, work or service by identifying the different cost elements relating to the product and taking into consideration its whole life cycle. It gives a baseline from which to work, allows a better communication of the benefits of new technologies, and helps define some general performance requirements for the new solutions (LCC Public Procurement Tool, not dated).

Thus, before tendering, the role of the analysis is to roughly assess different ideas put forward by the market or to narrow down the different techno-logical solutions envisaged. For instance, one of the recommendations of the European Commission working group on LCC in the construction sector is to carry out LCC at the early design stage, where the opportunities for modifying the costs of a project are the greatest (Estevan et al., 2018, p. 10). The same conclusion arises from the LCC Tool for emissions (LCC Public Procurement Tool, not dated).

LCA is possible to be taken into consideration at this stage in cases where the market players have already performed such an LCA for their products or services. It is harder to convey that public authorities may resort to a full LCA at this stage, due to its complexity. If producers have already carried out an LCA, this can inform the decision-making process of public authorities.

Technical specifications

Technical specifications can be drawn up using as a reference point LCT, or even based on an LCC calculation, in parallel with estimating the value of the procurement. The criteria can then be replicated in the contract performance clauses in order to be monitored.

The easier alternative is to refer to criteria already included in labels, in order to select or qualify the tenders. Many times procurers are buying 'sus-tainable' only as a result of requiring labels. In the policy paper *Buyin Green*, the European Commission's suggested strategy was for contracting authorities to use minimum requirements derived from eco-labels in the specifications and then to award extra points at the award stage of the procedure for tenderers who go the extra mile to offer green products or services or works (European Commission, 2011a, pp. 40–41).

Along the same lines, Recital 74 of the new Directive states that:

> The technical specifications drawn up by public purchasers need to allow public procurement to be open to competition as well as to achieve object-ives of sustainability. To that end, it should be possible to submit tenders that reflect the *diversity of technical solutions standards and technical specifications in the marketplace, including those drawn up on the basis of performance criteria linked to the life cycle* and the sustainability of the production process of the works, supplies and services.
>
> (Recital 74, our emphasis)

Award criteria: Life-cycle costing

According to Article 67 of the new Directive:

1. Without prejudice to national laws, regulations or administra-tive provisions concerning the price of certain supplies or the

remuneration of certain services, contracting authorities shall base the award of public contracts on the most economically advantageous tender.

2. The most economically advantageous tender from the point of view of the contracting authority shall be identified on the basis of the price or cost, using a cost-effectiveness approach, such as life-cycle costing in accordance with Article 68, and may include the best price–quality ratio, which shall be assessed on the basis of criteria, including qualitative, environmental and/or social aspects, linked to the subject-matter of the public contract in question. Such criteria may comprise, for instance:

   (a) quality, including technical merit, aesthetic and functional characteristics, accessibility, design for all users, social, environmental and innovative characteristics and trading and its conditions;

   (b) organisation, qualification and experience of staff assigned to performing the contract, where the quality of the staff assigned can have a significant impact on the level of performance of the contract; or

   (c) after-sales service and technical assistance, delivery conditions such as delivery date, delivery process and delivery period or period of completion.

The European Commission working group on LCC in construction explains that to carry out LCC during tendering means to compare the LCC and the anticipated CO_2 emissions of different offers during the evaluation phase (Estevan et al., 2018, p. 10).

One may observe that is not mandatory for contracting authorities to include all the different costs in their life-cycle cost analyses, except for the case when the method for the calculation of life-cycle costs has been made mandatory by a legislative act of the Union or where contracting authorities are bound by national regulations to use a certain method when calculating life-cycle costs (Inden, 2018, p. 661).

The advantages of using LCC as an award criterion are mostly related to two different arguments. First, the life-cycle costs over the life of an asset are widely acknowledged as a better indicator of value for money than the initial acquisition/construction costs alone. It is therefore clear that a greater focus on the maintenance and operating costs of assets, rather than on only capital costs, can deliver significant long-term financial and environmental benefits. Second, it provides a tool for the economic evaluation of alternative sustainability options exhibiting different capital, operating costs or resource usage. It also provides methods for evaluating the cost benefits of incorporating more sustainable options into different products/works/services.

The use of LCC raises the question of its place within the award criteria. Can LCC be used when the lowest price criterion is chosen, or only as part of MEAT (most economically advantageous tender)? In order to answer this question, a more in-depth discussion about which award criteria can be used under the new Directive, as opposed to the old legal regime, is required.

Under the 2004 Directive, a contract could be awarded based on the lowest priced criterion or based on MEAT. Criteria included in MEAT would be quality, price, technical merit, aesthetic and functional characteristics, environmental characteristics, running costs, cost-effectiveness, after-sales service and technical assistance, delivery date and delivery period or period of completion. Contracting authorities were responsible for creating the methodologies for assessing tenders under MEAT, on a contract-by-contract basis.

Under the 2014 Directive, at a first glance price is no longer an option for awarding public contracts. Article 67(1) states that contracting authorities shall base the award of public contracts on the most economically advantageous tender. The wording of the Directive is, however, rather misleading on this topic, as what the Directive actually did was to expand the scope of the 'most economically advantageous tender' to include the award of contracts on price or cost only (Semple, not dated; Hobson, 2016).

Under the 2014 Directive, a distinction is made between price and costs, the latter requiring the use of a cost-effectiveness approach, such as life-cycle costing. The new Directive also introduces a new concept, the best price–quality ratio, which can include qualitative, environmental and social aspects. Consequently, as opposed to the old Directive, currently the use of LCC is no longer restricted to tenders awarded on the price–quality ratio and it can be applied also to situations when the award is made exclusively on costs.

Resorting to LCC makes an award procedure based only on price as the sole award criterion a complex one. The difference from using the price–quality ratio will be that, in the case of an award based on the lowest price which, in its turn, is based on LCC, the price remains the only criterion for the award, so all the externalities have to be incorporated and monetized as elements of the price. In the case of an award on the basis of the best price–quality ratio, other criteria can be taken into account, but not as part of the costs. Externalities always have to be provided with a monetary value. Under the price–quality ratio, a weighting process needs to take place among the various criteria used.

Economic LCC

Initially, LCC was only an economic tool, with the aim of analyzing past, present and future costs in order to choose the most cost-effective option. Perhaps this is the main reason why the most common LCC methodologies used by governments are based on a purely financial valuation, considering the types of direct costs. Direct economic costs are easier to forecast and in most cases there is less uncertainty.

According to Article 68(1), the list of costs covered includes both direct costs, borne by the contracting authority or other users, as well as costs resulting from the monetization of the externalities linked to the product, service or work during its life cycle. The direct costs include costs relating to acquisition, costs of use, such as consumption of energy and other resources, maintenance costs and end-of-life costs, such as collection and recycling costs. Indirect costs, such as the cost of emissions of greenhouse gases and of other pollutant emissions, can be included only if their monetary value can be determined and verified.

Again, not all costs must be covered by LCC – contracting authorities have some freedom in choosing which costs are relevant to them. However, if contracting authorities choose to focus on certain parts of the life cycle, they must act in accordance with the general principles, such as the principle of equal treatment, both in terms of the choice and in terms of application of the criteria (Inden, 2018, p. 661).

Environmental LCC

Traditional LCC does not become an environmental tool just because it contains the words 'life cycle' (Gluch and Baumann, 2004). In order to become an environmentally relevant methodology, LCC needs to include external costs associated with the work/service/product (Dragos and Neamtu, 2013, p. 20).

The methodology best adapted to sustainable public procurement is environmental life-cycle costing (ELCC). This approach, on top of financial assessments (the 'economic LCC'), takes into consideration the external impacts on the environment, which may be based on LCA (Dragos and Neamtu, 2013, p. 20). Such an analysis may measure, for example, the external costs of global warming contribution associated with emissions of different greenhouse gases (European Commission, not dated). Environmental costs can be calculated also with respect to acidification (grams of SO_2, NO_X and NH_3), eutrophication (grams of NO_X and NH_3), land use (m^2*year) or other measurable impacts. For example, the SMART-SPP project developed and tested a tool for public authorities to assess LCC and CO_2 emissions and to compare bids (Smart SPP, not dated). The OECD also developed ten key environmental indicators derived from a larger set of major environmental issues (OECD, 2008). The selection was made based on their political relevance, analytical soundness and measurability. The indicators include: climate change, the ozone layer, air quality, waste generation, freshwater quality, freshwater resources, forest resources, fish resources, energy resources and biodiversity (OECD, 2008, p. 8). These indicators can constitute a base for developing a common framework for the use of ELCC by contracting authorities throughout the EU, taking into consideration the methodologies already developed at the national level.

The European Commission has provided some guidance for public procurement authorities wishing to use LCC in the International Reference Life Cycle Data System (ILCD) Handbook – a handbook for businesses, Life

Cycle Assessment (LCA) experts and public authorities on how to conduct life-cycle assessments to calculate a product's total environmental impact (European Commission, 2012).

However, the translation of environmental and social issues into monetary terms has never been an easy job (Gluch and Baumann, 2004; cited in Estevan et al., 2018, p. 17). The LCC calculation method proposed by the Clean Vehicles Directive, by the Regulation on office equipment, and by the Life Cycle Costing Public Procurement Tool, are notable attempts to standardize the LCC calculations. The latter (LCC Public Procurement Tool, not dated) is meant to help procurers calculate the life-cycle costs (LCC) and important emissions (CO_2, CO_2eq, NOx, SO_2, NMHC and PM) of different products, work and services to assist in procurement decision-making.

National contributions to the topic include the former Swedish Environmental Management Council (SEMCO), which has developed several tools for calculating life-cycle costs in public procurement. In addition to a general tool, specialized ones are available for cleaning and chemicals, office and textile, food, nursing and care, etc. Since 2015, the National Agency for Public Procurement has been in charge of Green Public Procurement (GPP) and criteria in Sweden (Swedish National Agency for Public Procurement, not dated).

Environmental labels are an alternative to ELCC. The idea is that if externalities are included in the criteria for some labels, the mere compliance with the label would be enough to insure a level of sustainability that would benefit the contracting authority.

Social LCC

Article 68 only refers to environmental externalities and provides examples of what they are. One question that arises in the context of LCC under the 2014 Directive is whether there are other types of externalities that can be factored in, for instance social costs, which are harder to assess but still important. While the literature refers to life cycle assessment incorporating social criteria (labor conditions, equal opportunities and accessibility criteria), almost no reference is made to the monetization of externalities pertaining to the social realm. One study (Perera et al., 2009, p. 3) refers to costs such as unemployment benefits the payment of which would have been necessary without the procurement of a given asset, or health care costs that would have been necessary if environmentally preferable alternatives would not have been procured and argues that they are difficult to forecast.

The 2014/24/EU Directive does not go far enough into this topic. From Article 68 it could be inferred that social and employment criteria are excluded from LCC, which definitely represents in our view a weakening of the full potential of LCC. Recital 96 of Directive 2014/24/EU, last paragraph, declares that:

the feasibility of establishing a common methodology on social life cycle costing should be examined, taking into account existing methodologies such as the Guidelines for Social Life Cycle Assessment of Products adopted within the framework of the United Nations Environment Programme.

It is not clear whether this declaration of intention is addressed to the Member States, it relates to the future endeavors of the Commission, or it is intended for the contracting authorities. At least in theory, contracting authorities may use the recital to justify the use of social LCC, and this would not be against the Directive.

Recital 97 of the Directive makes also reference to the social considerations in procurement:

> Furthermore, with a view to the better integration of social and environmental considerations in the procurement procedures, contracting authorities should be allowed to use award criteria or contract performance conditions relating to the works, supplies or services to be provided under the public contract in any respect and at any *stage of their life cycles* from extraction of raw materials for the product to the stage of disposal of the product, including factors involved in the specific process of production, provision or trading and its conditions of those works, supplies or services or a specific process during a later stage of their life cycle, even where such factors do not form part of their material substance. Criteria and conditions referring to such a production or provision process are for example that the manufacturing of the purchased products did not involve toxic chemicals, or that the purchased services are provided using energy-efficient machines. In accordance with the case-law of the Court of Justice of the European Union, this also includes award criteria or contract performance conditions relating to the supply or utilisation of fair trade products in the course of the performance of the contract to be awarded. Criteria and conditions relating to trading and its conditions can for instance refer to the fact that the product concerned is of fair trade origin, including the requirement to pay a minimum price and price premium to producers.
>
> (Fisher and Corbalán, 2013)

Contract performance conditions pertaining to environmental considerations might include, for example, the delivery, package and disposal of products, and in respect of works and services contracts, waste minimisation or resource efficiency.

However, the condition of a link with the subject-matter of the contract excludes criteria and conditions relating to general corporate policy, which cannot be considered as a factor characterising the specific process of production or provision of the purchased works, supplies or services. Contracting authorities should hence not be allowed to require tenderers to have a certain corporate social or environmental responsibility policy in place.

We can observe that social LCC is not referred to there, but nevertheless a form of LCA might be considered and performed at this level. The social considerations seem to find their place in the performance of the contract, and not in the award of the contract. However, as seen in the Max Havellaar case (*C-368/10 – Commission v Netherlands*), social criteria may be used as an award criterion as well.

Again, an alternative to social LCC is to resort to social labels such as fair trade labels (FAIRTRADE, 2015) or labels relating to work conditions such as the Fair Wear Foundation (not dated) and SA8000: Standard for Social Accountability (Social Accountability International, not dated).

LCC methodologies

Globally, there are various methodologies and software available for conducting LCCs, either for a fee or free of charge. The LCA Resources Directory for identifying such sources (in Europe and beyond) is available online (European Platform on Life Cycle Assessment, not dated). The link with LCT is clear as the website states that resources provided should facilitate the integration of 'Life Cycle Thinking into product development and into public policy making with structured, cost free and independent information'. At the EU level, the catch is that they need to be in line with Treaty principles: non-discrimination, free movement, but also environmental integration according to Article 11 TFEU.

Recital 95 of the Directive states that:

> It is of utmost importance to fully exploit the potential of public procurement to achieve the objectives of the Europe 2020 strategy for smart, sustainable and inclusive growth. In this context, it should be recalled that public procurement is crucial to driving innovation, which is of great importance for future growth in Europe. In view of the important differences between individual sectors and markets, it would however not be appropriate to set general mandatory requirements for environmental, social and innovation procurement.
>
> The Union legislature has already set mandatory procurement requirements for obtaining specific goals in the sectors of road transport vehicles (Directive 2009/33/EC of the European Parliament and the Council (16)) and office equipment (Regulation (EC) No 106/2008 of the European Parliament and the Council (17)). *In addition, the definition of common methodologies for life cycle costing has significantly advanced.*

It therefore appears appropriate to continue on that path, leaving it to sector-specific legislation to set mandatory objectives and targets in function of the particular policies and conditions prevailing in the relevant sector and to promote the development and *use of European approaches to life-cycle costing* as a further underpinning for the use of public procurement in support of sustainable growth.

(Recital 95, our emphasis)

Several conclusions might be drawn from these provisions:

- The Clean Vehicles Directive and the Regulation on office equipment provide for the only methodologies that are mandatory throughout the EU;
- The market should provide the rest of the methodologies, and it is providing some of them, although they are not identified in the Directive;
- The sector-specific regulations or directives are expected to further provide such methodologies.

Considering the above text in conjunction with Article 68 of the Directive, we can go further and say that:

- Member States are allowed to adopt mandatory methodologies – the question is whether these methodologies are mandatory in the case of joint cross-border procurement as well.
- If no such methodologies exist at the national level, contracting authorities may resort to existing methodologies developed by the market or by other governments; they may be used as such or adapted to the needs of the contracting authority. In any case, if a contracting authority chooses to apply a life-cycle cost approach in the award of a contract, it will, according to Article 68(2), be required to indicate in the procurement documents the data to be provided by the tenderers and the method which the contracting authority will use to determine the life-cycle costs on the basis of this data.
- Such methodologies are in conformity with the Directive, provided that the methods used for the assessment of costs imputed to environmental externalities are based on objectively verifiable and non-discriminatory criteria. In situations where such methodologies have not been established for repeated or continuous application, the principle is that they should not favor or disadvantage certain economic operators. A transparency obligation requires that the method should be accessible to all interested parties, and data required by contracting authorities for calculating LCC should be provided with reasonable effort by normally diligent economic operators, including economic operators from third countries party to the GPA or other international agreements by which the Union is bound (Article 68 (2)).

We consider that the mandatory use of a common methodology adopted at the EU level (or even at the national level) has the potential in the short term to encourage the use of LCC by contracting authorities. This can be achieved by limiting fragmentation and by increasing legal certainty in an already complicated field (Semple, 2012, p. 107). This is especially true for the Member States from Eastern Europe, whose institutions have low administrative capacities and less skilled procurement practitioners. However, in the long term and for governments that are more pro-active in this area, a common methodology is likely to prevent a contracting authority from using state-of-the-art approaches that would allow it to be more ambitious than the EU or national methodology. The usefulness of common EU methodologies will ultimately depend upon their quality (Semple, 2012, p. 107), but this is hard to assess at this moment since only one such methodology exists.

For certain contracts, an off-the-shelf LCC methodology, which adequately captures all internal and external costs, may not be available (either at the EU or another level). Under the existing provisions, it seems that contracting authorities can modify an existing methodology, and must strictly apply a pre-existing methodology only when it was adopted at the EU level. This means that contracting authorities may adopt their own methodologies as long as the European Commission (or the Member State that can supplement this absence internally) has not adopted one for a specific product or service. These methodologies may then be modified for the specific purpose of other tendering procedures, as they are not for repeated or continuous application.

A first conclusion is that this approach gives flexibility to contracting authorities, which is necessary in specific circumstances, but also may lead to abuses. The line between a methodology that is adapted to the needs of a specific procedure and one that is intended to favor a particular undertaking is a quite fine one. Such forbidden practices are hard to trace and remedy, because the right of undertakings to challenge the tender documentation is limited in time and the only option left for tenderers that did not challenge the methodology in due time is to play according to the rules already established. Moreover, it is difficult to state that a contracting authority has adopted a methodology that would favor one undertaking or another as long as this decision-making process is well within its discretion. The review performed by courts over this discretion will be not only technically challenging, but also a tough mission from a legal point of view.

For some contracts, the methodologies referred to above can be used as best practices or even incorporated into contracting authorities' operating manuals.

The European Commission has tried to develop, since 2015, a new LCC Tool, which includes direct costs (acquisition, use, maintenance and end-of-life costs) and indirect costs (environmental externalities as external costs). The tool initially assessed the four environmental impact categories: human health, ecosystems, resource availability and climate change. The relevant items of products' life cycle (e.g. electricity consumption) were first characterized by their resource/emission profile (using publicly available life-cycle inventory data) and then converted into environmental impacts applying a life-cycle impact assessment method (the method used in this tool is ReCiPe). Afterwards, the environmental impacts were converted into externalities applying monetization factors to the computed environmental impacts. However, the final version of the tool mentioned that there is still little consensus over the matter, especially for 'Human Health', 'Ecosystems' and 'Resources availability'. And thus,

> after further discussions and evaluations between the Commission and the project team, it was decided to take, at least for the first version of the tool, a cautious approach and use a monetization only for the impact category Climate Change. The calculations for the externalities Human Health, Ecosystems and Resources Availability were disabled.
>
> (Studio Fieschi & Soci srl and Scuola Superiore Sant'Anna, 2016)

The tool was expected to be delivered by 2016, but now the European Commission reports that the LCC calculation tools are delayed until the end of 2019 (European Commission, not dated).

Monitoring and performance clauses

During the performance of the contract, the supplier agrees to not exceed the life-cycle costs estimations of the contract. Penalties could also be applied if there are considerable deviations between the predicted LCC and the monitored one (Adell et al., 2009). One of the recommendations of the European Commission working group on LCC in construction is to use LCC after tendering in order evaluate and communicate the improvements of the purchased product in comparison to the current situation and/or other products and to communicate results (Estevan and Schaefer, 2017, p. 10).

Linking the LCC results with the contract performance clauses could be a possibility of reducing the risks associated to uncertainty. According to Lindholm and Suomala (2005), during the life cycle of a product, the focus of LCC should shift to cost monitoring and management so that at the end of a life cycle, the contracting authorities should have the complete cost history of a product tracked, reviewed and understood, thus enabling comparisons with original estimations. In this way, in time, the uncertainty of future analysis will be reduced.

However, in most of the cases, incurred costs and performance are not monitored adequately, the collected cost information is not analyzed systematically and comparison of actual costs with estimations are made only occasionally (Estevan and Schaefer, 2017, p. 33).

If a label was referred to during the tendering process, then the observance of the requirements of the label should be monitored during contract performance as well.

A combination of tools – life-cycle thinking?

As seen from above, there is no single stage of the procurement process where LCT is to be concentrated. Given the difficulties and challenges mentioned, a combination of tools could be one of the best solutions. LCC analysis would then be just one piece of a wider number of elements to take into account when preparing and evaluating a public procurement process. Environmental impacts, as well as social conditions or innovation could be other additional issues to take into account in the procurement process.

However, the practice of LCC is difficult to predict, as a crucial role will be played by the interpretation of the concept of 'normally diligent economic operator', against which the methodologies could be assessed, and this is subject to the discretion of the contracting authorities. Schebesta argues that the LCC approach, especially with regard to possible methodologies, is rather unspecified and unstructured and seems to legitimize a certain degree of experimentation with regard to public procurement (Schebesta, 2014, p. 135).

Sustainable versus cost-effective procurement

The central dilemma when using LCC in order to foster sustainable public procurement is whether the economic LCC results (thus without including the environmental impacts as externalities) point to an alternative that is not acceptable from an environmental point of view. In other words, 'whole-life costing methodology is necessary but not sufficient to guarantee sustainable procurement' (Westminster Sustainable Business Forum, 2008).

Several surveys across Europe suggest that greener products are perceived to be more expensive than non-green, conventional products (Adell et al., 2009). Procuring goods, services or works on the basis of life-cycle costing may mean paying more in the beginning (Min and Galle, 2001). In an ideal case, the higher initial price of the greener product is more than compensated by the much lower usage and disposal costs.

It has been argued that in developing countries, the production of sustainable and LCC-efficient goods and services is still emergent, which means that the only way to acquire sustainable alternatives will be through expensive imports or paying a very high cost premium to stimulate infant local industries. In lower income economies, this difference can be higher, as much as 10 to 50 percent (Perera et al., 2009, p. 3). The cited authors believe that over time, however, the large volumes demanded by public procurement contracts can make economies of scale more feasible, and the prices of these products can be expected to decrease as more producers enter the market. Also, public procurers can begin to use their strong market positioning to negotiate bulk discounts as the market begins to mature. In times of economic crisis, LCC may prove hard to be implemented effectively due to the existence of 'buy national' policies, given the fact that 'regular' public procurement gives preference to local companies over foreign suppliers (Brulhart and Trionfetti, 2004). Public authorities are more inclined to pursue sustainable procurement in contexts where they perceive win-win situations (Rao and Holt, 2005). It will be much harder to resort to the use of LCC and other sustainability tools when the outcomes are not very clear or documented properly, or fair competition concerns arise.

In conclusion, experiences show that LCC-efficient alternatives are not always the most environmentally and socially sustainable ones (Perera et al., 2009). While advocating the use of LCC in public procurement, one should keep in mind that the science behind LCC is far from perfect. Until now, LCC has been scarcely used in public procurement and studies show that it is not yet considered to be a critical component of sustainable public procurement worldwide (Perera et al., 2009, p. 3).

Final considerations

Once Einstein allegedly said that 'not everything that can be counted counts and not everything that counts can be counted'. This summarizes in a way the opportunities and challenges of LCC as a sustainability tool. However, LCC is only one element of LCT in public procurement – alternative routes such as the use of labels and technical specifications might be more effective in view of sustainability, as there are many sustainability considerations that are not easily monetized.

From the statistics presented in the report on LCC usage in the world, it emerges that the majority of procurers use LCC sometimes and only for some products, or rarely. Only 2 percent of the respondents confirmed that they are using LCC in all cases (UNEP, 2013, pp. 31–32).

In the EU, another study (Centre for European Policy Studies and College of Europe, 2012) showed that public authorities are still not frequently using (LCC) and Total Cost of Ownership (TCO) methods. The most commonly used award criterion was still the purchasing cost (64 percent), followed by a mix of the latter and LCC or TCO (30 percent); and finally, by the predominant use of LCC/TCO (6 percent) (2012, p. xv). In some countries, like Portugal and Romania, the use of LCC or TCO was still very limited, while Ireland was the country where LCC/TCO was most widespread. However, even in that case only 25 percent of respondents reported that they mostly make use of this evaluation criterion (2012, p. xvi).

It is quite evident that LCC was intended to be one of the pivotal elements of the new reform from 2014 and constitutes the core basis for LCT in public procurement (Dragos and Neamtu, 2014). The Procurement Directives are encouraging national governments to foster the use of sustainable public procurement and of LCC but they still rely in numerous situations on voluntary compliance. Due to legal uncertainties, especially in countries not used to the techniques of green procurement, contracting authorities choose not to implement LCC.

The administrative capacity is also a deterrent. Procurement professionals generally lack the skills and knowledge necessary to successfully implement LCT in procurement, LCC included. A recent report on LCC stresses that capacity building through permanent training and networking is needed to overcome the initial difficulties and complexities of applying LCC. Moreover, sharing experiences both within one organization and with other authorities is crucial for learning and exchanging best practices. In this way public procurers can stay in touch with the latest achievements and changes from the market (Estevan and Schaefer, 2017, p. 37).

In this context, the success of LCT in the future will heavily depend on the availability of methodologies prepared at EU or national levels for certain types of products in order to carry out LCC. Furthermore, the success of LCC will also depend on its scope (meaning the inclusion of environmental externalities and/or other externalities) and the methodology used, which in many cases is incomplete (Hochschorner and Noring, 2011) and based on experts' perceptions, not on hard scientific evidence (Korpi and Ala-Risku, 2008).

As an alternative, regulating certain environmental criteria as compulsory for some public procurements ensures that the result of the procurement process will fulfill a minimum environmental level, independently from the LCC results. Moreover, the final costs (and thus the LCC results) depend greatly on the tax policy, fees or subsidies of the different Member States, which are meant to foster sustainability.

One of the recurring deterrents in the application of LCC in public procurement is the fact that data in the public domain is often aggregated and incomplete, presented in different formats, thus making comparison and extrapolation difficult (Perera et al., 2009, p. 3). In addition to the lack of data, procurers in the public sector may also be confronted with high levels of uncertainty – for example due to fluctuations in commodity and electricity prices.

In the 2017 Life Cycle Costing: State of the Art Report, the numerous external factors that can affect enormously the outcomes of an LCC analysis are identified as well: market price variability of products and services; electricity, water and gas prices; taxes, subsidies and incentives; inflation, discount rate and other economic elements, and waste disposal regulations (Estevan and Schaefer, 2017, p. 37). Thus, the final result of an LCC can be highly dependent on these external factors, but this may be overcome by the establishment of a clear environmental policy, which can level out this variability, as well as other possible changes in the external conditions.

Another deterrent is that the public sector is often reluctant to embrace the multi-year accounting and budget frameworks that allow temporal flexibility to carry over or borrow against-the-future, a system that would encourage the payments based on life-cycle thinking. Also, in many instances the procuring agency is not the same as the agency that will operate/use the product/service (Perera et al., 2009, p. 1).

To end on an optimistic note, we believe that in the context of sustainable public procurement, LCT has the potential to become a very important element in the enterprise of shifting the paradigm beyond the confinement of the sole purchase price of a product. However, such an approach may be contested as representing interference with the 'good old reliable' judgment of value for money, especially during economic crises.

The 2014 Directives are a clear step forward towards advancing sustainability goals, at least in declaratory terms. Regardless, there is no sufficient empirical evidence that the tools envisaged by the new legal framework have brought more effectiveness or whether more decisive measures are necessary.

References

Adell, A., Esquerra, J., Estevan, H., Clement, S., Tepper, P., Acker, H. and Seebach, D. (2009) *Existing approaches to encourage innovation through procurement*, The SMART SPP consortium [Online]. Available at: www.smart-spp.eu/fileadmin/template/projects/smart_spp/files/SMART_SPP_D2.2_ExistingProcurementApproaches.pdf (Accessed: May 30, 2019).

Akenji, L. and Bengtsson, M. (2014) 'Making sustainable consumption and production the core of Sustainable Development Goals', *Sustainability*, 6(2), pp. 513–529.

Arnold, F.S. (1995) 'Why environmental life cycle assessment doesn't work', *Journal of Environmental Law and Practice*, 2(5), pp. 4–14.

Arnould, J. (2004) 'Secondary policies in public procurement: The innovations of the New Directive', *Public Procurement Law Review*, 13, pp. 187–197.

Arrowsmith, S. and Kunzlik, P. (eds.) (2009) *Social and environmental policies in EC procurement law*, Cambridge: Cambridge University Press.

Bratt, C., Hallstedt, S., Robert, K.-H., Broman, G. and Oldmark, J. (2011) 'Assessment of eco-labelling criteria development from a strategic sustainability perspective', *Journal of Cleaner Production*, 19(4), pp. 1631–1638.

Brulhart, M. and Trionfetti, F. (2004) 'Public expenditure, international specialisation and agglomeration', *European Economic Review*, 48, pp. 851–881.

Caranta, R. (2014) 'Sustainable procurement', in M. Trybus, R. Caranta and G. Edelstam (eds.), *European Union public contract law: Public procurement and beyond*, Brussels: Bruylant, pp. 165–190.

Caranta, R. and Trybus, M. (eds.) (2010) *The law of green and social procurement in Europe*, Copenhagen: DJOF Publishing.

Centre for European Policy Studies and College of Europe. (2012) *The uptake of green public procurement in the EU27* [Online]. Available at: http://ec.europa.eu/environment/gpp/pdf/CEPS-CoE-GPP%20MAIN%20REPORT.pdf (Accessed: May 30, 2019).

Cohen, M.A. and Vandenbergh, M.P. (2012) 'The potential role of carbon labeling in a green economy', *Energy Economics*, 34(S1), pp. S53–S63.

Council Regulation No. 880/92/EEC of 23 March 1992 on a Community eco-label award scheme, OJ: JOL_1992_099_R_0001_003.

Crespi, J.M. and Marette, S. (2005) 'Eco-labelling economics: Is public involvement necessary?', in S. Krarup and C.S. Russell (eds.), *Environment, information and consumer behaviour*, Northampton, MA: Edward Elgar, pp. 93–110.

Curran, M.A. (2016) 'Life-cycle assessment', in *Encyclopedia of Ecology*, 4, pp. 359–366.

Dalhammar, C. (2015) 'The application of "life cycle thinking" in European environmental law: Theory and practice', *Journal for European Environmental & Planning Law*, 12(2), pp. 97–127.

Danish Environmental Protection Agency. (2003) *An introduction to life-cycle thinking and management*, by A. Remmen and M. Munster [Online]. Available at: http://lca-center.dk/wp-content/uploads/2015/08/An-introduction-to-life-cycle-thinking-and-management.pdf (Accessed: May 30, 2019).

Directive 2014/25/EU of the European Parliament and of the Council of 26 February 2014 on procurement by entities operating in the water, energy, transport and postal services sectors and repealing Directive 2004/17/EC, *Official Journal L Series*, 94, 3.28.2014.

Directive 2014/24/EU of the European Parliament and of the Council of 26 February 2014 on public procurement and repealing Directive 2004/18/EC, *Official Journal L Series*, 94, 3.28.2014.

Directive 2014/23/EU of the European Parliament and of the Council of 26 February 2014 on the award of concession contracts, *Official Journal L Series*, 94, 3.28.2014.

Directive 2010/31/EU of the European Parliament and of the Council of 19 May 2010 on the energy performance of buildings, *Official Journal L Series*, 153, 6.18.2010.

Directive 2009/33/EC of the European Parliament and of the Council of 23 April 2009 on the promotion of clean and energy-efficient road transport vehicles, *Official Journal L Series*, 120, 5.15.2009.

Dragos, D. and Neamtu, B. (2015) 'Life cycle costing for sustainable public procurement in the European Union', in B. Sjåfjell and A. Wiesbrock (eds.), *Sustainable public procurement under EU law: New perspectives on the state as stakeholder*, Cambridge: Cambridge University Press, pp. 114–137.

Dragos, D. and Neamtu, B. (2014) 'Sustainable public procurement in the EU – Experience and prospects, in F. Lichere, R. Caranta and S. Treumer (eds.), *Modernising public procurement: The New Directive*, Copenhagen: DJOF Publishing, pp. 301–337.

Dragos, D. and Neamtu, B. (2013) 'Sustainable public procurement: Life cycle costing (LCC) in the new EU Directive proposal', *European Procurement & Public Private Partnership Law Review*, 8(1) pp. 19–30.

Ecolabel Index. (not dated) *Home* [Online]. Available at: www.ecolabelindex.com/ (Accessed: May 30, 2019).

Edler, J. and Georghiou, L. (2007) 'Public procurement and innovation: Resurrecting the demand side', *Research Policy*, 36, pp. 949–963.

Ekener, E., Hansson, J., Larsson, A. and Peck, P. (2018) 'Developing Life Cycle Sustainability Assessment methodology by applying values-based sustainability weighting – Tested on biomass based and fossil transportation fuels', *Journal of Cleaner Production*, 181, pp. 337–351.

Estevan, H. and Schaefer, B. (2017) *Life cycle costing. State of the art report*, ICLEI [Online]. Available at: www.sppregions.eu/fileadmin/user_upload/Life_Cycle_Costing_SoA_Report.pdf (Accessed: May 30, 2019).

Estevan, H., Schaefer, B. and Adell, A. (2018) *Life cycle costing. State of the art report*, ICLEI [Online]. Available at: file:///C:/Users/user/AppData/Local/Packages/Microsoft.MicrosoftEdge_8wekyb3d8bbwe/TempState/Downloads/Life%20Cycle%20Costing%20SoA%20Report%20(1).pdf (Accessed: May 30, 2019).

EUbusiness. (not dated) *EU Ecolabel: Background* [Online]. Available at: www. eubusiness.com/topics/environ/eu-ecolabel-1/ (Accessed: May 30, 2019).

European Commission. (2012) *International Reference Life Cycle Data System (ILCD) Handbook* [Online]. Available at: https://eplca.jrc.ec.europa.eu/uploads/ JRC-Reference-Report-ILCD-Handbook-Towards-more-sustainable-production-and-consumption-for-a-resource-efficient-Europe.pdf (Accessed: May 30, 2019).

European Commission. (2011a) *Buying green! A handbook on green public procurement*, Luxembourg: Publications Office of the European Union.

European Commission. (2011b) *Buying social: A guide to taking account of social considerations in public procurement* [Online]. Available at: https://publications.europa. eu/en/publication-detail/-/publication/cb70c481-0e29-4040-9be2-c408cddf081f/ language-en (Accessed: May 30, 2019).

European Commission. (2008) *Green public procurement and the European ecolabel*, Fact sheet [Online]. Available at: http://ec.europa.eu/environment/gpp/pdf/toolkit/ module1_factsheet_ecolabels.pdf (Accessed: May 30, 2019).

European Commission. (2003) *Integrated product policy: Building on environmental life-cycle thinking* [Online]. Available at: https://eur-lex.europa.eu/legal-content/ EN/TXT/PDF/?uri=CELEX:52003DC0302&from=EN (Accessed: May 30, 2019).

European Commission. (not dated) *Life-cycle costing* [Online]. Available at: http:// ec.europa.eu/environment/gpp/lcc.htm (Accessed: May 30, 2019).

European Platform on Life Cycle Assessment. (not dated) *Resources directory*. Available at: https://eplca.jrc.ec.europa.eu/ResourceDirectory/ (Accessed: May 30, 2019).

FAIRTRADE. (2015) *Fair trade labels* [Online]. Available at: www.vartotojai.lt/index. php?id=10343 (Accessed: May 30, 2019).

Fair Wear Foundation. (not dated) *Membership* [Online]. Available at: www.fairwear. org/about/membership/ (Accessed: May 30, 2019).

Fava, J. (2012) 'Framework for developing greener products', in A. Iannuzzi (ed.), *Greener products: The making and marketing of sustainable brands*. Boca Raton, FL: CRP Press, pp. 105–127.

Filimonau, V. (2016) *Life cycle assessment (LCA) and life cycle analysis in tourism. A critical review of applications and implications*, AG Switzerland: Springer.

Fisher, E. and Corbalán, S. (2013) 'Fair trade and European public procurement: legal principles and governance dynamics', *Social Enterprise Journal*, 9(1), pp. 11–27. Available at: https://doi.org/10.1108/17508611311329985.

Fuller, S. (2016) *Life cycle cost analysis (LCA)* [Online]. Available at: www.wbdg.org/ resources/life-cycle-cost-analysis-lcca (Accessed: May 30, 2019).

Gluch, P. and Baumann, H. (2004) 'The life cycle costing (LCC) approach: A conceptual discussion of its usefulness for environmental decision-making', *Building and Environment*, 39, pp. 571–580.

Guinée, J.B., Heijungs, R., Huppes, G., Zamagni, A., Masoni, P., Buonamici, R., Ekvall, T. and Rydberg, T. (2011) 'Life cycle assessment: Past, present and future', *Environmental Science & Technology*, 45(1), 90–96.

Gunningham, N. and Grabosky, P. (1998) *Smart regulation. Designing environmental policy*, New York: Oxford University Press.

Hobson, C. (2016) *Can the EU directive on public procurement encourage value-based procurement in healthcare?* [Online]. Available at: www.medtechviews.eu/article/can-eu-directive-public-procurement-encourage-value-based-procurement-healthcare (Accessed: May 30, 2019).

Hochschorner, E. and Noring, M. (2011) 'Practitioners' use of life cycle costing with environmental costs: A Swedish study', *International Journal of Life Cycle Assessment*, 16(9), pp. 897–902.

Hocking, M.B. (1991) 'Paper versus polystyrene: A complex choice', *Science*, 251(4993), pp. 504–505.

Hughes, R. (2017) 'The EU circular economy package: Life cycle thinking to life cycle law?', *Procedia CIRP*, 61, pp. 10–16.

Inden, T. (2018) 'Commentary to art. 68', in M. Steinike, and P. Vesterdorf (eds.), *Brussels commentary on EU public procurement law*, Munich: CH Beck, Hart, Nomos, p. 661.

ISO. (2006a) *ISO 14040: 2006. Environmental management – Life cycle assessment – Principles and framework*, Geneva, Switzerland: International Organization for Standardization.

ISO. (2006b) *ISO 14044: 2006. Environmental management – Life cycle assessment – Requirements and guidelines*, Geneva, Switzerland: International Organization for Standardization.

James, K. (2005) *A business guide to life cycle thinking and LCA* [Online]. Available at: www.helenlewisresearch.com.au/wp-content/uploads/2014/05/abusinessguideto lifecyclethinkingandlca.pdf (Accessed: May 30, 2019).

Karl, H. and Orwat, C. (1999) 'Environmental labelling in Europe: European and national tasks', *Environmental Policy and Government*, 9, pp. 212–220.

Keller, H., Rettenmaier, N. and Reinhardt, G.A. (2015) 'Integrated life cycle sustainability assessment: A practical approach applied to biorefineries', *Applied Energy*, 154, pp. 1072–1081.

Klöpffer, W. (2003) 'Life-cycle based methods for sustainable product development', *International Journal of Life Cycle Assessment*, 8(3), pp. 157– 159.

Koide, R. and Akenji, L. (2017) 'Assessment of policy integration of sustainable consumption and production into national policies', *Sustainability*, 6(4), 48.

Koroneos, C.J., Achillas, Ch., Moussiopoulos, N. and Nanaki, E.A. (2013) 'Life cycle thinking in the use of natural resources', *Open Environmental Sciences*, 2013, 7, pp. 1–6.

Korpi, E. and Ala-Risku, T. (2008) 'Life cycle costing: A review of published case studies', *Managerial Auditing Journal*, 23(3), pp. 240–261.

LCC Public Procurement Tool. (not dated) *When to use the tool* [Online]. Available at: http://tool.smart-spp.eu/smartspp-tool/registration/login.php (Accessed: May 30, 2019).

Lee, K.M. and Inaba, A. (2004) *Life cycle assessment. Best practices of ISO 14040 series* [Online]. Available at: www.apec.org/-/media/APEC/Publications/2004/2/Life-Cycle-Assessment-Best-Practices-of-International-Organization-for-Standardization-ISO-14040-Ser/04_cti_scsc_lca_rev.pdf (Accessed: May 30, 2019).

Life Cycle Initiative. (not dated) *Life cycle management* [Online]. Available at: www.lifecycleinitiative.org/starting-life-cycle-thinking/life-cycle-approaches/life-cycle-management/ (Accessed: May 30, 2019).

Lindholm, A. and Suomala, P. (2005) 'Present and future of life cycle costing: Reflections from Finnish companies', *Finnish Journal of Business Economics*, 2, pp. 282–292.

Min, H. and Galle, W.P. (2001) 'Green purchasing practices of US firms', *International Journal of Operations & Production Management*, 21(9), pp. 1222–1238.

Muralikrishna, I.V. and Manickam, V. (2017) *Environmental management: Science and engineering for industry*, Oxford: Butterworth-Heinemann.

Neamtu, B. and Dragos, D. (2015) 'Sustainable public procurement: The use of eco labels', *European Procurement and PPP Law Review*, 10(2), pp. 92–101.

Nygren, J. and Antikainen, R. (2010) *Use of life cycle assessment (LCA) in global companies*, Finnish Environment Institute [Online]. Available at: https://helda. helsinki.fi/bitstream/handle/10138/39723/SYKEre_16_2010.pdf?sequence=1 (Accessed: May 30, 2019).

OECD. (2011) *Environmental taxation. A guide for policy makers* [Online]. Available at: www.oecd.org/environment/tools-evaluation/48164926.pdf (Accessed: May 30, 2019).

OECD. (2008) *Key Environmental Indicators* [Online]. Available at: www.oecd.org/env/indicators-modelling-outlooks/37551205.pdf (Accessed: May 30, 2019).

Pelletier, N. (2015) 'Life cycle thinking, measurement and management for food system sustainability', *Environmental Science & Technology*, 49(13), pp. 7515–7519.

Perera, O., Morton, B. and Perfrement, T. (2009) 'Life cycle costing in sustainable public procurement: A question of value. A white paper from IISD', International Institute for Sustainable Development (IISD) [Online]. Available at: www.iisd.org/pdf/2009/life_cycle_costing.pdf (Accessed: May 30, 2019).

Quantis. (not dated) *Looking through a systemic lens* [Online]. Available at: https://quantisintl.com/metrics/frameworks/life-cycle-thinking/ (Accessed: May 30, 2019).

Rao, P. and Holt, D. (2005) 'Do green supply chains lead to competitiveness and economic performance?', *International Journal of Operations & Production Management*, 25(9), pp. 898–916.

Regulation (EC) No. 66/2010 of the European Parliament and of the Council of 25 November 2009 on the EU Ecolabel [2010] *Official Journal L Series*, 27(1), 1.30.2010.

Regulation (EC) No. 106/2008 of the European Parliament and of the Council of 15 January 2008 on a Community energy-efficiency labelling programme for office equipment, *Official Journal L Series*, 39, 2.13.2008.

Rete Italiana LCA. (not dated) *The 12th Italian LCA Network Conference* [Online]. Available at: www.reteitalianalca.it/attivita/organizzazione-convegni/new-the-italian-lca-network-conference-2018-university-of-messina (Accessed: May 30, 2019).

Rubik, F., Scheer, D., Stø, E. and Strandbakken, P. (2005) 'Background: Theoretical contributions, eco-labels and environmental policy', in F. Rubik and P. Frankl (eds.), *The future of eco-labelling: Making environmental product information systems more effective*, Sheffield: Greenleaf Publishing, pp. 16–45.

Sabapathy, J. (2007) *Sustainable production and consumption: A business premier* [Online]. Available at: www.cisl.cam.ac.uk/resources/publication-pdfs/sustainable-consumption.pdf (Accessed: May 30, 2019).

Schau, E., Traverso, M., Lehmann, A. and Finkbeiner, M. (2011) 'Life cycle costing in sustainability assessment: A case study of remanufactured alternators', *Sustainability*, 3(11), pp. 2268–2288.

Schebesta, H. (2014) 'EU green public procurement policy: Modernisation package, eco-labelling and framing measures', in S. Schoenmaekers, W. Devroe and N. Philipsen (eds.), *State aid and public procurement in the European Union*, Cambridge/Antwerp/Portland: Intersentia, pp. 129–144.

Semple, A. (2012) 'Mixed offerings for sustainability in a new European Union Procurement Directive', *Public Procurement Law Review*, 21, pp. 106–108.

Semple, A. (not dated) *New EU procurement directives and SPP: Opening the floodgates?* [Online] available at http://archive.sustainable-procurement.org/newsroom/special-features/new-eu-procurement-directives-and-spp-opening-the-floodgates/ (Accessed: May 30, 2019).

Sigma. (2016) *Brief 30: 2014 EU Directives: Public Sector and Utilities Procurement* [Online]. Available at: www.sigmaweb.org/publications/Public-Procurement-Policy-Brief-30-200117.pdf (Accessed: May 30, 2019).

Smart SPP. (not dated) *Tool for calculating life-cycle costs and CO_2 emissions* [Online]. Available at: www.smart-spp.eu/index.php?id=7633 (Accessed: May 30, 2019).

Social Accountability International. (not dated) *SA8000® Standard* [Online]. Available at: www.sa-intl.org/index.cfm?fuseaction=Page.ViewPage&pageId=1689 (Accessed: May 30, 2019).

Sonnemann, G., Gemechu, E.D., Sala, S., Schau, E.M., Allacker, K., Pant, R., Adibi, N. and Valdivia, S. (2018) 'Life cycle thinking and the use of LCA in policies around the world', in M. Hauschild, R. Rosenbaum and S. Olsen (eds.), *Life Cycle Assessment*. Cham: Springer, pp. 429–463.

Stavropoulos, P., Giannoulis, C., Papacharalampopoulos, A., Foteinopoulos, P. and Chryssolouris, G. (2016) 'Life cycle analysis: Comparison between different methods and optimization challenges', *Procedia CIRP*, 41, pp. 626–631.

Stripple, H. (2013) Life Cycle Assessment (LCA) and Life Cycle Cost (LCC) evaluation of Rockdrain and a conventional tunnel drainage system [Online]. Available at: www.ivl.se/download/18.343dc99d14e8bb0f58b763f/1449742836097/B2067.pdf (Accessed: May 30, 2019).

Studio Fieschi & Soci srl and Scuola Superiore Sant'Anna. (2016) Update on Life Cycle Costing (LCC) project [Online]. Available at: http://ec.europa.eu/environment/gpp/pdf/20_04_2016/6_LCC_Tool.pdf (Accessed: May 30, 2019).

Swedish National Agency for Public Procurement. (not dated) *Sustainability criteria* [Online]. Available at: www.upphandlingsmyndigheten.se/en/sustainable-public-procurement/sustainable-procurement-criteria/ (Accessed: May 30, 2019).

Symposium on Sustainable Consumption. (1994: Oslo, Norway) & Ofstad, Sylvi & Norway. Miljøverndepartmentet 1994, *Symposium: Sustainable consumption, 19–20 January 1994, Oslo, Norway*, Oslo: Ministry of Environment.

UNCED. (1992) *Rio Declaration Principle 8: Reduction of unsustainable patterns of production and consumption* [Online]. Available at: www.unesco.org/education/pdf/RIO_E.PDF (Accessed: May 30, 2019).

UNEP. (2013) *Sustainable public procurement: A global review* [Online]. Available at: https://globalecolabelling.net/assets/Documents/unep-spp-report.pdf (Accessed: May 30, 2019).

UNEP. (2012a) *Greening the economy through life cycle thinking: Ten years of the UNEP/SETAC life cycle initiative* [Online]. Available at: www.unep.fr/shared/publications/pdf/DTIx1536xPA-GreeningEconomythroughLifeCycleThinking.pdf (Accessed: May 30, 2019).

UNEP. (2012b) Global outlook on SCP policies: Taking action together [Online]. Available at: www.unep.fr/shared/publications/pdf/DTIx1387xPA-GlobalOutlookonSCPPolicies.pdf (Accessed: May 30, 2019).

UNEP. (2011) *Towards a green economy: Pathways to sustainable development and poverty eradication – A Synthesis for Policy Makers* [Online]. Available at: https://sustainabledevelopment.un.org/content/documents/126GER_synthesis_en.pdf (Accessed: May 30, 2019).

UNEP. (2010) *Green economy developing countries success stories* [Online]. Available at: www.minambiente.it/sites/default/files/archivio/allegati/rio_20/unep_developing_countries_success_stories_eng.pdf (Accessed: May 30, 2019).

UNEP/SETAC. (2004) *Why take a life cycle approach* [Online]. Available at: www.unep.fr/shared/publications/pdf/DTIx0585xPA-WhyLifeCycleEN.pdf (Accessed: May 30, 2019).

United Nations. (2015) *Transforming our world: The 2030 Agenda for Sustainable Development A/RES/70/1* [Online]. Available at: www.un.org/ga/search/view_doc.asp?symbol=A/RES/70/1&Lang=E (Accessed: May 30, 2019).

United Nations. (2002) *World Summit on Sustainable Development Johannesburg, South Africa 26 August–4 September 2002. Draft plan of implementation of the World Summit on Sustainable Development* [Online]. Available at: www.un.org/ga/search/view_doc.asp?symbol=A/CONF.199/L.1&Lang=E (Accessed: May 30, 2019).

UNOPS. (2009) *A guide to environmental labels – for procurement practitioners of the United Nations system* [Online]. Available at: www.ungm.org/Areas/Public/Downloads/Env_Labels_Guide.pdf (Accessed: May 30, 2019).

Verma, S. (2015) 'Life cycle costing in defense acquisition: The challenges of transforming complex aspirations into factual ground realities', *Trade, Law and Development*, 7(1), pp. 120–136.

Westminster Sustainable Business Forum. (2008) *Costing the future: Securing value for money through sustainable procurement* [Online]. Available at: www.policyconnect.org.uk/wsbf/sites/site_wsbf/files/report/370/fieldreportdownload/costingthefuture.pdf (Accessed: May 30, 2019).

3 LCC and GPP

Competing or complementary approaches?

Áurea Adell Querol, Bettina Schaefer and Josep Esquerrà i Roig

Introduction

The use of life-cycle costing (LCC) in public procurement is not a new idea. However, in recent years LCC has become more prominent in the framework of sustainable public procurement, and green procurement advocates are promoting its use for its potential to foster the acquisition of "green" solutions.

The rationale is that green solutions have higher acquisition costs (are more expensive upfront), which is a barrier to their procurement, but their green attributes – in terms of higher durability, lower resources consumption during use, lower disposal costs, etc. – can offset those upfront higher prices when considering costs during the whole life of the solution. That could be even more so if the costs of externalities, that is, of environmental and social impacts during the whole life of the "green" solution, are included in the calculations. Unfortunately, that is not always the case (neither before nor after adding externality costs).

LCC can be a useful tool for Green Public Procurement (GPP) if the costs savings during the "product" lifespan compensate the price premiums linked to the green alternatives or if there is a validated correlation between low life-cycle costs and low environmental impact. If that cannot be guaranteed, other measures have to be put in place to ensure a green output.

This chapter, in line with a previous paper tries to briefly present the environmental dimension in LCC and aspects to consider when using LCC to ensure that it does not compete but rather complements GPP.

LCC in public procurement

The use of life-cycle costing or life-cycle cost assessment in public procurement is not a recent idea. Already in the 1960s the Department of Defence of the US Government applied LCC in the procurement of military equipment (Epstein 1996) as they found that acquisition costs only accounted for a small part of the total costs of weapon systems, while operation and support costs represented up to two-thirds of overall costs (Asiedu and Gu 1998).

LCC is a method of calculating the costs of products, services or works (hereafter "products") throughout their life cycle. This allows for visualising "hidden" costs beyond the acquisition price and brings them into the procurement decision-making process to foster the cost-effectiveness of the procurement.

The EU recognises its value and has included it in the latest Directive on public procurement, Directive 2014/24/EU (hereafter Procurement Directive[1]) as one of the approaches to determine the "*most economically advantageous tender*" (our emphasis) in combination with other quality, environmental and/ or social criteria, whenever relevant:

Article 67. Contract award criteria

1. *Without prejudice to national laws, regulations or administrative provisions concerning the price of certain supplies or the remuneration of certain services, contracting authorities shall base the award of public contracts on the most economically advantageous tender.*
2. *The most economically advantageous tender from the point of view of the contracting authority shall be identified on the basis of the price or cost, using a cost-effectiveness approach, <u>such as life-cycle costing</u> in accordance with Article 68, and may include the best price-quality ratio, which shall be assessed on the basis of criteria, including qualitative, environmental and/or social aspects, linked to the subject-matter of the public contract in question. [...]*

According to the Procurement Directive, Article 68, and applying the terminology used in ISO 20400 on Sustainable Procurement, LCC can cover:

*   The total cost of ownership (TCO) of the product, service or work, as well as
*   The costs imputed to environmental externalities generated during their whole life cycle, that is from its research and development to resources extraction or generation, production, trading, transport, use, maintenance and end-of-life or service management (as defined in Article 2 of the Procurement Directive).

Article 68. Life-cycle costing

1. *Life-cycle costing shall to the extent relevant cover parts or all of the following costs over the life cycle of a product, service or works:*
    (a) costs, borne by the contracting authority or other users, such as:
        (i) costs relating to acquisition,
        (ii) costs of use, such as consumption of energy and other resources,

(iii) *maintenance costs,*

(iv) *end of life costs, such as collection and recycling costs.*

(b) *costs imputed to environmental externalities linked to the product, service or works during its life cycle, provided their monetary value can be determined and verified; such costs may include the cost of emissions of greenhouse gases and of other pollutant emissions and other climate change mitigation costs.*

In practice, introducing LCC in the tendering process might not only affect the financial part of the awarding criteria, but the whole awarding structure of the tender. According to the new *User Guide to the LCC Tool for Green Public Procurement of Computers and Monitors* of the European Commission (Ecoinstitut and ICLEI, 2019) when using LCC as an award criterion, all aspects included in the LCC calculation should not be duplicated elsewhere in the award criteria. In the procurement of computers, for example, given that they are energy-consuming products, operational costs based on energy consumption will be included in the LCC and thus considered as part of the cost award criterion. Therefore, energy consumption of computers should not be duplicated elsewhere in the award criteria; what could be done, however, is to define minimum energy efficiency specifications in combination with LCC for the awarding phase. This is important when analysing if LCC is the best approach to fostering green public procurement (GPP) or not.

However, that is not the only stage in a procurement process when LCC can be applied. LCC can be used at different stages (Ecoinstitut and ICLEI 2019):

- **Before tendering**: To assess the LCC of the current situation and evaluate different solutions to narrow down options or to help guide pre-tendering market engagement activities.
- **During tendering**: To compare offers during the evaluation and award of contracts, as long as the conditions set in the Procurement Directive are met.
- **After tendering**: To evaluate the performance of the awarded solution in comparison to the previous situation or other offers, to monitor and communicate results and to help prepare future tenders.

The environmental dimension of LCC

The environment in "internal" costs

The first approaches to LCC were purely economic, more in line with the concept of TCO, thus focused on analysing "internal" costs, that is, costs borne directly by any of the actors in the "product" life cycle (be it the producer, supplier, procurer, user/beneficiary, end-of-life manager) such as production, acquisition, operation, maintenance or end-of-life costs (Rebitzer and Hunkeler 2003). As Gluch and Baumann (2004, p.571) emphasise "*[...]* *"traditional" LCC does not become an environmental accounting tool just because it contains the words* life cycle".

However, certain environmental attributes of "products" can influence "internal" life-cycle costs in favour of greener solutions. This is one of the reasons why LCC is being promoted by green procurement advocates. Green solutions might have higher acquisition costs (be more expensive upfront), which is a barrier to their procurement, but their green attributes – in terms of higher durability, lower resources consumption during use, lower disposal costs, etc. – could offset those higher upfront prices when considering costs during their whole lifespan, thus, achieving both financial savings as well as reductions in the environmental impacts. In those cases, LCC can be a complementary approach to support green public procurement; but that is not always the case.

For example, in 2013 the Montréal Transport Society (STM) conducted a study to evaluate the possibility of acquiring 11 electric rail tractor units to replace the existing diesel ones which were reaching the end of their lifespan. Many different benefits were expected in terms of: reduction of the immobilisation rate, increase in productivity, improvement of work conditions, reduction of pollutants emissions, etc. In the pre-tendering study, STM analysed the total cost of ownership of the two options, taking into consideration acquisition costs, energy consumption costs, maintenance costs, associated costs (for managing the technology shift, infrastructure changes, training) and financial elements (such as the lifespan of the different solutions, subsidies and grants, etc.). Data and estimates were obtained from STM's departments as well as preliminary market consultations with manufacturers. The results for a planning horizon of 60 years are shown in Figure 3.1:

The positive results of the study (an estimated saving of CAD 25 million in 60 years) resulted in a call for tenders in 2016 for the acquisition of 17 electric rail tractor units. In the tendering process the final acquisition costs of the electric units were lower than initially estimated, being even lower than those for diesel units (Devault and Malouin 2018).

The environment in "external" costs

The environmental component of LCC was made explicit when the scope of the methodology broadened to include not only "internal" costs but also "external" costs or costs of externalities in an attempt to internalise in the economic system the effects on the environment of "products". "External" costs are the costs of the monetised effects of environmental impacts that a "product" causes during its production, use or handling but for which no one is directly paying (Rebitzer and Hunkeler 2003).

When considering externalities in LCC, the Procurement Directive, Article 68, establishes certain conditions to ensure transparency, equal treatment,

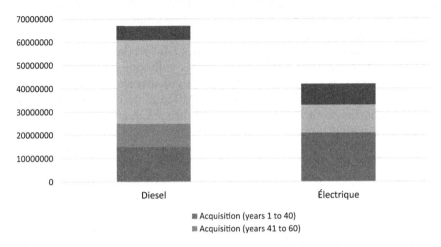

Figure 3.1 Total cost of ownership during 60 years for 11 rail tractor units.
Source: Devault and Malouin (2018).

non-discrimination and objectivity in the method to quantify and monetise impacts; and makes it compulsory to use common LCC methods if defined as mandatory in other EU regulations. The only common method listed so far is the one defined in Directive 2009/33/EC[2] on the promotion of clean and energy-efficient road transport vehicles (known as the Clean Vehicles Directive).[3]

However, the evaluation of environmental impacts and its translation into monetary terms is not an easy task. For example, in 2014 the European Commission launched a first tender for the development of an LCC tool to promote the use of LCC in public procurement and to contribute towards a common methodology to use in LCC.[4] The tool had to include both "internal" and "external" costs and be designed for energy-using products, namely IT equipment, office and street lighting, white goods, vending machines and electrical medical equipment.

The tool initially assessed four environmental impact categories: human health, ecosystem, resource availability and climate change. However, taking into consideration the sensitive nature of monetisation, the little consensus over the matter, especially for three of the four impact categories assessed (namely Human Health, Ecosystems and Resources availability), and other methodology limitations (Studio Fieschi et al. 2016), it was agreed that the proposed method for the evaluation and monetisation of externalities was not robust enough to meet the requirements of Article 68 of the Procurement Directive and that the tool should perform calculations only for the impact category Climate Change and only related to the use phase of products (Pretato and Rillo 2016).

This approach has been maintained in the follow-up of the LCC Tool project and, in the second tender for the development of LCC tools for use in GPP, the EC reiterates that:

> *The tool should mainly look at elements linked with the phase of ownership of the product by the contracting authority, thus not covering the whole life cycle of a product because of the difficulties to account for the early stages of the life cycle.* (our emphasis)[5]

So the tools will consider only the impact category of Climate Change and only related to the use phase of products, as in the previous tool.

However, even in those cases where externalities are monetised, it does not guarantee the selection of a greener option, as shown in the examples below. In those cases, the use of LCC in a tendering process might hinder rather than foster the selection of a greener option, which could have been achieved if the environmental criteria included in the LCC had been considered as independent award criteria and not as part of it.

For example, in order to test the effectiveness of the methodology of the Clean Vehicles Directive (Directive 2009/33/EC) to promote the purchase of cleaner vehicles, that is, energy-efficient vehicles with lower pollutants emissions, the authors used the Clean Fleets LCC calculator to compare the life-cycle costs of two small cars, one diesel and one electric. The LCC included acquisition costs, fuel consumption costs, maintenance costs and externality costs – operational lifetime costs monetised according to the Clean Vehicles Directive. Based on average market data for Spain, the results when comparing a small diesel car with the equivalent electric version are shown in Figure 3.2 below. Even though the electric vehicle has lower maintenance

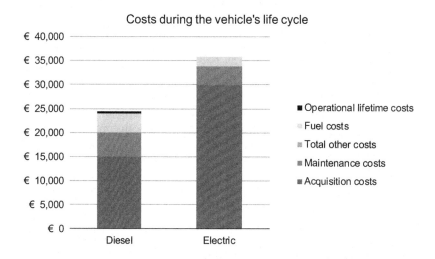

Figure 3.2 LCC comparison of a diesel and an electric small car over 8 years.

Table 3.1 Procedure results for the financial score of received offers

	Supplier 1	*Supplier 2*	*Supplier 3*	*Supplier 4*
Mini cars				
Car cost	8297.38	10064.76	9526.01	8821.76
Fuel cost	5724.18	4336.50	4336.50	5463.99
Maintenance cost	5884.29	4765.62	4892.03	3373.95
Ecological cost	298.83	232.72	232.72	552.03
Cost for 18 vehicles	20204.68	19399.60	18987.26	18211.73
Small cars				
Car cost	10467.55	11687.76	10331.21	10583.76
Fuel cost	8920.80	6442.80	6442.80	8920.80
Maintenance cost	6769.99	3954.39	5152.40	3381.51
Ecological cost	447.90	358.60	357.58	631.21
Cost for 18 vehicles	26606.24	22443.55	22283.99	23517.28
Score				
Financial score (max.50)	44.2	48.6	49.5	50
Rank considering the other awarding criteria	4	1	2	3

Note: Values are in Euros.

and operational costs, these are not enough to compensate the higher pur-chasing costs, not even after including the externalities associated to the CO_2 and other pollutants emissions during the use phase, as they only account for less than 2 per cent of the overall costs (Adell 2018).

In the case of an actual procurement by the city of Niort, France, results were similar. Niort has a car procurement strategy that includes the use of LCC in the procurement process. In a call for tenders for the procurement of 18 mini cars and seven small cars, the administration used LCC to cal-culate the financial score of offers. The LCC included acquisition costs, fuel consumption costs, maintenance costs and externality costs (monetised according to the Clean Vehicles Directive). The results are shown in Table 3.1. Based on all awarding criteria, supplier 2 was awarded the con-tract. However, if only LCC results would have been used to award the contract, the awarded supplier would have been supplier 4, which had the second highest fuel costs and proposed the more polluting vehicles (highest ecological costs) (Tarris 2016).

Directive 2009/33/EC on the promotion of clean and energy-efficient road transport vehicles obliges Member States to consider the energy consumption and gas emissions (namely CO_2, NO_x, NMHC and particulate matter) during use when purchasing road transport vehicles. This requirement can be fulfilled by setting, for each of those elements, technical specifications or by including them as award criteria (as such or through their monetisation using the meth-odology and impacts monetisation factors provided in the Directive).

In 2015, a report evaluating the implementation and results of the Directive was published. In it the authors highlighted the lack of coherence of the regulation with respect to air quality policies and with the objective of the 2011 Transport White Paper to phase out conventionally fuelled cars, given that the use of the monetisation methodology in procurement results in the selection of diesel vehicles, whose use can be detrimental to air quality objectives (Brannigan et al. 2015).

In 2017, a review of the Directive was proposed in which the mandatory use of a common LCC methodology was removed, though still encouraged, and a more effective approach for clean vehicles procurement was proposed by clearly defining what qualifies as a clean vehicle and setting minimum clean vehicle procurement targets, in the form of a minimum share of vehicles below defined emissions thresholds (CO_2 and air pollutant emissions) for light duty vehicles, and a share of alternative fuel vehicles for heavy duty vehicles.

As stated in the proposal:

> Setting minimum procurement targets can effectively reach the objective of impacting market uptake of clean vehicles in comparison to relying on the internalisation of external cost into overall procurement decisions, while noting the relevance to consider environmental aspects in all procurement decisions.
>
> (European Commission 2017a)

In fact, the externalities component of LCC is seldom included in existing LCC tools for procurement developed in the European Union (Table 3.2), and when included, it refers only to the impact during operation rather during the whole life cycle of the "product".

Challenges and solutions from a GPP perspective

As several EU studies show, LCC and TCO methods are still seldom used in tendering processes and purchasing costs are still the main criteria when evaluating costs in tendering procedures (PricewaterhouseCoopers, Significant and Ecofys 2009; Centre for European Policy Studies and College of Europe 2012). When analysing it worldwide, results are quite similar (United Nations Environment Programme 2013). However, as a recent survey shows, LCC is one of the topics becoming more prominent in respondents' organisations and this may increase in the future although its use is not without challenges (United Nations Environment Programme 2017).

Some of the challenges relate to the methodology itself in relation to complexity, lack of knowledge and basic data, etc. When considering the use of LCC to support the procurement of environmentally friendlier "products", additional aspects have to be taken into consideration to avoid making LCC a competing rather than a complementing tool.

Table 3.2 Existing LCC tool for public procurement in the European Union

Tool	Categories covered	Monetised externalities included
European Commission LCC tool	Office IT equipment Indoor and outdoor lighting Household appliances Vending machines Electrical medical equipment	CO_2 during operation
Danish Environmental Protection Agency TCO calculators	Office IT equipment Vending machines Bulbs and lighting systems Refrigerators and freezers Bidet toilet seats	No
Swedish National Agency for Public Procurement LCC tool	General tool Vehicles Indoor and outdoor lighting Household appliances Vending machines Professional fridges and freezers	No
German Federal Environmental Agency LCC tool	Office IT equipment Data centres Household appliances Flooring	No
Latvian Ministry of Environmental Protection and Regional Development LCC tool	Office IT equipment Light bulbs Household appliances	No
SMART-SPP EU project LCC-CO2 tool	General tool	No
Buy Smart EU project costing tool	Office IT equipment Vehicles Lighting Household appliances Electricity	No
Clean Fleets EU project LCC tool	Vehicles	CO_2, NOx, NMHC and particulate matter during operation

In this section we present some of the main ones in relation to GPP, and the possible approaches for dealing with them, expanding on information already gathered in a previous publication by the authors (Estevan and Schaefer 2017).

General lack of knowledge and perceived difficulty to apply LCC

The lack of knowledge and perceived complexity and difficulty to apply LCC by procurement practitioners and other users is one of the challenges reported in many LCC-related studies and reports (Gluch and Baumann 2004; Perera et al. 2009; Hochschorner and Noring 2011; Brannigan et al. 2015; SPP Regions: LCC Workshop 2016).

Regular training, information exchange, support services, working groups and community of practices are key to overcoming these initial and recurring difficulties. The use in the pre-tendering/planning phase, instead of in the actual call for tenders, was also mentioned as a way to mitigate some of the difficulties in applying LCC (SPP Regions: LCC Workshop 2016).

For example, within the Study Group on sustainable procurement of the French government (*Groupe d'étude des marchés du développement durable et de l'environnement (GEM-DD)*), a working group was established to discuss about its use, given the explicit mention in the Procurement Directive, and try to clarify this approach and the differences and complementarities with already existing concepts and practices (Ministère de la Transition écologique et solidaire 2017).

Similarly, the Forum on Sustainable Procurement, a platform promoted by the Danish Government to promote sustainable procurement amongst both public and private professional buyers, established a working group on the topic of TCO to provide information and practical experience exchange amongst participants (Forum for Bæredygtige Indkøb n.d.a).

Lack of standards and data availability, especially for some environmental aspects

One of the steps when planning to conduct LCC is to identify, on the one hand, the specific standard analysis parameters for the LCC, and on the other, the cost drivers of the "product" to be purchased and the parameters to transform them in costs, as this information will have to be required in the procurement process.

However, the availability and reliability of some of this data is one of the main challenges to LCC (Perera et al. 2009; Adell et al. 2009; UNEP-SETAC 2011; Hochschorner and Noring 2011). This is especially true for certain environmental cost drivers that often cannot be transformed into reliable, objective, measurable and verifiable cost parameters.

For example, the European Commission is developing a set of LCC tools to be used in conjunction with the EU GPP criteria, one of which is for computers and monitors. When analysing the different cost drivers to include in the tool, criteria related to energy consumption and durability and performance of the equipment were identified as relevant cost drivers.

Energy-efficient equipment consumes less energy compared to an equivalent non-efficient product, contributing to lower operational costs and avoiding environmental impacts due to energy savings. Products with higher performance and durability are expected to have a longer useful life. The longer that equipment can be used, the longer it will be before it needs replacing, thus life-cycle costs will be lower; and so will the environmental impact in terms of the use of natural resources and waste generation. For energy, the Energy Star is the most widespread standard to estimate energy consumption (in kWh/year), which can easily be transformed into costs with the energy price of the contracting authority. However, for durability, even though there are standards to test it (in terms of resistance to fall, vibrations, etc.), there are no standards or agreed references to transform those qualities into an expected longer lifespan, which is the parameter needed for LCC. Therefore, durability and performance considerations have not been included in the LCC Tool. Nevertheless, these aspects are important for the overall environmental impact of IT equipment and should be included in the tender as technical specifications or award criteria (Ecoinstitut and ICLEI 2019).

When using LCC estimations in the planning phase, authorities can be more flexible and accept a certain degree of inaccuracy as long as the level of uncertainty is acceptable, given that those estimations are for solutions or technology selection rather than to compare specific "products". However, when used in a tendering process, the main procurement principles must be observed and robustness of LCC parameters is required.

If that cannot be guaranteed for relevant environmental cost drivers, authorities should ensure that they are still considered as either technical specifications or independent award criteria outside the LCC. Environmental ecolabels and existing GPP criteria should be used as sources, as has been done so far.

Inherent deficiencies of environmental externalities evaluation and monetisation

The internalisation of externalities is a way to consider environmental aspects beyond those related to the usual LCC elements of operational, maintenance and end-of-life costs. However, the conversion of environmental impacts into a monetary dimension has several deficiencies due to the methodologies themselves. For example, environmental impact estimations are always an oversimplification of reality (e.g. synergy effects are rarely considered) and existing impacts and costing methodologies still fail to incorporate certain environmental impacts such as the irreversible changes or consequences in life, habitats or ecosystems, unknown future environmental problems and costs, or how to deal with items without the owner (Gluch and Baumann 2004).

On the other hand, requiring full life-cycle assessments or environmental product declarations with the estimated cradle-to-grave environmental impacts of "products" to monetise them afterwards, might not fulfil condition (c) of Article 68 of the Procurement Directive: "(c) the data required can be provided with reasonable effort by normally diligent economic operators, including economic operators from third countries party to the GPA or other international agreements by which the Union is bound".

However, even if we were to overlook these aspects and accept a high degree of uncertainty, the monetisation of externalities might not support the selection of greener products, as shown in the examples for clean vehicles presented before.

Therefore, public authorities should evaluate in the pre-tendering phase if the LCC, including externalities, will support the selection of greener options or not. If the weight of externality costs is too low in comparison to the other cost elements, it might be wiser to consider them outside the LCC either as technical specifications or as award criteria, to better reflect the relevance of the environmental dimension for the authority.

Most environmental versus most cost-efficient results

Finally, as reflected in the report Costing the future: Securing value for money through sustainable procurement (Westminster Sustainable Business Forum 2008, p.23):

> [...] *whole-life costing is primarily an economic tool and that, while it may have positive implications for sustainable procurement, it is not a panacea. As such the application of whole-life costing methodology is necessary but not sufficient to guarantee sustainable procurement.* (our emphasis)

As a management tool, LCC allows unveiling and being aware of all expenses associated to a "product". Therefore, its estimation – at least with the scope of total costs of ownership – should be standard practice from a management and planning point of view. However, cost-effectiveness should not be the only guiding principle. As stated in the European Commission's public procurement strategy (European Commission 2017c), a substantial part of public investment is spent through public procurement and authorities should lever this more strategically to obtain better value for euro spent and contribute to a more innovative, sustainable, inclusive and competitive economy, given that Europeans expect a fair return on their taxes in the form of high-quality public services. This is also expressed in several paragraphs of the Procurement Directive preamble.

As a market driver and key actor in achieving sustainable development goals, public authorities need to ensure that their decisions pull in the right direction even if it means a cost premium.

LCC can be a useful tool if the costs savings during the "product" lifespan compensate the price premiums linked to the green alternatives (Perera et al. 2009) or if there is a validated correlation between low life-cycle costs and low environmental impact (Rebitzer and Hunkeler 2003). If that cannot be guaranteed, the best solution, is to define environmental technical specifications strict enough to ensure a green result and use LCC (with or without externalities) as an economic award criterion to select amongst already green alternatives. This is also recommended in all the TCO guides produced by the Danish environmental protection agency.

For example, in 2012, the Danish national procurement agency (SKI) tendered a framework agreement for the supply of computers to 40 Danish municipalities. In the tender, SKI defined minimum compulsory environmental requirements based on the green procurement guidelines of the Danish environmental protection agency, to ensure a minimum environmental quality of computers (Forum for Bæredygtige Indkøb n.d.b, 2018). For the evaluation of the economic offer, SKI evaluated offers based on estimated TCO considering acquisition costs as well as operational costs linked to energy consumption (based on "on", "standby" and "off" energy consumption according to the Energy Star standard) for a period of three years, which is the typical average lifetime for computers according to the Danish environmental protection agency (Miljøstyrelsen 2016). The combination of the compulsory energy efficiency requirements in the technical specifications and the TCO evaluation ensure competition amongst the most energy-efficient products in the market.

Also in 2012, the City of Rotterdam published a tender for the procurement of lighting fixtures for the city street-lighting system with the objective to reduce and standardised the type of light fixtures and lamps, minimise energy consumption and light pollution and simplify maintenance and repair works. As compulsory technical specifications, the administration required LED-fixtures only and other requirements based on reparability and durability, amongst others. Offers were evaluated based on TCO results as well as other social and environmental criteria. TCO evaluation was based on a fictional street section complying with the Dutch street-lighting guidelines for which bidders had to provide: the number of fixtures to properly illuminate the fictional street section; the price of the fixture, LED light source and driver; and the energy consumption and maintenance costs over a period of 20 years (European Commission 2017c).

Summing up from a GPP perspective

LCC stayed for many years a secondary topic in public procurement. This is changing and is becoming a more prominent topic in organisations, promoted, amongst others, by green procurement advocates. In the European Union, the legal clarity provided by its inclusion in the latest Procurement Directive is contributing to this process too.

Nevertheless, LCC is first and foremost an economic tool, which may or may not support GPP. LCC can be a useful tool for GPP if the costs savings during the "product" lifespan compensate the price premiums often linked to green alternatives or if there is a validated correlation between low life-cycle costs and low environmental impact. If that cannot be guaranteed, to avoid LCC being a competing rather than a complementary tool, a mixed approach should be followed.

One option is to define strict environmental technical specifications to ensure a green result and use LCC (with or without externalities) as an award criterion to select amongst already green alternatives. Another possibility is to analyse the weight and influence of environmental parameters in the LCC calculation and assess their inclusion in the LCC or as separate award criteria to ensure a green procurement result.

In any case, this will require a case-by-case evaluation prior to the tendering process and critical thinking in relation to the impacts assessment and impacts monetisation methodologies.

Notes

1 Directive 2014/24/EU of the European Parliament and of the Council on public procurement and repealing Directive 2004/18/EC [2014] OJEU L 94/65.
2 Directive 2009/33/EC of the European Parliament and of the Council on the promotion of clean and energy-efficient road transport vehicles [2009] OJEU L 120/5.
3 This Directive is currently under review.
4 European Commission 2014, Call for tenders ENV.F.1/SER/2014/0032rl. Service contract for the Development of a life-cycle cost (LCC) calculation tool.
5 European Commission (2017b), Call for tenders ENV.B.1/SER/2017/00XXMV. Service contract for the Development of life-cycle costing (LCC) tools for use in green public procurement (GPP).

References

Adell, A. 2018, *Les avancées et outils utilises par les administrations européennes leaders en achat durable* (Progress and tools used by leading European public authorities in sustainable procurement), presentation at ICLEI World Congress, 18 June, Montréal.

Adell, A., Esquerra, J., Estevan, H., Clement, S., Tepper, P., Acker, H. and Seeback, D. 2009, *Existing approaches to encourage innovation through procurement*, ICLEI – Local Governments for Sustainability, European Secretariat, Freiburg, Germany.

Asiedu, Y. and Gu, P. 1998, 'Product life cycle cost analysis: State of the art review', *International Journal of Production Research*, 36 (4), pp. 883–908.

Brannigan, C., Luckhurst, S., Kirsch, F., Lohr, E., and Skinner, I. 2015, *Ex-post Evaluation of Directive 2009/33/EC on the promotion of clean and energy efficient road transport vehicles – Final report*. European Commission – Directorate-General for Mobility and Transport, Brussels.

Centre for European Policy Studies and College of Europe. 2012, *The uptake of green public procurement in the EU27*, (online) CEPS.

Devault, C. and Malouin, E. 2018, *Coût total de propiété – exemple de l'étude sur l'électrification des véhicules de travaux de la STM* (Total cost of ownership – exemple of the case on electrification of works vehicles of STM). Presentation at ICLEI World Congress, 19 June, Montréal.

Ecoinstitut and ICLEI. 2019, *User Guide to the Life Cycle Costing Tool for Green Public Procurement of Computers and Monitors* (online), available at: www.iclei-europe.org, European Commission, Brussels.

Epstein, M. J. 1996, *Measuring corporate environmental performance: Best practices for costing and managing an effective environmental strategy*, Chicago, IL: Irwin Professional Publishing.

Estevan, H. and Schaefer, B. 2017, *Life Cycle Costing State of the Art report*, (online), available at: www.iclei-europe.org, ICLEI –Local Governments for Sustainability, European Secretariat.

European Commission. 2017a, Proposal for a Directive of the European Parliament and of the Council amending Directive 2009/33/EU on the promotion of clean and energy-efficient road transport vehicles, Brussels 8.11.2017, COM(2017) 653 final, 2017/0291 (COD).

European Commission. 2017b, Communication 'Making public procurement work in and for Europe', COM(2017), 572 final.

European Commission. 2017c, 'Purchasing energy efficient street lighting', *GPP in Practice*, Issue no. 68, February, European Commission, viewed 29 August 2018, http://ec.europa.eu/environment/gpp/pdf/news_alert/Issue68_Case_Study_137_Rotterdam.pdf.

Forum for Bæredygtige Indkøb. n.d.a, *Temagruppe: TCO-beregninger som værktøj i udbudsprocesser* (Theme group: TCO calculations as a tool in tender processes), viewed 30 August 2018, www.ansvarligeindkob.dk/forummet/arbejdsgrupper/temagruppe-tco-beregninger-som-vaerktoej-udbudsprocesser/.

Forum for Bæredygtige Indkøb. n.d.b, *TCO-beregninger giver store besparelser på belysning i Syddjurs Kommune* (TCO calculations provide great savings on lighting in Syddjurs Municipality), viewed 30 August 2018, www.ansvarligeindkob.dk/cases/miljoebesparelse-paa-ca-7-250-mwh-med-forpligtende-indkoebsaftale-paa-computere/.

Gluch, P. and Baumann, H. 2004, 'The life cycle costing (LCC) approach: A conceptual discussion of its usefulness for environmental decision-making', *Building and Environment*, 39, pp. 571–580.

Hochschorner, E. and Noring, M. 2011, 'Practitioner's use of life cycle costing with environmental costs: A Swedish study', *The International Journal of Life Cycle Assessment* 16, pp. 897–902.

Miljøstyrelsen. 2016, *Total Cost of Ownership tool for computers*, viewed 30 August 2018, https://mst.dk/media/133148/danish_epa_tco_tool_computers.xlsm.

Ministère de la Transition écologique et solidaire. 2017, *Le coût du cycle de vie dans l'achat public (Life cycle costing in public procurement)*, viewed 30 August 2018, www.ecologique-solidaire.gouv.fr/cout-du-cycle-vie-dans-lachat-public.

Perera, O., Monton, B. and Perfrement, T. 2009, *Life cycle costing in sustainable public procurement: A question of value* (online), IISD, Winnipeg, Manitoba, Canada.

Pretato, U. and Rillo, E. 2016, *Update on Life Cycle Costing (LCC) project*, presentation at GPP Advisory Group meeting, 20 April, Amsterdam.

PricewaterhouseCoopers, Significant and Ecofys 2009, *Collection of statistical information on Green Public Procurement in the EU. Report on data collection results* (online), PricewaterhouseCoopers, The Netherlands.

Rebitzer, G. and Hunkeler, D. 2003, 'Life cycle costing in LCM: Ambitions, opportunities, and limitations', *International Journal of LCA*, 8 (5), pp. 253–256.

SPP Regions: LCC Workshop. 2016, Procura+ Seminar, 13–14 October, Rome.

Studio Fieschi and soci Srl and Scuola Superiore Sant'Anna. 2016, *LCC calculation tool. Technical Specifications* (online), available at: https://ec.europa.eu/environment/gpp/pdf/LCC_tool_user_guide_final.pdf, European Commission – Directorate-General Environment, Brussels.

Tarris, B. 2016, *Life cycle Cost for passenger cars purchase*, presentation at Procura+ Seminar, 14 October, Rome.

UNEP-SETAC. 2011, *Towards a life cycle sustainability assessment: Making informed choices on products*. United Nations Environment Programme, Paris.

United Nations Environment Programme. 2013, *Sustainable Public Procurement: A Global Review*. United Nations Environment Programme, Paris.

United Nations Environment Programme. 2017, *Global review of Sustainable Public Procurement 2017*. United Nations Environment Programme, Paris.

Westminster Sustainable Business Forum. 2008, *Costing the future: Securing value for money through sustainable procurement*. Westminster Sustainable Business Forum, London.

Part II

Calculating costs and savings of public procurement

Public procurement is a key tool for the improvement of the effectiveness of government spending. Good public procurement makes the best use of public money, delivering goods, services and works that are beneficial for the economy as a whole. This is the main reason why being able to increase the productivity of public spending through efficient and effective procurement processes should be pursued by governments all over the world.

Within this framework, costs and savings are fundamental measures for the effectiveness of the overall purchasing process and, at the same time, represent a big challenge to be addressed because they should be able to account for factors such as, for example, time and quality.

In their debate, Glas and Spagnolo achieve an interesting synergy of reinforcing views between an expert of the economics of procurement field of studies and one of its management. As pointed out by Spagnolo in his contribution, it could happen that "if you buy cheap, you buy twice", meaning that the search for a cost cut in the short run could result in cost increases in the long run especially if the development of techniques able to capture dimensions such as quality improvements, innovations in productive methods, urgency in the execution of the procurement orders, are not given proper attention. Consequently, these become crucial issues to be measured and are in need of special attention by procuring institutions and auditors. According to Glas, what is called Cost and Savings Measurement and Management (CSMM) plays an important role in the evaluation of public procurement, while he also agrees with Spagnolo that in the absence of full information/ verifiability, quality degradation is more likely with savings and this reduces the advantages of high-powered incentive schemes like competitive tenders or performance-based contracts. The debate goes directly to the heart of the multifaceted issue of how to properly measure savings, highlighting monetary but also non-monetary components, elements such as the quality of goods, services and works procured, but also the fundamental quality of data and of competencies needed to use available data and/or to better collect them.

The other two contributions complement the analysis of this chapter with the empirical perspective; the first one, by Åslundh, presents what the Stockholm Public Transport Administration is doing to obtain valuable cost analysis of procurement procedures with the aim of describing learning outcomes and methods used. One method, shadow price calculation, and the example of the commuter train system in Stockholm, are described to help the reader gauge the key elements that need to be included in the cost analysis for such services. The second, by Sbicca, introduces the concept of reference prices of goods and services, as developed in Italy, explaining how they should be taken as benchmark fair values in public tenders and how they can be used by anti-corruption authorities also for the identification of corruption risk indicators (red flags).

4 Calculating the costs and savings of public procurement

Colloquium

Giancarlo Spagnolo and Andreas H. Glas

Opening remarks – *Giancarlo Spagnolo*

"You can't manage what you can't measure" (William Edwards Deming)

Measuring the effectiveness of public procurement is challenging because procurement policy is often used to achieve different, changing objectives besides that of maximizing value for money.[1] Because of this complexity of objectives, in most cases procurement evaluation has been focusing only on the most basic indicators, such as "savings", typically intended as improvements in the value for money obtained through procurement. Value for money remains a central element of public procurement performance, although the presence of many other important effects and objectives of public procurement must always be kept in mind. Realizing costs savings will always be an important government objective, particularly with the tight budgets and high debt after a financial crisis. Even in the private sector, savings remain a crucial objective of the procurement function, even though they may sometimes conflict with long-term investments and future savings. For these reasons, even though it is an extremely partial measure of procurement performance, how to properly measure savings is an important issue. Furthermore properly defining and measuring procurement cost savings is not at all easy. Even just measuring changes in purely monetary costs – abstracting from how to account for potential simultaneous and future changes in the many quality dimensions – is not as easy as it may seem at first glance. *Data* on all types of purchasing costs linked to the object of a procurement should be factored in to obtain the so-called "total cost of ownership", including all types of ex post renegotiations, and add-ons more or less explicitly linked to the initial purchase. In addition, all types of ex ante and ex post procurement transaction and contract management costs, including time and administrative costs of tender preparation and advertisement, renegotiations/amendments, procedure, administration and contract management costs, and typically data on all these costs, are not collected. To gain an idea of how significant these previously mentioned types of costs can be, note that Bajari et al. (2014) estimate that the transaction costs of ex post contractual adaptation, mostly bargaining and legal contracting costs of adaptation/renegotiation[2] in US Highway Procurement contracting, range between 7.5 and 14 percent of the total value of procurement.[3]

Even in the very best case where all quality dimension and dynamic effects are properly taken into account and all data on all types of monetary costs incurred at all phases of the procurement process are available, producing a meaningful measure of purely monetary savings may be a challenge. This is because even in this best-case scenario *a good counterfactual* to use as a benchmark against which to measure the pure change in monetary costs is typically lacking. Past prices and costs may be poor references to what could have been achieved today with a different procurement design. Even if past procurements were not different in terms of quantity and quality, many things may have changed in between the procurements. Such changes can range from drastic cost-reducing innovation in the production of the procured good or service to drastic innovation in market structure due, for example, to the entry or exit of crucial potential suppliers. In few cases, rules for the construction of reservation prices help in generating some type of benchmark, but these are exceptions rather than the norm.

Assuming that all issues linked to the pure changes in monetary expenditures have been taken into account with appropriate methodologies, and that potential differences in quantity, cost-reducing innovation, market structure and procurement methods are controlled for, a crucial remaining issue for the calculation of "savings" is controlling for differences in *quality*. The rest of this chapter will be focusing on this issue.

Governments around the world increasingly rely on private contractors for the provision of goods and services in the hope of enjoying cost savings from the stronger incentives for productive efficiency linked to private ownership and competition. However, precisely because of these much stronger incentives to cut costs, maintaining an appropriate quality level from private providers is difficult. Let us distinguish among what economists call contractible and non-contractible quality dimensions of a procured good or service.

Contractible (or verifiable) quality includes all the dimensions of a good or service that can be objectively measured at reasonable cost by a third party. The agreed upon levels of these quality dimensions (think of delivery time) are in principle easy to guarantee through legally binding contractual clauses that can be enforced by a court, precisely because their level is easily measured by a third party, hence the name "contractible". We know well that even when contractible, these quality dimensions are very often under-provided by suppliers, because they were poorly specified in the contract, or because of poor contract management, poor contract enforcement by the legal system, or a number of other factors (see e.g. Decarolis et al., 2016). However, the fact that these quality dimensions can be objectively measured at low cost by a third party means that reliable performance data may be collected (or is already available) and that changes in these quality dimensions occurring together with monetary expenditures can be accounted for to obtain a more meaningful measure of "savings" in terms of improvement in (observable) value for money.

While this is possible, it is typically not done in reality. In many cases of non-academic evaluation of public procurement savings, even the most basic and easily measured quality dimensions are not (or are very poorly) taken into account. Savings are then wildly exaggerated, for the pleasure of the politician in turn, because existing data on these easily measured quality dimensions are strategically ignored to claim success, or because the data are poor or not collected at all, or because they are not made easily accessible to the entities able to properly evaluate them.[4]

Observable but non-contractible quality dimensions are those that cannot be measured objectively (cannot be verified) at a reasonable cost by a third party, such as an independent auditor working for a court of law. The risk of degradation is, of course, much higher for quality dimensions that are hard to measure/verify, and hence cannot be described and enforced through a legal contract. For this very reason (difficulty to measure by third parties, courts or evaluators) it is difficult to control for degradation of these quality dimensions, which is often connected to strong monetary savings from intense procurement competition (for a detailed discussion of these measurement problems and an attempt to overcome them for a specific class of services see Bergman et al., 2016).

Failing to measure quality degradation of all types makes measurements of monetary savings entirely uninformative and often highly misleading. Both measurable and non-measurable quality is costly to produce and therefore tend to increase the price, but also the value of the procurement. When 20 percent of monetary savings is realized through increasing procurement competition, but, taken all together, the most important quality dimensions of the procured goods or services, worth 80 percent of the total value fell 25 percent, the apparent 20 percent of monetary savings is accompanied by a 20 percent fall in the value procured, and 0 percent savings.

Things get more complicated when even the most basic additional objectives of the procurer (other than the characteristics of the purchase) become important in the calculation of the value of procurement. Consider, for example, the case of an emergency, say an earthquake (or a financial crisis requiring a swift increase in public demand), where the urgency of the problem makes the speed at which the procurement is executed and the unobservable quality of the services procured, the main crucial determinants of its value that *must* be taken into account in the calculation of "savings". Suppose a benevolent/honest public buyer switches to faster, simpler and more discretional awarding procedures to meet these needs. For example, it switches to using restricted auctions with pre-selection of suppliers invited to participate and a minimum but limited number of invited bidders. These faster and simpler procedures, if used well, may both meet the need to speed up the procurement linked to the emergency and the need to maintain higher quality standards by only inviting highly reputable suppliers and excluding suppliers that performed poorly in the past (Calzolari and Spagnolo, 2009).

Of course, these procedures are tools (like, say, a scalpel in a hospital) that, as any other tool, can be misused to obtain less honorable outcomes than the original ones, such as favoring local or politically connected firms or extorting bribes (killing or threatening and robbing someone rather than saving a patient in the case of the scalpel). Therefore, any such policy change that increases public buyers' power/discretion should always be accompanied by a strengthening of ex post contract performance measurements and controls, to deter the abuse of the increased power/discretion without slowing down emergency procurement.

How should we measure "savings" from such a policy change? We know well that the potential costs of such a policy change (the cost of buying the scalpel) include at a minimum:

C1)   *Higher procurement costs*, because of the reduced competition and the connected potentially poorer contractor selection in terms of production costs.[5]

C2)   *More favoritism/corruption* that is likely again to induce even *higher procurement costs and lower levels of all forms of quality.*[6]

These are the costs of the tool. Of course, one should then consider the value of the benefits, the very reason why the tool was introduced (the reason why we bought the scalpel in the first place, saving the life of a patient):

B1)   *Lower costs and suffering for the population hit by the earthquake* linked to the faster relief.

B2)   *Higher non-contractible quality* in the relief brought to the population because of the improved incentives to perform, not to be excluded from future procurements (possibly also through the exclusion of the very low quality firms). High quality is costly to produce, so it will also come with an – in this case very welcome – increase in total procurement cost.

Suppose C1 and C2 are large and increase procurement cost by 10, but that B1 and B2 are ten times as large, causing a reduction of costs and suffering of 100, although it is harder to measure them. In standard (mal-)practice procurement, savings would mean measuring price increase linked to C1 and C2, which would of course result in concluding that savings from the new policy were highly "negative", -10, and that the reform – moving to a restricted auction with pre-selection of suppliers invited to participate – was ill-conceived.

But does it make any sense to say that incurring the cost for buying a scalpel reduced savings when the scalpel allowed the saving of several patients' lives? Of course not, one should evaluate total savings, as (B1+B2)-(C1+C2), and then conclude that the total savings from the new policy were *huge*, 90 (100–10), even if C1 and C2 did increase.

Many similar stories can be told. A first conclusion for this note is therefore that – given the current low standards in amount and quality of procurement data and in the poor methodologies typically used to turn this data into measures of procurement "savings" – we should discount the importance of such measures and be extremely careful in taking any serious policy decision based on them. A second conclusion is that we should work much harder in collecting more and better data and improving the methodology for calculating savings to account for as many as possible of the complications discussed earlier, as good performance measurement is an essential ingredient of the receipt for improvement.

Opening remarks – *Andreas H. Glas*

Savings as a performance indicator of public procurement

Irrespective of the industry sector, the size of an enterprise or the maturity of the procurement discipline, realizing cost savings will always be one of the most important objectives of the procurement function. This is hardly a surprise. In most organizations the percentage of revenue or budget that is spent on procurement has grown to 50 to 70 percent, depending on the type of business. The most important reason for this growth is the continuing trend of outsourcing tasks that were formerly performed within the organization (Putters, 2013). Hence, savings in procurement have a huge impact on the overall performance of an organization and cost control is an important shared responsibility of both procurement and finance functions.

This topic becomes urgent in the context of public organizations, as in many countries the major public procurement projects (infrastructure, defense, public transport) often exceed their already small and constrained budgets. This intensifies the ongoing and project-to-project repetitive public debate on cost overruns and increases the existing tensions between procurement performance, legal compliance, and political leadership in public procurement (Schapper et al., 2006). In the debate during the Symposium, at least some prominent projects were briefly mentioned for illustrative purposes (A400M military aircraft transport; Berlin airport; Elbphilharmonie Hamburg a.o.). However, getting good value out of public procurement is not just a question of getting goods at the best price, but also involves considerations of the costs incurred during the procurement process (Burger and Hawkesworth, 2011).

Overall, the economic benefits of cost savings in procurement are enormous and in public procurement this would provide political leeway to allocate resources. Vogel (2009) found that macroeconomic benefits are approximately linear for savings in public procurement and referred to an increase in GDP, employment or other macroeconomic measures, such as public investment.

Therefore, Cost and Savings Measurement and Management (CSMM) plays an important role in the evaluation of public procurement. However, savings measurement faces some special challenges. For example, in many cases, it is not possible to compare the actual price with previous prices, as is typically done for production materials in an industrial context, and follow-up costs during the life-/usage cycle are partially higher than the pure purchase price. Besides, CSMM can be influenced by several tactics of buyers in order to manipulate savings measurement results (Emiliani et al., 2005). Still, a majority of organizations are not completely satisfied with their CSMM implementation (Maucher and Hofmann, 2013) with typical problems of understating and overstating savings, manipulability and a missing trust in the results.

In public procurement, some more challenges arise. So process costs refer to procedures that are determined to a large extent by public procurement law, and the contract is awarded to the most economically advantageous tender (MEAT). Process costs or award savings are not considered in public procurement law per se, but are the subject of other laws, for example, budget law and the principle of austerity in public budget management. There are also some other challenges, for example, the danger that expiring budgets ("savings throughout the year") leads to wasteful year-end spending (Liebman and Mahoney, 2017).

Overall, CSMM has received too little attention from practitioners and academics, making it a topic for future research in particular in the context of public procurement.

Savings measurement in procurement – status quo

The debate can aim to address the issues that are illustrated in Figure 4.1.

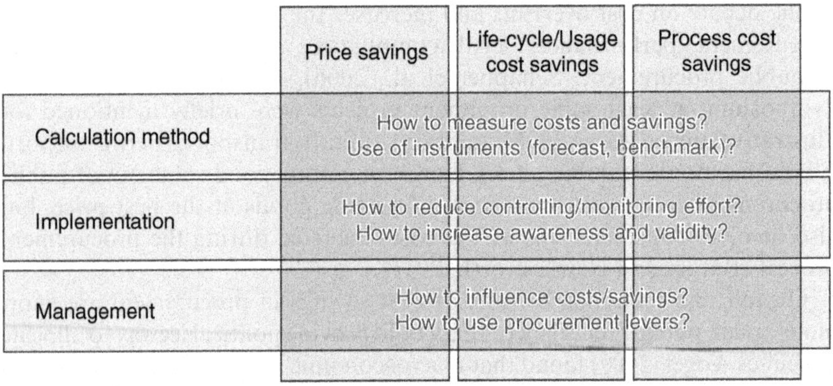

	Price savings	Life-cycle/Usage cost savings	Process cost savings
Calculation method	How to measure costs and savings? Use of instruments (forecast, benchmark)?		
Implementation	How to reduce controlling/monitoring effort? How to increase awareness and validity?		
Management	How to influence costs/savings? How to use procurement levers?		

Figure 4.1 Framework for the debate of savings in public procurement.

It is shown that the scope of measurement (price, usage costs, process costs) and its analytical model (calculation method), its measurement through, for example, automatic systems (implementation), and the approach to influence the size of savings (management) are interlinked.

There are already a number of propositions how calculation and implementation might be enhanced: (1) use of multi-dimensional inputs on cost data; (2) consideration of benefits and qualitative aspects; (3) calculation of savings at different phases in the project; (4) establishment of guidelines on how to proceed in savings measurement; (5) audits of results that should be performed by an independent party; (6) formulation of a realistic savings target.[7]

One major problem in public procurement is the management perspective of this model. While price, life-/usage cycle, or process costs can be calculated, and while in many procurement organizations there is at least cost-controlling management implemented, the active management of costs and savings is a gap in theory and practice. First, many drivers of process costs are fixed on the short term (IT systems, personnel, infrastructure) and are only the subject of reforms in the long run. Second, price and usage costs in public tenders for products and services are awarded and then there is the "fundamental transformation" (Williamson, 1985, p. 61). Public buyers can compare price and cost information ex ante the award of contract on the basis of proposals, forecasts, or benchmarks, but ex post there is a strong bilateral monopoly situation in which the buyer can hardly use new or additional management instruments to incentivize cost savings. Maybe both aspects are an issue for debate, but I want to highlight pathways to incentivize cost reduction efforts in public contracts.

Innovative CSMM: Contractual implementation

At Bundeswehr University Munich one applied research project is concerned with performance-based contracts in defense. In this area, contracts use functional and outcome-oriented performance indicators and monetary bonus incentives to influence the behavior of the supplier. In one peculiar case, a formula connects cost savings in a long-term contract with performance. The cost savings achieved by the supplier are split up in a pain–gain share (50 percent if performance goal is achieved). If the supplier manages to overachieve performance then that distribution changes to a share of 70:30 for the supplier. That example provides one case insight into how CSMM could be implemented in public contracts.

Response to Andreas H. Glas – *Giancarlo Spagnolo*

In his three-pages debate memo, Glas raises a number of important issues, distinct and complementary to those I raised in my opening remarks above. In my reading, focusing on the state of the art way of calculating costs savings and on the most common process of costs and savings measurement and management, the main issues raised in Glas's memo are the following:

(a) The issue of costs and savings measurement in public procurement is very important and more complex than usually perceived; these complexities have received too little attention from both practitioners and academics, making it a topic for future research in particular in the context of public procurement.
(b) The costs linked to the procurement process may be substantial and need to be taken into account in the calculation of costs and savings.
(c) In many cases, it is not possible to compare the actual price with previous prices, and it becomes difficult to calculate an appropriate benchmark.
(d) Costs and savings measures can be influenced by several tactics of the buyers in order to manipulate savings measurement results.
(e) It may be difficult to provide incentives to reduce costs within a procurement because many costs are fixed and, after the contract is awarded, the buyer loses bargaining power with the fundamental transformation. But of course incentives should be incorporated in the contract, as in the savings-sharing example of the Bundeswehr.

Here are my reactions/comments point by point.

(Response to a) I fully agree that the issue is important and way more complex than typically understood. There is a large literature on "measuring public bodies' performance" that adds many other sources of complexity. As clarified in my opening remarks, I believe another major source of complexity in the measurement of costs and savings in public procurement that Glas did not emphasize is linked to the many quality dimensions that are difficult to measure, and that may fall together with costs, making the standard measures of savings a very poor measure of real changes in value for money.
(Response to b) I also fully agree with this, as also mentioned in my note. Unfortunately I am not aware of a simple methodology to estimate these costs that may also differ across buying organizations.
(Response to c) I also agree on this point, which I raised in my note as well. There are sophisticated econometric techniques that allow for estimating such benchmarks, but data are often unavailable and there is a need for simpler methodologies for evaluating institutions that lack the skills required to perform advanced econometric studies.
(Response to d) Manipulation of costs and savings measures is a pervasive problem in many environments, both in the private and public domain (think of well known stories of managers "cooking the books"). Third party auditing is the "standard" solution to these problems, provided the auditor has the necessary incentives, capabilities, and integrity, which is

unfortunately often not the case. Arranging for auditing institutions with the appropriate skills, including statistical and econometric ones, which would allow the uncovering of such manipulations, is an issue for most of the countries I am aware of.

As in my response to (a), when talking about ways to incentivize savings for the case of public procurement, at point (e), one thing that Glas does not emphasize is the risk of degradation of poorly measurable but important quality dimensions to obtain measurable cost savings. This has been a major drawback of the use of high-powered incentives, and is widely recognized as intense competition at the tendering stage as a source of a very high-powered incentive, able to generate large benefits in terms of innovation and savings, but at the same time large damages in terms of difficult to measure but important quality dimensions.

Response to Giancarlo Spagnolo – *Andreas H. Glas*

My debate memo distinguishes between CSMM challenges in general and peculiar CSMM challenges in public procurement; CSMM is also linked to a model that distinguishes cost content (price costs, usage costs, and process costs) and controlling (method, measurement, management). These thoughts are highly interlinked with the remarks and conclusions of Spagnolo, who discusses some challenges more deeply, and also discusses contractibility of quality. While reading both debate contributions, I became aware that they are based on the same perception of the situation with only slight differences. Commonalities of both are (1) the high relevance of Cost and Savings Measurement and Management (CSMM) in the public sector, (2) problems in CSMM practice, and (3) the claim that legal procurement procedures is a dilemma situation referring to CSMM. In the following sections, I will point out the perspectives and the differences.

The relevance of CSMM in the public sector

Spagnolo puts stronger emphasis in pointing out that value for money (cost saving) is only one of many other objectives of public procurement policies. I fully agree with this and think that this adds another perspective to my reasons why CSMM is of high relevance. These are mainly the high share of already outsourced tasks to industry (high procurement volume), while procurement cost savings performance is low, as many projects exceed their budgets. Together, I can refer to the German examples (A400, Berlin Airport etc.), which are illustrating that public procurement considers other relevant objectives in the award decision.[8] Because the (political) focus might be on those other objectives, the challenges of CSMM are not always sufficiently regarded in public procurement projects.

The problems in CSMM practice

While in my debate memo, I refer to a couple of practical challenges to measure costs and savings (forecasts uncertainty, lacking trust in results, limited scope of calculation etc.), Spagnolo also addresses some practical measurement problems, such as that data are often poor, not collected at all or hardly accessible, but refers to the quality of the procurement object. If the quality is different, this must have an impact on any cost savings calculation. Mainly he refers to qualities and if these are contractible or not. This is highly related to information, experience or credence qualities of a product or service (Nelson, 1970; Darby and Karni, 1973), as specific qualities are measureable ex ante or ex post, while some qualities are not measurable at all (credence qualities). I understand this reasoning very well, as my research on complex services procurement is addressing the contractibility aspects. However, I would be happy, if we could align in the debate, that this is a call for the development of an integrated quality and CSMM approach (MEAT-LCC). We should work on the development of not only a CSMM but also on improved quality measurement instruments to reduce uncertainty and to become aware of the interdependencies.

The claim that legal procurement procedures are a dilemma situation to CSMM

In my paper I refer to the fundamental transformation to point out that legal procedures are posing a dilemma situation to CSMM. It starts with highly regulated procedures to increase competition and to get the best MEAT offer. It ends in a (long-term) relationship with a supplier, who then is in a monopoly-like and typical principal situation against the agent of the public procurement office. The management instruments to influence quality or costs ex post the award of contract are limited. But there is hardly any alternative, as this would mean to reduce competition or to reduce transparency with the hope that this will increase agility, flexibility and overall performance in the contract execution phase.

Spagnolo also addresses this dilemma, but argues with public tasks and the requirement of agile and robust processes in the face of immediate relief and emergencies. This is highly interesting, as my research addresses military and security projects. I often hear the argument, that we need more robustness but often there is no budget to plan and implement reserves for "uncertain" or "unlikely" events. The price for having no or low reserves (in case of, let's say, river flooding), prices for urgently required equipment (sandbags, walls, boats etc.) go up. But the price is paid, as the public task must be fulfilled due to public, media, and political pressure (at any costs).

So I think, that we both conclude on the same core-CSMM challenge for public procurement: The use and the outcome of a specific procedure (e.g. speed in case of emergency) must be tied together and weighted against potential negative effects such as higher costs or reduced competition. This is not a question of CSMM, but a question of the alignment of policy goals. Therefore, this would bring us to the wider question of which dimensions of quality, costs and performance shall be considered in public procurement.

A concluding remark could be that we need to distinguish different procurement situations. Let's say a normal case in which a CSMM is executed for "market-common" goods or services and a second case in which more critical/emergency goods or services are procured. The latter approach is already allowed to choose exceptions, but could be even freer to use negotiated procedures and faster processes. This could maybe prevent a situation in which a public agency could not provide urgently required public services due to a lack of an "insignificant" supply item.

Conclusions – *Giancarlo Spagnolo*

In his reply Glas suggested to focus on the development of an integrated quality and CSMM approach (MEAT-LCC), and to work on the development of not only a CSMM but also on improved quality measurement instruments to reduce uncertainty and to become aware of the interdependencies. I think we converge on this topic. My point is to focus on the typically poorly measured quality changes, while far too often practice focuses on calculating monetary costs that are much easier to measure "effective costs", which should include the costs of quality reduction, when relevant. This potential "hidden cost" is not equally relevant for all purchases, but the tradition in the past has been one of disregarding it also where potentially highly relevant.

My example of "urgent needs" was not intended to point out the different objectives of procurement, for example, costs versus flexibility, but at the "hidden costs" that may be highly relevant even when calculating the standard cost of a purchase. If an urgent purchase is obtained with a long delay, at a much lower monetary cost, the "effective cost" should account for the "cost of late delivery" that can be substantial in some situations, potentially reversing the message coming from standard measures of the purely monetary cost of procurement. In practice, I was trying to point out the partial and potentially misleading measure of costs that only focus on monetary costs when other aspects of procurement change, thereby generating increases (or decreases) in other dimensions of the procurement (quality, speed, flexibility) that could or should effectively be accounted for as part of the change in the procurement costs in different procedures.

In the end, what I am arguing for is for a more encompassing concept of cost that, besides administrative costs of the procurement process, tries to incorporate as many other hidden costs linked to changes in non-monetary procurement outcomes as possible. I understand that this is challenging, for example in terms of increased scope for ad hoc costs adjustments and manipulations. But I believe that the damages in the past practice of only focusing on monetary costs have been large enough to justify the attempt to develop broader measures of costs and savings.

Conclusions – *Andreas H. Glas*

Spagnolo responded point by point to the key issues I raised in my opening remarks, while I tried to focus my response on three main areas (relevance, practical (data) problems, public performance /quality aspects). Overall, I feel that we are very close in our reasoning, but both are highlighting different sides of the same medal.

If I get Spagnolo right, his key argument focuses on the difficulties to measure price, cost, and in particular numerous performance dimensions in an appropriate way. At the same time, he is skeptical about the effectiveness of relational coordination mechanisms (e.g. incentives) as these are often badly implemented in practice. This could cause damages to low-incentivized goals of public procurement.

Of course, I can understand this side of the medal. But in this final response, I want to raise the question, what can business research do to improve the situation to the better?

Business research in the past succeeded in developing a range of CSMM benchmarks (to previous paid prices, previous paid prices adjusted to market index developments, catalogue prices, planned prices (e.g. budget), target prices, average bids, bids of the selected supplier and prices paid by administration units). At the same time, we see the development of a wide range of multidimensional performance evaluation tools (scoring tables, balanced scorecards, key performance indicator systems etc.). Third, business research developed a range of methods to award a contract to the "best" offer (tendering, auctions, framework contracts, negotiations etc.) Finally, business research developed customized relationship management. Richard Thaler ("Nudge"[9]) and other scholars deeply focus on behavior and how this affects (buying) decision-making.

The bilateral discussion made me realize that the core problem is to integrate and implement the aforementioned facets of business research to public procurement practice. My summary is a call for developing a more fine-grained method toolbox for public procurement with integrated instruments for cost, savings and performance measurement. It is also a call to provide public procurement with relationship management strategies that allow the influence of behavior (=cost, savings, performance) of suppliers to safeguard goal achievement in the face of contract dynamics.

Notes

1 These have ranged, depending on the time period, from stimulating the economy through public demand to ensuring market transparency and equal opportunities for suppliers, from supply assurance for public buyers to static and dynamic

allocative efficiency, from long-term market development and connected small firms participation/protection, to the amount of cross-border deals (in the EU), up to the more recently fashionable ones of fostering innovation, social inclusion, and environmentally sustainable technologies.

2　See Williamson's "haggling costs" (Williamson, 1985).

3　Moreover, contract modifications are sometimes done for good reasons, to obtain additional useful performance, and sometimes for bad ones, linked to a poor initial tendering process. Contract modifications in terms, for example, of cost overrun, must be added to the total cost of the procurement, but in an appropriate way. When cost overrun is caused by a very useful, unexpected adaptation that greatly increases the value of the overall good or project, this increase in value must be accounted for.

4　Or, because the entity having the data and trying to measure procurement savings does not have the capability to calculate how quality underprovision affected real savings in value for money, which is the case for most national audit offices I am aware of.

5　Though this is only likely to happen if the number falls to a very small number of bidders, say five or less; if instead the new policy puts a high minimum to the number of bidders, and the number of bidders falls, say, from 30 to 15, this may be beneficial even for selection and overall costs, not to mention the fall in transaction costs, particularly if the excluded firms play the 'underbidding/going-for-broke/renegotiation' strategy.

6　If the policy change, that is, is not accompanied – as it always should be – by a strengthening of proper ex post performance measurement of contractors and contracting authorities and related enforcement/incentives, sufficient to prevent the abuse of the increased discretion.

7　Similar to Maucher and Hofmann (2013).

8　A400M military transport aircraft is also a support project for a European Defence Industrial Base. It is plausible to believe that the European decision to develop a new aircraft in contrast to buy an existing transporter from the Ukraine competitor company Antonov is mainly based on wider economic objectives, but not on cost and savings perspectives. At Berlin Airport a new and unique technique for fire protection has been installed. That equipment was highly innovative, but failed in practice. Innovation had a higher relevance in the award decision than (cheaper) existing fire protection installments.

9　See, for example, Thaler and Sunstein (2008).

References

Bajari, P., Houghton S. and Tadelis, S. (2014) "Bidding for Incomplete Contracts: An Empirical Analysis of Adaptation Costs". *American Economic Review*, 104 (4): 1288–1319. www.aeaweb.org/articles?id=10.1257/aer.104.4.1288.

Bergman, M., Johansson, P., Lundberg, S. and Spagnolo, G. (2016) "Privatization and Quality: Evidence from Elderly Care in Sweden". *Journal of Health Economics*, 49 (September): 109–119. Freely available for download from www.sciencedirect.com/science/article/pii/S0167629616300492.

Burger, P. and Hawkesworth, I. (2011) "How to Attain Value for Money: Comparing PPP and Traditional Infrastructure Public Procurement". *OECD Journal on Budgeting*, 11: 91–146.

Calzolari, G. and Spagnolo, G. (2009) "Relational Contracts and Competitive Screening". CEPR, Discussion Paper No. DP7434, https://ssrn.com/abstract= 1484466.

Darby, M. R. and Karni, E. (1973) "Free Competition and the Optimal Amount of Fraud". *Journal of Law and Economics*, 16 (1): 67–88.

Decarolis, F., Pacini, R. and Spagnolo, G. (2016) "Past Performance and Procurement Outcomes". NBER Working Paper No. 22814, www.nber.org/papers/w22814.

Emiliani, M. L., Stec, D. J. and Grasso, L. P. (2005) "Unintended Responses to a Traditional Purchasing Performance Metric". *Supply Chain Management*, 10 (3): 150–156.

Liebman, J. B. and Mahoney, N. (2017) "Do Expiring Budgets Lead to Wasteful Year-end Spending? Evidence from Federal Procurement". *American Economic Review*, 107 (11): 3510–3549.

Maucher, D. and Hofmann, E. (2013) "Savings Measurement for Capital Equipment Purchasing: Challenges and Conceptual Model". *International Journal of Productivity and Performance Management*, 62 (5): 490–513.

Nelson, P. (1970) "Information and Consumer Behaviour". *Journal of Political Economy*, 78 (2): 311–329.

Putters, M. (2013) "How To Measure Procurement Savings?" www.capgemini.com/consulting/2013/09/how-to-measure-procurement-savings/.

Schapper, P., Veiga Malta, J. N. and Gilbert, D. L. (2006) "An Analytical Framework for the Management and Reform of Public Procurement". *Journal of Public Procurement*, 6 (1): 1–26.

Thaler, R. H. H. and Sunstein, C. L. (2008) *Nudge: Improving Decisions about Health, Wealth, and Happiness.* London: Yale University Press.

Vogel, L. (2009) "Macroeconomic Effects of Cost Savings in Public Procurement", European Economy: Economic Papers 389, available at: http://ec.europa.eu/economy_finance/publications/pages/publication16259_en.pdf

Williamson, O. E. (1985) *The Economic Institutions of Capitalism: Firms, Markets, Relational Contracting.* New York: Free Press.

5 Challenges and methods for cost analysis in public procurement

Lessons from the procurement of public transportation services in the Stockholm region

André Åslundh

Introduction

To perform cost analysis that is sufficiently detailed and insightful to be of value in the procurement of public transportation services is difficult. However, a number of methods supporting the execution of cost analysis can be implemented – methods that will also mitigate the continuous deterioration of cost awareness that otherwise tends to happen when the organization outsources its operation and therefore loses its direct connection to the service delivery. The purpose of this chapter is to provide some insights into what the Public Transport Administration (PTA) in Stockholm, Sweden, is doing to make sure that cost analysis that is sufficiently valuable can be made when procuring service operators for its public transport services. One method that will be specifically described is shadow price calculation, together with some special considerations and intricacies that one must consider when doing such calculations. The commuter train system in Stockholm is further used as a specific example when describing key costs that need to be included in the cost analysis for such services.

In Sweden there has been a strong trend in the last decades where public service operators have been moving from own operations to outsourcing. This makes Sweden today one of the few countries in the EU with the highest number of reported public procurement projects as indicated by the data presented in Figure 5.1.[1,2]

It is not the intention of this chapter to further study the underlying factors for this, but it is an important aspect for understanding the highly outsourcing-centric procurement climate for public services and the state of the legal framework for procurement in Sweden. It is also in this context that the Public Transport Administration of the Stockholm County Council (Stockholm PTA), the organization from which lessons learned are presented in this case study, is operating.

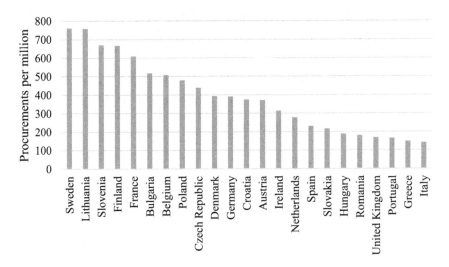

Figure 5.1 Number of procurements published in TED 2015 relative to the population (in millions) for EU countries with a population larger than two million inhabitants.

Outsourcing has been an important strategic component of the Stockholm PTA since the early 1990s and the organization is now relying solely on external suppliers to provide public transport services.

The Stockholm PTA is the largest buyer of public transportation in Sweden, spending 1.3 billion Euros on the procurement of public transport services every year.[3] This includes, as shown in Figure 5.2, services for various means of transport such as buses, metro, commuter trains, local rail services and passenger ferries in the Stockholm archipelago.

The Stockholm PTA is providing transport services with the aim of making them easily accessible, reliable and environmentally friendly and, as can be seen in Figure 5.3, the customers are quite content with the quality delivered.[4]

In addition to the travelers being rather satisfied, a recent study made by Arthur D. Little, and sponsored by UITP, found Stockholm to be one of the highest ranked public transport systems, second only to Singapore.[5]

The most important trends that are having an impact on the current strategy evolution of the Stockholm PTA are related to the following factors:

- Digitalization of both customer services and internal processes
- Stockholm is growing quickly, and the transportation system therefore has areas with capacity problems or areas undergoing a lot of development
- Costs are increasing at a higher rate than the population of the Stockholm County, as can be seen in Figure 5.4.[6]

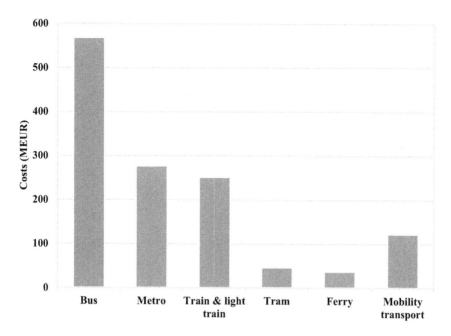

Figure 5.2 Costs 2017 in the Stockholm County for different types of public transportation.

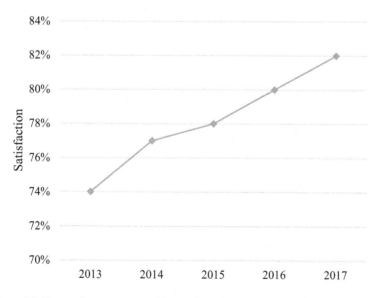

Figure 5.3 Share of passengers stating in onboard surveys that they are satisfied with the transport service provided.

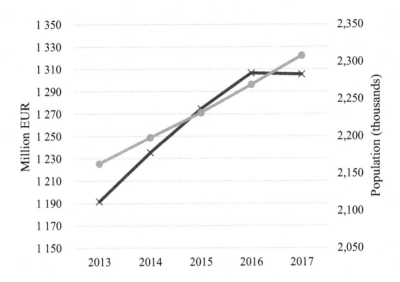

Figure 5.4 Population of the Stockholm County (•) and total costs (×) for transport operators providing transport services for the Stockholm PTA.

The dent in the curve for the cost in 2017 is to a large extent the result of passengers moving from bus contracts, with passenger volume-based compensation models, to other types of transportation like the commuter train, with a production-based compensation model, where the increase in passenger volume is not having a direct impact on the costs for the buyer. The transfer of passengers between the types of transport is, to a large degree, the result of the recent introduction of a major infrastructure upgrade to the commuter train system called the Stockholm City Line.[7]

Other factors like improved infrastructure for biking and the increased usage of electric bikes is also expected to start to have an impact on the traveling behavior. However, the overall cost trend is negative, and it is how cost analysis can play a role in mitigating this situation that will be further discussed in this chapter.

Challenges when performing cost analysis

Cost analysis has always been an important part of the procurement process of the Stockholm PTA. In particular for financial prognosis purposes but also in order to make sure that bids received are neither overly expensive, so that a too-high price is paid, or underfinanced, making it difficult for the supplier to provide sufficient quality in the services provided.

In the early years of outsourcing cost analysis was rather straightforward. The level of cost awareness in the organization was high, the operational information that had been acquired when performing the operations in-house was still relevant, and the competence of the staff of the buyer was still more or less the same as that of a supplier.

However, over time actual in-house cost awareness deteriorated. Partly due to the natural turnover of staff, and partly due to the recruitment of more procurement-oriented competence rather than resources with operational transport service skills.

This has made it increasingly difficult to maintain the detailed understanding of costs needed to chase the increasingly narrower margins for cost efficiency improvements.

One important way of increasing cost awareness is by benchmarking with other providers of public transportation. The Stockholm PTA is interested in performing such analysis but has few or no other similar operations in Sweden with which to compare, either due to being so much larger than other buyers of similar services or in some cases being the only buyer. Operations of a similar size can be found in other countries but then the cost conditions are so different that it becomes difficult to compare cost indicators.

During the process of becoming more efficient as a buyer, the Stockholm PTA has spent a lot of time and effort on evolving its processes for requirement management. In the early phases of outsourcing, the requirements tended to be detailed and specific for what the actual solution should be. Over time the requirements have been made more functional.

This is a feasible strategy because it provides the suppliers with more freedom to maneuver and to offer the best solution depending on the procurement situation. It is also rational from a cost efficiency point of view. However, it generates problems for the buyer in the long run, because it creates a larger distance between the buyer and the operations, resulting in difficulties maintaining knowledge about the operational details, including costs.

In addition to what has already been mentioned, cost analysis has turned out to be difficult in a constantly changing organization. Examples of hurdles for cost analysis created by organizational changes are:

• Re-organization leading to new cost structures that create a disturbance in accounting records kept over time, making it difficult to monitor trends in a good way
• Movement of responsibilities and thus costs between different contracts generates problems when trying to monitor trends and to keep track of contract performance
• New ERP systems; Information loss when changing between ERP systems and re-mapping of accounts makes historical cost mining tricky
• Changes to the way of performing financial control; Changes in accounting rules and regulations is an additional factor that tends to distort cost data.

Examples of methods in cost analysis

One of the most important kinds of cost analysis in public procurement is made to figure out if the prices received in bids are reasonable, that is, to do what is called a shadow price calculation. It is not the purpose of this chapter to provide a complete description of how to do a shadow price calculation for the procurement of public transportation but, rather, to provide some highlights of important aspects to consider.

General aspects of a shadow price calculation for public transportation

Depending on the strategy selected, the distribution of risk and responsibility for different cost areas can be different between PTAs. This will have an impact on the scope of the shadow price analysis since the calculation should be on the responsibilities given to the supplier of the contract in question.

Investments, for instance, can be treated in various ways. The model chosen by the Stockholm PTA is, to as large a degree as possible, responsible itself for investments with economical life length longer than multiple contract periods. The Stockholm PTA therefore invests in infrastructure such as tunnels, tracks and stations (e.g. metro and light train), which can have depreciation periods of up to 100 years and in trains, which are having depreciation periods of around 30 years. Buses that are having operational lifespans of eight to ten years are instead made the responsibility of the traffic operators in contracts of similar agreement periods.

Once the distribution of responsibility is decided upon, the analysis can be made for the key areas, which, in the case of the Stockholm model, typically consists of the cost categories listed in Figure 5.5.

Examples of main cost components when providing commuter train services

In order to highlight some specific aspects of cost analysis, the Stockholm commuter train system is further used as an example. The Stockholm commuter train system is a public transportation system running on the national railway infrastructure provided by the Swedish railway authority. Every day 300,000 passengers are travel on the Stockholm commuter train. As already mentioned, the Stockholm PTA invests in and owns the trains as well as the part of the infrastructure that is not already provided by the government railway authority.

Examples of key non-investment-related cost areas for this kind of system are:

- Train drivers, support staff on trains and customer support and sales staff in stations
- Maintenance of trains

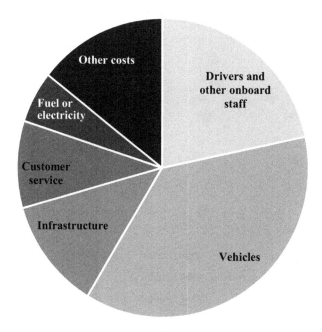

Figure 5.5 Key cost categories for a commuter train transport operator and the sche-
matic share of cost per category.

- Electricity
- Fees for running on the shared railway infrastructure.

*Train drivers, support staff on trains and customer support and sales staff in
stations*

Costs for drivers and other onboard resources are difficult to assess. They
depend, in a very complex way, on the timetable and the effect it has on the
resulting overall duty list for the trains. The trains then also need to be staffed
based on a complex set of rules listed in the Collective Labor Agreement
(CLA) (see Figure 5.6). These CLAs also provide rules for salaries and other
benefits.

Considering all these factors, the efficiency for a train driver (measured as
the ratio of time driving a train with passengers over total paid time) can be as
low as 40 percent due to the time lost in scheduling and the activities needed to
prepare and transport non-passenger carrying trains. This can be compared
with an efficiency of 60 percent for a bus driver who is not as engaged in preparing the buses. Bus drivers are also employed with CLAs containing less
scheduling constraints. Scheduling of resources is an area where much digitalization is taking place with the transport operators implementing IT systems

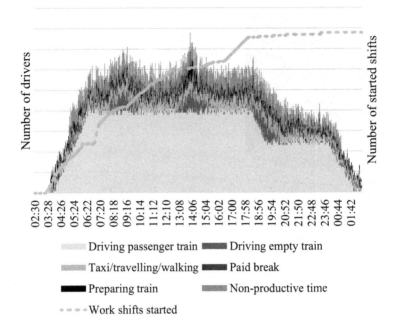

Figure 5.6 Number of drivers needed to perform different tasks during a weekday and the number of cumulative work shifts started. Based on simulations in a traffic scheduling planning system.

that are increasingly capable of preparing efficient plans for utilizing both trains and staff in a good way.

Another important factor with an impact on resource costs are compensation levels. For drivers of transport types who do not need high educational attainment, such as bus drivers and taxi drivers (needed for the provisioning of mobility transport), the Swedish PTAs have, together with their suppliers, been so successful in maneuvering the labor market so that for some types of traffic the overall compensation package has been reduced to levels where it is now starting to become difficult to acquire the resources needed to perform the traffic services.

This will most likely have a long-term effect on cost levels as salary levels bounce back when suppliers need to increase the attractiveness of the profession to secure staff for its operations.

Maintenance of trains

Another area with a complex cost structure is maintenance of trains. Trains are large and complex heavy-duty machines running almost all day on tight schedules and operating under the high security requirements applied to passenger trains running on railway infrastructure. Due to the complexity of the trains and the varying types of maintenance needed, both preventive and corrective, it is very difficult to do a detailed calculation on costs. One must therefore rely instead on statistics for historical costs.

This dependency on statistics for cost analysis can be reasonably managed during steady state operation. However, when larger upgrades are implemented or when completely new models of trains are introduced into the fleet it is very difficult to make a prognosis on what the actual costs will be since the statistics lose their relevance. This means that lead times for collecting new and updated statistics play an important role and therefore need to be minimized.

Electricity and fees for running on the shared railway infrastructure

Compared to the cost areas already described, calculating costs for electricity and the fees for running on the railway infrastructure is rather straightforward. The consumption of electricity of a train in relation to average speed and load is something that can be measured fairly easily. Driver behavior and time schedule will have some, but comparatively limited, impact.

As for the infrastructure fees, there is a price list provided by the Swedish National Transport Administration that can be applied to the movement of trains to calculate the resulting fees. These costs are more related to issues of making long-term forecasts for the fees since they are governmentally controlled and therefore impacted by political decisions that are difficult to predict.

Estimating and controlling risk and profitability

Although not part of the actual cost structure of a service, it is nevertheless important to understand how risk factors and profitability requirements among the suppliers will add to the final price for the buyer. On the one hand it is not in the interests of the buyer, the end customers, and the taxpayers to pay too much for the services procured. On the other hand, it is also not a good strategy to make the margins too small for the suppliers since it will reduce the overall attractiveness of the business, which might have a long-term impact on the competition. Small margins might also reduce the ability of the suppliers to provide sufficient quality and ability to invest in the development of the services provided.

This chapter will not further discuss feasible levels of risk and profitability and the results in the market for public transportation in Sweden. However, having sufficient awareness of these factors is very important in the final negotiations of a procurement project in order to be able to close the deal in a way which in the end is favorable both for the buyer and the supplier.

Dealing with cost evolution

To lower the risk margin needed for the supplier to manage cost changes that are out of its control, it is common among the Swedish PTAs to take as large a part of the risk for general cost changes as possible. A common criterion when distributing risk is that it should be made the responsibility of the party with the best means to control it. For the Stockholm PTA this has resulted, for instance, in the situation where it is itself responsible for the fees for the infrastructure for passenger-carrying trains since it is responsible for making the overall time schedule and therefore in control of the volume of traffic.

The traffic operator is, instead, responsible for the consumption of electricity, since it is the drivers who can have an impact on how much electricity is used based on driving skills and behavior. The price variation of electricity is, however, a risk taken by the PTA since it is very difficult for both parties to make a reasonable prognosis over the length of a contract. Depending on the overall cost structure of the service a few feasible indices, such as the consumer price index (CPI) and labor cost index (LCI), are selected as proxies for inflation or other more general factors that have an impact on the cost evolution.

Additional tools and activities to support cost analysis

The actual cost analysis depends not only on the knowledge about the underlying cost structures and drivers. It is also crucial to have up-to-date information on prices and cost levels for the cost components of the service in question. A common problem shared between all buyers, not only ones in public procurement, is the difficulty in closing the information gap to the suppliers. The information gap not only makes it more difficult to define the proper scope and requirements of the services to be procured, but it also makes the suppliers stronger in negotiations.

One way of mitigating this information deficit is to implement several ways of acquiring cost information from ongoing contracts. The main flow of information is generated by processing invoices and the information on invoices. This has its challenges because it is usually tricky to manage a detailed invoicing and accounting structure and make sure that the quality of the process is maintained at the same time.

In addition to the information generated by the flow of invoices, structured flows of financial or cost-related information from the suppliers to the buyer can also be implemented. This is not always easy because it has an impact on how people are working and therefore requires a lot of planning and preparation when setting up the process. However, the evolution and digitalization of business support systems provides lots of tools in this area, the use of which is important for PTAs.

In addition to this, one can also try to improve the general flow of input needed for cost analysis, such as increasing the dialogue with other buyers to collect benchmark and other cost-related information. The dialogue with the market in between procurement projects should also be sufficiently frequent in order to understand how different cost areas are developing.

Conclusions

Generating cost awareness that is sufficiently detailed and up to date is proving to be increasingly difficult over time. This is the result of the procurement organization maturing and becoming increasingly distant from the original operational activities.

Cost awareness can be regained or even increased but it requires a lot of hard work in changing both the internal ways of working as well as the interaction with the actors in the supply chain.

Key factors in this work for the Stockholm Public Transport Authority have been to:

- Develop and maintain competence and methods for comprehensive shadow price calculation
- Engage in close and frequent dialogue with both the suppliers as well as other buyers
- Start the development of the internal processes and system tools needed to not only perform invoicing and accounting in an efficient way but also to be able to monitor and store more detailed financial data needed for cost analysis, collecting them immediately as costs occur as well as later when cost analysis might be needed in order to prepare for upcoming procurement projects.

Implementing these methods might make it possible to improve the detail and accuracy of the cost analysis performed in procurement projects.

Improved skills in cost analysis are likely to increasing the overall performance and cost efficiency, resulting in a larger savings potential for public procurement performed in this area.

Notes

1 Graph prepared based on procurement data collected by the European Commission as published by the Swedish National Agency for Public Procurement, www.upphandlingsmyndigheten.se/verktyg/statistik-om-offentlig-upphandling/europeiska-jamforelser/, together with population statistics for the EU in 2015 as published by Eurostat.
2 Using the metric of procurements published in TED should only be seen as an indication for the degree of outsourcing since it does not take the total value of the individual procurements into consideration.
3 Annual reports for the Stockholm Public Transport Administration, 2013–2017
4 Statistics provided by Transport Analysis, a Swedish government agency for transport policy analysis, www.trafa.se

5 The future of Mobility 3.0, Arthur D Little, March, 2018, www.adlittle.com/sites/default/files/viewpoints/adl_uitp_future_of_mobility_3.0_1.pdf
6 Statistics about the population per county in Sweden as provided by the Statistics Sweden Agency, www.scb.se/en/
7 The Stockholm City Line, Trafikverket (Swedish Transport Administration), www.trafikverket.se/en/startpage/projects/Railway-construction-projects/The-Stockholm-City-Line/

6 Reference prices and Italian spending review

Fabrizio Sbicca

Introduction

In recent years, the Italian Anti-Corruption Authority (ANAC) has calculated, following specific statistical surveys, numerous "reference prices" of goods and services selected among ones with the greatest impact on national public expenditure.

Reference prices have been introduced in Italy starting from the second half of 2012 with the aim of containing public spending. For this purpose, the legislator assigned ANAC the task of preparing and publishing these prices. ANAC determined reference prices as benchmark values in public tenders: they represent, essentially, price constraints imposed on contracting authorities. It is important to clarify that reference prices, on which ANAC is responsible under Italian law, are different concepts than standard costs on which to base state funding on local government of the public activity concerning the supply to citizens of the main social rights (health, social assistance and education, as well as local public transport). These standard costs are, in fact, the result of an applied methodology of monetization of the "industrial" product, borrowed from the business economy (in particular, cost accounting) and from the theory of public finance.

A reference price represents, instead, a sort of "fair" price to pay for the purchase of certain goods and services in the context of public procurement. To fulfill its task, in particular about healthcare purchases, ANAC has faced the need to acquire extremely detailed information on contracts concerning specific types of services/products with the aim of determining these reference prices.

The analysis of the efficiency of public contracts, made possible by the abundance of information gathered to support this regulatory activity, also allows the development of "price overspending" indices, capable of signaling potential anomalies of public contracts.

Understanding the information potential of the acquired data, ANAC has extended the use of such information for the identification of corruption risk indicators (*red flags*) constructed from such information elements.

Their publication and application, in addition to directly reducing economic extra income (due to higher prices), which is the main incentive for corruption, also favors transparency and accountability of public administration purchases, thus preventing inefficiency and any corrupting behavior.

Refe rence prices in the health sector: A general overview

Reference prices for the health sector have been introduced in Italy as a spending review measure. In particular, the Italian law established that ANAC must prepare reference prices at the conditions of greater efficiency of goods and services among those with the greatest impact in terms of cost to the National Health Service. The same rule also provided for publication on the Authority's website of the unit prices paid by local health authorities for the purchase of goods and services for which reference prices are processed (ANAC, 2015).

Reference prices have regulatory value (they represent a sort of price ceiling) aimed at reducing public spending on public contracts related to the purchase of goods and services in the health sector. Starting from 2012, the Authority has therefore proceeded to determine and publish on its own website the reference prices in the health sector relating to multiple product categories, for the hospital laundry, catering and cleaning services, as well as for the supply of some medical devices and drugs.

In carrying out this activity, ANAC found itself fundamentally enriched by two extremely relevant instruments: the first concerning the availability of an information asset with a very high level of detail and the second concerning the methodological experience developed in the determination of statistical-econometric models developed specifically for the purpose.

It is necessary to clarify that the reference price is a tool for the synthesis of complexity; it allows the comparison between highly complex contracts, each of which relates to heterogeneous goods or services. Thanks to the use of the statistical-econometric methodology developed by the Authority, it has been possible to identify a rather precise synthesis measure: the reference price. It allows summarizing in a single "number" all the different characteristics, making purchases with different contractual specifications easy to compare.

It is possible to summarize in these terms the idea underlying the identification of reference prices: given a specific good (or service), through a survey of the public contracts market, it is also possible to identify the most convenient price for the Public Administration.

This process is like a market research, not far from the logic of finding the lowest prices viable with the current specialized search engines on the web. Once the range of prices available for the specific product has been identified, we could abstractly use the lowest price as a reference for purchases by the Public Administration.

However, also taking into account the fact that this (lowest) price, determined by the matching of supply and demand in a specific context, could be the result of particular conditions not necessarily replicable in all situations, the legislator introduced the use of the percentile to give substance to the concept of "conditions of greater efficiency of goods". The Italian legislator has decided to identify values a little less challenging of the lowest price detected, or one of the 5th, 10th, 20th or 25th percentile. ANAC has therefore collected a number – for example 100 – of contracts relating to a specific good/service and then, after having ordered it in ascending order, has selected the 5th, 10th, 20th or 25th percentile as the reference price.

The percentile method contains the implicit (necessary) forecast to draw up reference prices on goods (services) that have a certain degree of homogeneity, that is, it is necessary to identify comparable goods/services. The comparison of prices of different goods would lead in fact to completely misleading results.

The homogeneity of goods or services, if not inherent in the product or service itself (for example, some drugs), can be induced through a process that can be defined as "standardization". This process, which therefore has the purpose of "constructing" comparable goods/services, can be carried out ex ante (before data collection) or ex post (after data collection). In the first case – ex ante standardization – the expert merchandiser selects and gives a value to the characteristics considered relevant to identify homogeneous products on which to go to collect prices and then calculate the percentiles (a more practicable technique in the field of goods than services).

For the second case (ex post standardization), which happens in situations where the ex ante standardization procedure is not applicable, as in the case of services which, by their nature, have a higher degree of complexity, it is necessary to proceed with an empirical standardization mechanism, based on the statistical analysis of the information collected. In this case, data analysis, conducted through statistical considerations, selects potentially relevant characteristics provided by the expert merchandiser, which actually impact on prices.

Obviously, the identification of a sufficiently high number of characteristics, on the one hand, helps to increase the complexity of the analysis; on the other it allows a thorough analysis of the service. In fact, wanting to represent in a stylized way the link between the price of service and the – potential – relevant features we could write that

$$P_S = f(V_1, V_2, \ldots, V_i, \ldots V_n, \boldsymbol{h})$$

That is, the price of the service (P_S) can be represented as a function (f) of a certain number of observed variables (features) (V_i) and of a certain number of unobserved ones (the vector $\boldsymbol{h}$). Clearly, the non-prior knowledge of exactly what the characteristics relevant in determining the price of the service induces the expert merchandiser to introduce a significant number of characteristics. This choice contributes, among other things, to making the informative content of the unobserved characteristics negligible. ANAC used a methodology based on a variable selection procedure to identify the subset of characteristics that have a statistically significant influence on the price.

Once this subset of variables has been selected – $(V_{j_1}, V_{j_2}, ..., V_{j_k}) \subseteq (V_1, V_2, ..., V_i, ... V_n, h)$ – two regression functions are computed: a function that provides for the modification of the intercept of the ordinary OLS model (1) and one through a quantile regression (2).

$$P_s^{mOLS} = f^{mOLS}\left(V_{j_1}, V_{j_2}, ..., V_{j_k}\right) \tag{1}$$

and

$$P_s^{Quant} = f^{Quant}\left(V_{j_1}, V_{j_2}, ..., V_{j_k}\right) \tag{2}$$

The reference price is the maximum of the values that emerge from these two – (1) and (2) – regression functions (3).

$$P_s^{ref} = MAX\left(P_s^{mOLS}, P_s^{Quant}\right) \tag{3}$$

Relating to the choice of which percentile to consider (5th, 10th, 20th or 25th), according to Italian law, a reference price in the health sector, at the most efficient conditions, is a percentile of the prices recorded for each good or service being analyzed on the basis of statistical significance and the heterogeneity of the goods and services. Then, in general, higher heterogeneity and lower statistical significance must correspond in principle to higher percentiles.

An example of ex ante standardization: Drugs and medical devices

As aforementioned, homogeneity of goods can be guaranteed, if not inherent in the product itself, through a preliminary identification of the relevant features by the expert(s) of the good(s). The expert merchandiser selects and gives a value to the characteristics considered relevant to identify homogeneous products on which to go to collect prices and then calculate the percentiles. We used to call this process ex ante (before data collection) standardization.

Example: "Hypodermic needles for syringe". The expert merchandiser identifies which characteristics are essential for obtaining comparable products. In the specific case are the material, the tip type, the gauge, and the presence/absence of phthalates, latex and the safety device.

Subsequently he also indicates the "values": "*in lubricated stainless steel, triple sharp point, gauge* G18 ÷ G 25, without phthalates, latex free, with safety device".

Precisely on this product so punctually identified – "*Hypodermic needles for syringe in lubricated stainless steel, triple sharp point, gauge G18 ÷ G 25, without phthalates, latex free, with safety device*" – are collected unit prices and the subsequent calculation of percentiles (5°, 10°, 20° and 25°) is performed, including the one that will represent the reference price. Tables 6.1 and 6.2 shown below contain some examples of reference prices for some drugs and medical devices.

An example of ex post standardization: The sanitary cleaning service

The survey involved 283 public administrations operating in the health sector as well as regional purchasing centers with expertise in healthcare. Considering the sanitary cleaning service, since the ex ante standardization was not possible, the questionnaire was set up to acquire data relating to a very large number of characteristics (about 50 for each contract) potentially relevant to the price of the service, which, specifically, is the "monthly rent per square meter" (ANAC, 2016a).

Only some of them (13 out of 50) proved effectively influential on the price based on ANAC's statistical procedure.

Then, given the choice of the 25th percentile, five reference price functions, one for each risk area, were designed and put together as a weighted average (4).

$$P_{cleaning}^{ref} = \sum_{i=1}^{5} \left(P_i^{ref} \times Surface_i \right) / \sum_{i=1}^{5} \left(Surface_i \right) \tag{4}$$

In this regard, it is indeed important to specify that, commonly, cleaning service contracts in the health sector are categorized according to the area of infectious risk (Very high risk, High risk, Medium risk, Low risk, External area). A higher price corresponds to a higher level of infectious risk.

Only for instance, we can observe the High-risk area formula:

$$P_2^{ref} = Max \left(\hat{P}_{25}, \hat{P}_{25}^{quant} \right): \tag{5}$$

$\hat{P}_{25} = 0.856345548 - 0.00013401 \times Surface_2 + 0.07676 \times Employees + 0.13779 \times Freq + 0.07281 \times clean2 + 0.69507 \times S2included + 0.85663 \times S5included + 1.25419 \times S9included + 2.11109 \times S18included,$

$\hat{P}_{25}^{quant} = 1.0478 - 0.0000492 \times Surface_2 + 0.0205 \times Employees + 0.165 \times Freq + 0.0857 \times clean2 + 0.5529 \times S2included + 0.2651 \times S5included + 0.3468 \times S9included + 1.0731 \times S18included$

Table 6.1 Some reference prices for drugs

ATC	Active pharmaceutical ingredient	Dosage	Pharmaceutical form	Reference price (VAT excluded)		
				P10	P20	P25
A16AB03	Algalsidasi Alfa	1 Mg/Ml Ev	Phial	1,538.84		
A16AB07	Alglucosidasi Acida Umana Ricombinante	50 Mg + 1 Phial 20 Ml	Phial	508.25		**2.05**
B01AB01	Eparina Sodica	25000 Ui 5 Ml	Phial	145		
B01AB02	Antitrombina Iii Umana	1000 Ui	Flacone			
B01AB04	Dalteparina Sodica	Ui Axa	Phial/Syringe	0.000499		
B01AB05	Enoxaparina Sodica	Ui Axa	Phial/Syringe	0.00018875		
B01AB06	Nadroparina Calcica	Ui Axa	Phial/Syringe		0.000270	
B01AB07	Parnaparina Sodica	Ui Axa	Phial/Syringe		0.000216	
B01AB08	Reviparina Sodica	Ui Axa	Phial/Syringe		0.000563	
B01AB12	Bemiparina Sodica	Ui Axa	Phial/Syringe		0.000314	
B01AC11	Iloprost	20 Mcg 2 Ml Soluzione	Phial	24.652		
B01AC13	Abciximab	2 Mg/Ml 5 Ml	Phial		231.74	
B01AC17	Tirofiban	0,25 Mg/Ml 50 Ml	Phial	157.71		
B02BD08	Eptacog Alfa	1 Mg Polvere	Phial	653.84		
B02BD08	Eptacog Alfa	2 Mg Polvere	Phial	1,307.7		
B03XA01	Eritropoietina	Ui	Phial/Syringe	0.0018		
B03XA02	Darbepoetina Alfa	Mcg	Phial/Syringe/Bottle	1.15		
B03XA03	Eritropoietina Pegilato	Mcg	Phial/Syringe	1.16		

Source: Italian Anti-Corruption Authority – www.anticorruzione.it.

Table 6.2 Some reference prices for medical devices

Type	Cnd_Code	Description	Technical specifications	Intended use	Reference price (VAT excluded) P25
Patches	M050101	Patches on spool band	Nonwoven, height 2.5 cm, length ≥ 9 m	For fixing medications, probes and catheters	0.18000
Patches	M050101	Patches on spool band	Canvas, height 2.5 cm, length ≥ 9 m	For fixing medications, probes and catheters	0.26000
Patches	M050101	Patches on spool band	Silk, height 2.5 cm, length ≥ 9 m	For fixing medications, probes and catheters	0.45000
Patches	M050101	Patches on spool band	Nonwoven, height 5 cm, length ≥ 9 m	For fixing medications, probes and catheters	0.34900
Patches	M050101	Patches on spool band	Canvas, height 5 cm, length ≥ 9 m	For fixing medications, probes and catheters	0.52000
Patches	M050101	Patches on spool band	Silk, height 5 cm, length ≥ 9 m	For fixing medications, probes and catheters	0.87200
Patches	M050102	Medicated patches	ca. mm 19 x 75 mm	For small wounds	0.00900
Patches	M050201	Nonwoven stretch patches	Height 5 cm, length ≥ 9 m	For fixing medications	0.64590
Patches	M050201	TNT stretch patches	Height 10 cm, length ≥ 9 m	For fixing medications	1.21630
Patches	M050201	Nonwoven stretch patches	Height 15 cm, length ≥ 9 m	For fixing medications	1.79280
Patches	M050201	TNT stretch patches	Height 20 cm, length ≥ 9 m	For fixing medications	2.47000

Source: Italian Anti-Corruption Authority – www.anticorruzione.it.

Where *Surface₂*, *Employees*, *Freq*, *clean2* are quantitative variables, and *s2included*, *s5included*, *s9included*, *s18included* are dichotomous variables:

> **Surface₂:** *Total area of risk area in square meters;*
> **Employees:** *Number of employees per day made available by the company;*
> **Freq:** *Weekly frequency;*
> **clean2:** *Weekly further clean intervals;*
> **s2included:** *Emergency response team for spot operations on request;*
> **s5included:** *Disposal of special waste;*
> **s9included:** *The provision of a continuous monitoring;*
> **s18included:** *Porterage.*

Reference prices and spending review

From a general point of view, the activity of determining reference prices is the expression of a regulatory power, able to have a very marked impact on public contracts and on the behavior of the contractors and the companies participating in the contracts, which allows at the same time to pursue objectives of control and revision of public spending. Moreover, the application of reference prices is a mechanism that is certainly preferable to the so-called "linear cuts", often criticized because they are not based on efficiency considerations in establishing the various areas in which to intervene to rationalize spending.

In fact, while the linear cuts affect indifferently the various public administrations regardless of the analysis of merit of the expense, the reference prices have the effect of promoting a virtuous process of improvement of the purchasing performance, aligning the performance of the less-efficient contractors to the results of the most virtuous ones.

In this regard, the two graphs shown below compare, by way of example, the various distribution effects derived from the savings obtainable from an alignment with the reference prices, compared to the equivalent reduction in expenditure obtainable with a linear cut (ANAC, 2016b).

In particular, the first graph (Figure 6.1) shows how an alignment with the reference prices of contracts of the contracting authorities that present an excess of expenditure would imply, for the sanitary cleaning service, a significant cost saving, in the order of 17.5 percent. The estimates have been drawn up by applying to each contracting authority the reference price that is determined by taking into consideration the relevant characteristics present in each specific contract. Therefore, the realization of these savings, in addition to not feeding undesirable effects such as those typical of linear cuts, should allow the maintenance of the same levels of service, a very important aspect especially for those typically labor-intensive services, where price reductions very often translate into staff cuts.

Coming to the explanation of the graph, on the abscissa axis there are (anonymously) the contractors examined. On the axis of the ordinates, the

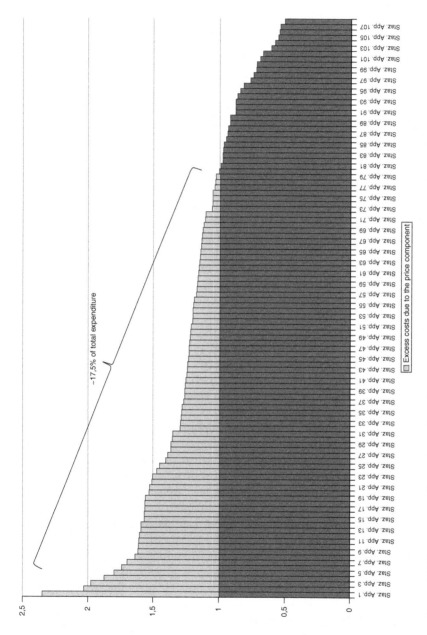

Figure 6.1 Excess expenditure due to the price component – estimates for the sanitary cleaning service.

expenditure is expressed as a percentage of the reference price. The height of each bar therefore represents the expense of each contracting station, ordered from left to right in descending order, from the less "virtuous" health structures to the more "virtuous" ones. In the first graph, the bottom part (from 0 to 1) therefore represents the expenditure not higher than the reference price (represented by 1), while the top part constitutes the excess expenditure with respect to the bottom part, the so-called "overspending". In this case, if all contracts were aligned with the reference price, this excess expenditure would be zero. The entire top part of the chart, equal to 17.5 percent of the total expenditure, should be cut. In the next graph (Figure 6.2) the criticalities related to the linear cuts are highlighted.

The size of the graph is the same as the previous one, but in this case, the distribution effects of a linear cut are highlighted, aimed at obtaining the same savings in expenditure attainable with the reference price, equal to 17.5 percent. The individual bars of the graph have in fact the same height and the colored area is the same as the first graph. In other words, the sum of the bottom and top areas of the first chart is identical to the sum of the bottom, middle and top areas of the second chart. More precisely, the top area of the first graph is the same size (17.5 percent of the total expenditure) as the top area in the second graph. In this second case (linear cut), however, the reduction of the excess expenditure of 17.5 percent is obtained cutting to all the contractors the same percentage of expenditure, represented by the top area. The new total expenditure, following the cut, is in the second chart (the sum of the bottom and middle areas). In other words, while the overspending in the previous graph is the top area, in this case the cut is overall the same, but evenly distributed in the percentage of 17.5 on the contractors regardless of their efficiency. The "waste" is not eliminated but only reduced (it remains a middle area), while the most efficient health structures are penalized. Linear cutting is less effective for the most inefficient and unfair for the most efficient.

The reference prices, in addition to representing an "intelligent" tool for reviewing spending that can generate savings in an equitable manner, identifying and reducing inefficiency spaces, are at the same time instruments to assist in the identification and prevention of corruption phenomena, often closely related to the misuse of public money. Regarding this last aspect, the reference prices, limiting the discretion of contractors by identifying price limits, prevent upstream and, in a direct way, possible inefficiency and/or corruption phenomena.

The availability of this informative patrimony also makes it possible to identify, through the construction of one or more ranking systems, those contractors that could be the subject of a possible preliminary investigation. For example, it is possible to construct a simple indicator of excess expenditure attributable to the price component:

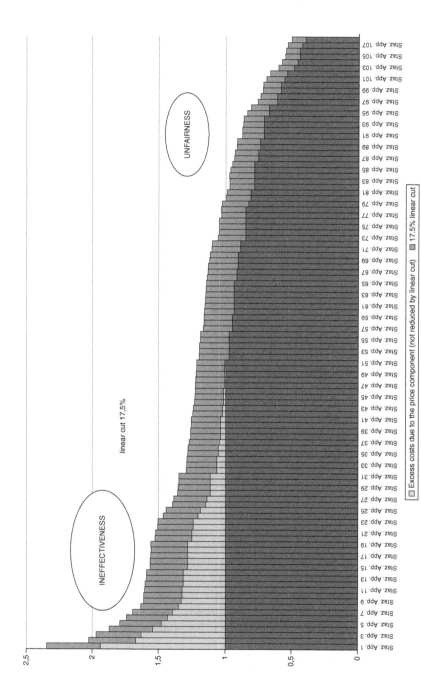

Figure 6.2 Excess expenditure due to the price component and linear cuts – estimates for the sanitary cleaning service.

Price overspending

Indicator of excess expenditure due to the price component, defined as (ANAC, 2017):

$$\text{Pos} = \frac{P_{eff} \times Q_{eff} - P_{Ref} \times Q_{eff}}{P_{Ref} \times Q_{eff}} \times 100$$

P_{eff} = actual price
Q_{eff} = actual quantity
P_{Ref} = reference price

The indicator calculates the excess of expenditure due to the difference between the price actually paid and the reference price (Sbicca and Conforti, 2018). In general, very high values of this index can be symptomatic of anomalies.

In this way, it is possible to draw up a ranking of the less performing contractors and, therefore, more deserving of attention from a standpoint of vigilance. The following chart (Figure 6.3) shows the values of this indicator, always related to the data of the sanitary cleaning service.

In particular, the values of the indicator are shown in descending order for the first 50 less-efficient contractors, starting from the first one, which has an excess of 57 percent. In general, it is easy to understand how extremely high values of this index can be symptomatic of pathological situations, not necessarily related to inefficiency alone (on the possibility of constructing objective indicators of corruption on the basis of the analysis of purchasing behavior of public administrations, see for example Di Tella and Schargrodsky (2003). With particular reference to the Italian case, see Bandiera et al. (2009) where excess spending on public purchases of goods and services is conceptually distinguished between "passive" waste (which does not benefit anyone, but is the result of pure inefficiency) and "active" waste (which benefits the bureaucrat, that is, it is the result of corruption).[1]

The availability of information concerning the successful tenderer also allows for an in-depth knowledge of the market in question, while at the same time producing indicators that combine, for example, information regarding the price practiced and the market share held. In this regard, in the pie chart below (Figure 6.4), you can see the companies' market shares (anonymously).

Combining the information relative to the market shares with those of the prices calculated previously, it is possible to construct the graph below (Figure 6.5), in which the winning companies, represented on the abscissa axis, are ordered in relation to the excess price, represented on the axis of the ordinates.

This chart provides useful information for an interpretation of both the market mechanisms and its possible pathologies, deserving further insights

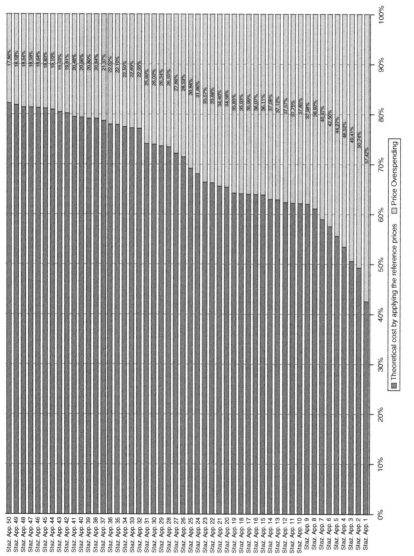

Figure 6.3 Price overspending ranking – sanitary cleaning service.

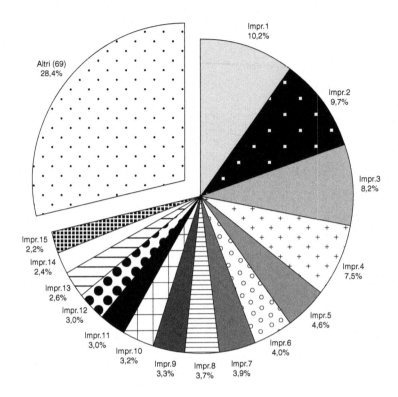

Figure 6.4 Supply side – companies' market shares.

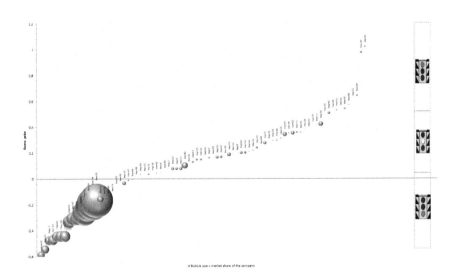

Figure 6.5 Price overspending and companies' market shares.

and developments, both in terms of analysis and in terms of construction of indicators of inefficiency and/or corruption. On the one hand, the hypothesis of economies of scale in the provision of cleaning services seems confirmed, on the other the remarkable diversity of performance is evident, in this case of the single companies supplying the service about the price offered and awarded in the tender. In other words, if only the excess price can abstractly be an indicator of corruption on the demand side, the combination with the information on the bidders can represent an indicator of corruption on the supply side, as represented graphically by the traffic lights on the right of the graph.

The methodological innovation aimed at homogenizing the characteristics of a service by its complex and heterogeneous nature has therefore resulted in a positive contribution in terms of comparability of situations that would otherwise be difficult to compare. It is a contribution to achieving a less formal and more substantial objective of transparency. On the other hand, an analysis that goes beyond the price paid by the contracting stations for a good/service could also be very useful: an analysis that considers both components of public spending, not only the price, but also the quantity purchased, as well as, possibly, other parameters (for example, the population served, the number of patients treated, etc.). All of these elements are suitable for the identification of more complex and detailed indicators, to guarantee a more effective and lasting control of public spending and the prevention/identification of inefficiency, corruption and collusion.

The possibility of having separate information for the price and quantity components offers opportunities for analysis that are difficult to conduct using pure "expense" data (typical of analyses based on financial statement data). In these analyses, in fact, it is much more complicated to differentiate the "waste" attributable to the price factor from that relating to the quantity purchased. This valuable information asset, in terms of collected data and methodological evolution, can be the starting point for analysis whose aims, as mentioned, go beyond the spending review objectives.

The development of further indicators concerning the same contracts based on other useful information collected (relating, for example, to the contractors, the territorial context, the dimensional data of the contract, the contractor selection procedure, the use of extensions/renewals), further increases the information contained in price overspending indicators (Sbicca and Marino, 2018). The combined use of all the indicators, in an organic "red flags" system, considerably strengthens their effectiveness, since their simultaneous analysis makes it possible to identify situations that are even more anomalous in a more targeted way, especially in cases where the different indices converge in the same direction. In this way it is possible to direct the supervisory activity towards potentially more critical situations, in order to verify if the administrative action is really affected by situations of inefficiency and/or even corruption (ANAC, 2018).

Note

1 With reference to public infrastructure spending in Italy, see finally Golden and Picci (2005).

References

ANAC – Autorità Nazionale Anticorruzione. 2015, *Relazione annuale*, Roma.

ANAC – Autorità Nazionale Anticorruzione. 2016a, *Prezzi di riferimento in ambito sanitario servizio di pulizia e sanificazione – Documento tecnico*, Roma.

ANAC – Autorità Nazionale Anticorruzione. 2016b, *Relazione annuale*, Roma.

ANAC – Autorità Nazionale Anticorruzione. 2017, *Relazione annuale*, Roma.

ANAC – Autorità Nazionale Anticorruzione. 2018, *Relazione annuale*, Roma.

Bandiera, O., Prat A., and Valletti, T. 2009, "Active and passive waste in government spending: Evidence from a policy experiment", *American Economic Review*, 99 (4), pp. 1278–1308.

Di Tella, R. and Schargrodsky, E. 2003, "The role of wages and auditing during a crisis in the city of Buenos Aires", *Journal of Law and Economics*, 46 (1), pp. 269–292.

Golden, M. and Picci, L. 2005, "Proposal for a new measure of corruption illustrated using Italian data", *Economics and Politics*, 17 (1), pp. 37–75.

Sbicca, F. and Conforti, D. 2018, "Sviluppo di indicatori di rischio corruttivo sulla base dei prezzi di riferimento. Il caso dei servizi di pulizia e sanificazione in ambito sanitario". Autorità Nazionale Anticorruzione – Rapporti e Studi.

Sbicca, F. and Marino, G. 2018, "Efficienza dei contratti pubblici e sviluppo di indicatori di rischio corruttivo". Autorità Nazionale Anticorruzione – Rapporti e Studi.

Part III

Corruption and probity in public procurement

Whenever talking about corruption in public procurement, an interdisciplinary debate cannot avoid focusing on the definition of the phenomenon, which typically has clear boundaries from the legal side, which are instead more blurred from the economist's point of view. In fact, from this latter perspective, a clear definition of corruption in the context of public procurement is offered which distinguishes between active and passive waste, as determinants of public services' costs and where corruption is a typical example of active waste, as it entails a "direct or indirect benefit for the public decision-maker", while passive waste does not (e.g. red tape).

In the debate presented in this chapter the two authors discuss EU rules and the tools currently available to combat corruption, surveying what the existing literature has to say about the efficacy of these tools, and then moves on to mention the problem of how to implement these tools in the absence of reliable data, keeping in mind the need to find methodologies to fight corruption that are themselves not too costly. Tünde Tátrai on one side, moving from the prescriptions of EU rules on combating corruption through debarment of suppliers involved in criminal organizations, highlights the urgent need for proper forms of transparency, in relation to data of companies and persons concerned, as a necessary condition for prevention and monitoring activities, especially in the phase of contract execution. She suggests a solution not necessarily relying on expensive controlling organizations: a governance model of public procurement that relies on an Internet-based "reputation system" which is in line with the significance of the role of society in combating public procurement corruption. Francesco Decarolis, on the other side, reminds us that we might be missing the elephant in the room: corruption in the early stages of the administrative (or political) decision to purchase a certain type of good/service/infrastructure. Even if both awarding and execution stages are impeccable, the very existence of a public contract might be the result of initial corruption involving the choice of using public funds for this contract instead of something else. So, while cost–benefit analysis can be an important tool to make decisions sound and transparent, it is likely that corruption at this stage is, and will remain, larger economically and harder to combat than other forms of corruption.

The other two contributions bring in the empirical side of the central theme. Both works look at Municipalities' behaviors in public procurement. Chabrost and Saussier study the impact of opening a public investigation into French municipalities' choice of award procedures. They observe that an allegedly corrupt municipality will not significantly tend to use more transparent and open procedures once under suspicion. However, they observe that neighboring municipalities will use more transparent calls for tenders to dismiss any suspicions when under a local spotlight on corruption. Uenk, Telgen, and Wind analyze tender documents of Dutch municipalities for adult social care services, looking at commissioning approaches and opportunistic behavior by providers. They find that there is no model where each of the stakeholders is completely protected against care provider opportunism, keeping in mind that the fact that there is an opportunity for opportunistic behavior does not mean care providers necessarily make use of this opportunity.

7 Corruption and probity in public procurement

Colloquium

Tünde Tátrai and Francesco Decarolis

Opening remarks – *Tünde Tátrai*

Why is ensuring transparency a strategic issue in combating procurement-related corruption?

I begin to answer this question by providing a background analysis of the European Directives. The goal is to learn how the regulator envisages combating corruption.

In an article in 2002, Tina Sorreide highlighted three criteria in relation to procurement-related corruption. The first includes problems that often arise if this type of corruption is common, the second relates to the mechanisms through which this illegal activity is actually carried out, and finally there is the strategy to combat corruption. Below I would like to go into the details of the third issue in view of the European public procurement directives.

As the Directive 24/2014/EU particularly underlines combating the criminal offense, it is worthwhile exploring what solutions are offered for combating it. The main rule is exclusion from public procurement, also set forth in the preamble to the Directive:

> Directive 24/2014/EU. (100) Public contracts should not be awarded to economic operators that have participated in a criminal organisation or have been found guilty of corruption […]

The first answer is including corruption among the reasons for exclusion and declaring bids irregular, as follows:

> Directive 24/2014. Art. 57 (1) Contracting authorities shall exclude an economic operator from participation in a procurement procedure where they have established, by verifying in accordance with Articles 59, 60 and 61, or are otherwise aware that that economic operator has been the subject of a conviction by final judgment for one of the following reasons: […]
>   (b) corruption…

Art. 26 (4) b) and Art. 35 (5):

> [...] tenders which do not comply with the procurement documents, which were received late, where there is evidence of collusion or corruption, or which have been found by the contracting authority to be abnormally low, shall be considered as being irregular.

In other words, a legal solution already exists, the sanction of exclusion and declaring bids irregular can truly be a restraining force. What is really missing is transparency in relation to the data of the companies and persons genuinely concerned, who need to be excluded from the procedure. The solution could determine the list of deterrents – which Auriol (2006) also called for in his article in order to make the information truly available – for the purposes of exclusion.

The answer to the question of how and what sort of strategy should be applied directly and actively appears only in one place and on one occasion in the normative text when the Directive calls attention to ensuring transparency.

> Dir. 24/2014. (126) The traceability and transparency of decision-making in procurement procedures is essential for ensuring sound procedures, including efficiently fighting corruption and fraud. Contracting authorities should therefore keep copies of concluded high-value contracts, in order to be able to provide access to those documents to interested parties in accordance with applicable rules on access to documents. Furthermore, the essential elements and decisions of individual procurement procedures should be documented in a procurement report. [...]

Accordingly, the Directive's approach of reducing corruption with the power of transparency is not suitable for enabling the contracting authority to quickly access information in the course of the tendering procedure.

Hunsaker (2009)[1] says: "Public procurement professionals must keep abreast of not only the laws that govern their practice, but be aware of the need for transparency in the way they conduct their transactions."

If based upon the above, the strategy is to exclude companies concerned in corruption and it is not really realistic for the contracting authority to examine every single economic operator concerned, one by one. Particularly not in the way Article 57 (1) of Directive 24/2014/EU suggests, as it also refers to non-legal persons, when it sets forth the following:

> The obligation to exclude an economic operator shall also apply where the person convicted by final judgment is a member of the administrative, management or supervisory body of that economic operator or has powers of representation, decision or control therein.

If any list is drawn up of those concerned, that public list must surely not include non-legal persons, in contrast to the economic operators concerned. This, however, presupposes the setting up of a database, which also pays attention to the non-legal persons concerned and their points of contact with the economic operators, as well as the changes therein. If a list of this kind is not drawn up and the contracting authority will continue to have to rely on the statements of the economic operators themselves, which the bidders are required to make in the European Single Procurement Document, in actual fact, this exclusion ground loses its significance in the fight against corruption.

As to how the monitoring required by Article 83 (3) of Directive 24/2014/EU will be implemented, this depends, to a large extent, on the format in which the data provided by the individual Member States can be made easily accessible and controllable.

> By 18 April 2017 and every three years thereafter, Member States shall submit to the Commission a monitoring report [...] about prevention, detection and adequate reporting of cases of procurement fraud, corruption, conflict of interest and other serious irregularities [...]

According to Greenwood and Klotz (2009), the key principles of best anti-corruption practices in public procurement are as follows:

* transparency,
* good management and the prevention of misconduct,
* monitoring compliance, accountability and enforcement.

If the connection between transparency, prevention and monitoring is omitted, transparency cannot play its role, because if the contracting authority does not have access to the "corruption status" of economic operators prior to or during the procedure, it will not be possible to check whether they are involved in corruption and they will have to accept the statements they make.

The regulatory environment is stuck at the level of ensuring general transparency, while it stipulates exclusion and irregularity as legal consequences. In the absence of an unambiguous possibility to control, the strategy of transparency in combating corruption can be implemented only to a moderate degree.

So Auriol (2006) will continue to be right as he expounds: if there is no list of debarred suppliers, firms that have been found guilty of active corruption are allowed to bid for new public contracts.

Opening remarks – *Francesco Decarolis*

The role of corruption in procurement

Given the general framework, theory has discussed various ways in which corruption may arise, the most important one being favoritism (see, for example, Arozamena and Weinschelbaum, 2009; Burguet and Perry, 2007; and Koc and Neilson, 2008 for a discussion of ex ante favoritism; or Lengwiler and Wolfstetter, 2010; and Menezes and Monteiro, 2006 for ex post favoritism). Overall, theoretical models predict that corruption entails both a transfer of rents from the principal to the official and efficiency costs, in particular in terms of lower quality of the good/service provided. Some papers also discuss potential measures to reduce the risk and/or costs of corruption in public procurement. In a model with bribe competition and favoritism, Burguet and Che (2004) show that, when contracts are awarded according to the scoring rule, putting less emphasis on quality (relative to price) in the scoring rule can reduce the effect of bribery. Compte et al. (2005) instead suggest that a form of "handicap" of the ex ante most efficient supplier may destabilize the collusive outcome that would otherwise emerge (with all the bidders bidding the highest acceptable price and the official extracting all rents in form of bribes paid by the lowest cost supplier). More recently, Auriol and Søreide (2017) discuss the use of debarment as a tool to deter corruption, and its consequences for collusion.

Rather than looking at partial mechanisms, other papers adopt a mechanism design perspective and try to identify the optimal procurement mechanism in presence of risk of bribery. Celentani and Ganuza (2002) assume a procurement setting in which the principal has preferences defined over ex ante quality and price, and there are a number of potential bidders with private information about their production costs. Delivered quality is certified by a public supervisor that can manipulate his report for a bribe. The optimal mechanism entails the use of a scoring rule in which the higher the probability of corruption, the lower the discretion left to the supervisor. The probability of corruption is endogenously determined by the choice of the supervisor, which, in turn, depends on the level of discretion. Supervisor and Official thus play a game where the optimal discretion level is decreasing in the expected corruption and the optimal corruption level is increasing in the expected discretion.

In this setting, higher market competition may lead to higher corruption for two reasons. First, more competition decreases the expected cost of quality and thus raises the expected quality being supplied. Second, higher competition allows for the selection of a better supervisor, thus the opportunity cost of reducing his discretion is higher. Since higher discretion implies higher profits, higher corruption may arise.

The *empirical literature* had an earlier blossoming more than a decade ago with the pioneering studies of Rose-Ackerman[2] and others bolstered by the new availability of data on corruption (cross-country perception indices). This older literature focused on whether corruption influences growth. The view that has emerged from it is that corruption significantly hurts growth (see Ades and di Tella, 1997). Motivated by this negative result, the current wave of studies has focused on the next set of questions: How prevalent is corruption? How does it take place? How can it be curbed? Progress on all these questions has been achieved through the use of more sophisticated data (e.g. Fisman and Miguel, 2007). Nevertheless, there are surprisingly few findings of this literature that have direct applicability to procurement. This is clearly acknowledged by the studies mentioned above.

Olken and Pande (2012), for instance, write

> [...] if we were asked by a politician [...] or the head of an anti-corruption agency what guidance the economic literature could give them about how to tackle the problem, we realized that, beyond a few core economic principles, we had more questions to pose than concrete answers.

What is missing is the empirical evidence in support of the main policy alternatives.

Among the limited set of aspects that the empirical literature has been able to address, there are four areas that have received particular attention. The first is the role of discretion: following the lines of theoretical literature stressing the importance of delegation and negotiation, a growing number of papers try to assess empirically the effects of discretion in public procurement (Branzoli and Decarolis, 2015; Chever and Moore, 2012; Chever et al., 2017; Coviello and Gagliarducci, 2017; Decarolis et al., 2016, 2019; Lalive and Schmutzler, 2011; Szucs, 2017), but overall the results are ambiguous. The second is favoritism. A growing literature is investigating the role of political favoritism in procurement. This does not necessarily entail corruption, but it can lead to similar effects in terms of efficiency costs (Baltrunaite, 2016; Brogaard et al., 2015; Coviello and Gagliarducci, 2017; Goldman et al., 2013; Muraközy and Telegdy, 2016; Schoenherr, 2019). Looking at financial transactions data from Russia, Mironov and Zhuravskaya (2016) show that firms dependent on public procurement increase tunneling around regional elections, whereas neither tunneling of firms without procurement revenue, nor legitimate business of firms with procurement exhibit a political cycle. Data are consistent with the corruption channel: cash is tunneled to politicians in exchange for procurement contracts. A third element is how corruption is related to monitoring and bureaucrats' compensation. This is a key economic theme as the efficiency wage theories pushed forward by the labor economics literature suggest that raising wages of bureaucrats may be an effective way to reduce the temptation of corruption. However, evidence is mixed and with very few works focusing specifically on procurement. Di Tella and Schargrodsky (2003) analyze corruption activities related to procurement in the hospitals of Buenos Aires, showing that higher public wages are effective against corruption only if there is enough auditing intensity. This, however, entails high costs, which may not be sustainable over time. The fourth is the impact of organized crime. Recent studies using micro-data to estimate the impact of corruption and organized crime on firms include Montoya (2016), Rozo (2014) and Fenizia (2018). Acconcia et al. (2014) exploit the random timing of the dismissal of local city councils for mafia connections in Italy.

They document that external commissioners, who replace the public elected officials after dismissal, cut public investment. Along the same lines, Galletta (2016) finds evidence of spillovers on neighboring municipalities: neighbors reduce spending as a result of city council dismissal, and he attributes this effect to an increase in law enforcement.

Response to Francesco Decarolis – *Tünde Tátrai*

Data availability and corruption

There is no question about the new directions that research into the relationship between public procurement and corruption is taking. Although definitions could be made more accurate, the weakness lies primarily in the management of prevention and the underdeveloped nature of monitoring activities.

Data availability invoked earlier by Rose-Ackerman[3] is only the beginning because having an exceedingly great deal of information may be in vain if we are unable to channel and compare all this information. There is a possibility of finding cases smacking of corruption by data mining; this is one of the objectives of the Digiwhist project (www.digiwhist.eu), which aims at rendering the data accessible and manageable in a structured way by collecting national public procurement databases (www.opentender.eu).

The www.redflags.eu project of Transparency International Hungary, whose objective was to develop red flags for the announcements launching the procedure, also uses an existing database to point out risks of corruption. These are innovations of the recent past and important European initiatives, which can lay the foundations for what Rose-Ackerman and their followers rightfully missed.

It is, however, worthwhile to refer again to the requirements of the European directives, which require as the pre-condition to a uniform monitoring system that the individual Member States disclose the necessary information with the appropriate data structure. One of the significant limitations of the Digiwhist project was precisely that the data structures of the individual national databases were totally different, that they keep changing and their reliability is far from identical. As relatively large sets of data are missing, it is only natural that it is impossible to aim for perfect results. In this case, the project itself, its existence and the fact that they managed to channel in the individual national databases is indeed a historic deed. It is also the lack of data, which may cause problems for the redflags.eu project. If, for instance, contracting authorities in the individual Member States do not complete the announcements appropriately, those researching the database will not even have a chance to compare the data.

If we were to explore the relationships between estimated values and contract values in the TED database (tenders.europa.eu), the comparison cannot be made in the case of several Member States because so many of the data are missing, particularly with regard to contract data. The limitations on arranging prices disclosed in different formats, or of the evaluation criteria into a database, give rise to such data problems, which render research impossible. The quantity of the available data does not necessarily guarantee the achievement of better results in exploring cases suspicious of corruption. That is why the uniform structure of available data content is so important and accordingly preparation plays a key role already when defining data requirements. If Member State data are of the same content, are comparable and accurate, it will be possible to measure corruption risks much more accurately and the power of the public may urge contracting authorities to publish more uniform announcements with better structured content. Short of this, we will not know who acquired what and for how much, nor will we be able to track the processes that are obviously taking place in the European public procurement scene.

Making electronic public procurement mandatory does not mean that corruption risks would automatically decline. Just consider the phase following the procedure, the phase of performance, which is at least as much concerned in corruption. Currently, the disclosure of contracts and data related to performance do not constitute parts of mandatory electronic public procurement.

Accordingly, the availability of contract registers is, as yet, limited. The report of the EXEP Contract Register Subgroup (EXEP CR Report, 2017) deals with ensuring transparency by way of building up contract registers in detail. As this subject matter has practically no literature, it is useful to take this report as the basis when developing the fundamental definitions. The definition that experts have developed is the following:

> A contract register is a function, or module, of a public procurement system that gathers structured data and unstructured information throughout the lifecycle of the contract, at a level relevant for governance (e.g. country-level, regional level). This function, or module, is also used to disclose information. The degree of disclosure depends on national preferences.
>
> As regards the scope, CRs are repositories of information and data on all public contracts awarded under the national public procurement legal framework. CRs should contain information of the complete life cycle of the contract (planning, pre-awarding and post-awarding).
>
> (EXEP CR Report, 2017, p. 7)

Accordingly, public procurement registers contain not only all the contracts, but they are excellently suited to becoming subject matters of statistical analysis through their search functions. To that end, the purpose of public procurement registers is the examination of the planning, contents and performance of contracts based on available structured data.

In general, it holds that the value limits of the Member States are in line with the national value limits for disclosing contracts and contract data.

Frequently, registers disclose both information in relation to the invitation to tender and the information on the results of the procedure. Many registers also contain information related to contract amendments. There are very few registers that include details on payments or the conclusion of contracts. In some 40 percent of the Member States, sanctions are applied in the case of failure to comply with disclosure obligations. One of the most frequently applied conditions of ensuring the validity of contracts is, for instance, the obligation to disclose information on the results or the contract documents.

The subject matter of contract registers is a good example for demonstrating that there are yet unexplored areas where we do not utilize available data and accordingly the phase of the performance of public procurement contracts tends to be neglected in the fight against corruption. In this sense, ensuring the transparency of contracts in a structured manner not only implies the possibility of control, but also the more efficient consideration of the main areas, which were identified in Decarolis's opinion.

Response to Tünde Tátrai – *Francesco Decarolis*

Combating corruption

In her initial assessment of the relevant legal aspects concerning corruption in public procurement, Tátrai has focused on the use of transparency to combat corruption. In particular, she pointed out what prescriptions the Procurement Directive 24/2014 contains on combating corruption through debarment of suppliers involved in criminal organizations or corruption activities. There she lamented that, despite the potential efficacy of this tool, the lack of transparency on the set of firms (and connected individuals) who have been involved in such criminal conducts prevents the full applicability of debarment since it would be complex (if at all feasible) for public procurers to access information on all companies (and their relevant owners and members of the administrative, management or supervisory bodies).

In my first document, I had not entered into the specifics of what the economics literature has to say about combating corruption. Therefore, I will use the chance of answering to Tátrai's document to illustrate what lessons can be learned from the economic analysis on how to combat corruption. First, I want to remark on the obvious difficulty in quantitatively assessing what policies work to combat corruption: if credible policy evaluations are hard to obtain in general, when they involve illegal behaviors they are even more complex. It is therefore noteworthy to mention a study by Olken (2007), which represents the gold standard of what can be done. He conducted a field experiment to both measure corruption and evaluate alternative strategies to combat it. The setting is that of Indonesia's road-building projects. Some 608 villages were involved in this experiment that lasted between 2003 and 2004. The evaluation tested two types of anti-corruption policies: encouraging community participation in the projects and increasing the probability of centrally administered audits. Testing is made possible by the fact that the two policies are randomly assigned across villages. The results point to the greater efficacy of top-down monitoring and showing that corruption can be reduced.

Second, and more to Tátrai's point about the provisions in the Procurement Directive, recent evidence about Italy is strongly indicative of the effectiveness of a debarment system based on transparent lists of corrupt and criminal organization-affiliated firms. Since 2011, Italy underwent a series of legislative interventions all aimed at increasing transparency and enhancing the ability of public procurers to identify and exclude risky firms from public tenders. The most significant legal interventions have been: (a) the Antimafia Code (d.lgs. 159/2011); (b) the Severino Reform (l. 190/2012 and adoption procedures enacted in 2012 and 2013); (c) D.l. 90/2014, later transformed into l. 114/2014 (prescriptions on soundness and transparency in public contracts); (d) L. 69/2015 (harsher punishments for crimes against public administrations and for mafia associations); (e) new Code of Public Contracts (d.lgs. 50/2016, implementing in Italy the Procurement Directive 24/2014); (f) L. 103/2017 (lengthening of the prescription terms for corruption crimes). Although the rollover of these reforms did not follow such a clean pattern as that of the experimental design implemented in Indonesia by Olken (2007), it is nevertheless possible to try to quantitatively assess their effects. This is what I do in ongoing work (Decarolis and Giorgiantonio, 2020; Decarolis et al., 2019) by looking at novel data on the probability that contracts are awarded to firms whose owners and managers have been signaled to the Italian police forces for potential crimes related to corruption, collusion or criminal organizations. Among the results that we observe, in the context of the procurement of public works for roads and buildings in the period between 2000 and 2017, is that the probability of awarding the contract to these suspicious firms declines from nearly 27 percent at the beginning of the sample to around 20 percent toward the end of it. Our analysis also underscores a marked fragility of the more discretionary awarding mechanisms (namely the use of negotiated procedures and of the most economically advantageous tender criterion) under which suspect firms are about twice as likely to be awarded the contract relative to open auctions based on price only.

The above findings indicate that the anticorruption policies have likely been effective in limiting the corruption risk. But at what cost? Within the Italian context, there is concern voiced by both firms and public administrations that the fight against corruption has hindered the proper functioning of the public procurement sectors. The procedures that firms have to follow to demonstrate they are legitimate bidders in an auction are cumbersome as additional controls by public buyers. Both parties lament that there has been a substantial increase in the number of days that it takes to arrive at the awarding of a contract.

Albeit there are no studies that I am aware of that properly quantify both the cost and the benefits of the current fight against corruption in Italy, what the above discussion suggests is that it might be useful to consider whether the target of zero corruption is desirable and attainable. The answer to this question, however, is certainly dependent on the costs that a society has to incur to lower corruption and, in this respect, it is important to ask whether the policy of debarment put forward by the Procurement Directive is indeed the right policy to achieve a zero-corruption target.

I would argue that this is unlikely to be the case. Debarment can certainly serve a twofold role in the fight against corruption. First, for firms already involved in corruption episodes, by keeping them out it enforces a punishment. Second, it acts as a deterrent: a firm considering the short-term benefits of adopting some type of corruption practice should weight them against the long-term costs of being excluded from future contracts. But for how long into the future? Here immediately the limits of the debarment solution appear clear: an excessively long punishment might induce firms to try to shut down and reopen in disguise, but an excessively short period of exclusion might not create a sufficient incentive for proper behavior. Striking the right balance is not simple and, most likely, from a social welfare point of view, conditions of the market and the firms should matter in defining this optimal timing. Suppose, for instance, that a market with high entry barriers has only two players, then debarring one transforms this market into a monopoly, which might cause the public administrations to face procurement costs even higher than those faced when the two firms competed, despite the extra costs of corruption. More generally, debarment seems a rather risky policy to adopt in those markets that are already rather concentrated.

Moreover, it seems only fair that debarment ends when the ties are broken between a firm and its members who have been involved in corruption activities. In Italy, for instance, it is extremely rare that corruption charges are moved against a legal entity like a firm; they are nearly always moved against individual members of the firm. The conclusion of any formal relationship between these individuals and the firm rehabilitates the firm. But the evidence clearly shows signs of potential abuses: for instance, in Conley and Decarolis (2016), we look at the case of one of the largest criminal trials for collusion and corruption involving more than 300 auctions held by both the Municipality and County of Turin. In 2008, the Criminal Court convicted a large number of individuals belonging to nearly 90 firms (organized in eight different cartels). But nearly all firms kept on bidding and winning public contracts: their solution was that ownership and management was transferred from fathers to sons and daughters.

All this leads me to propose serious consideration of alternatives to debarment. One in particular, despite its simplicity, has been shown to be quite powerful: the use of a pledge or sign to confirm honesty, associated with moral reminders and clear guidelines of what is legitimate behavior and what is not. In contrast to the classical theory of rational crime by Becker (1974), the strength of what is proposed above has been experimentally shown by Arieli (2012). The Italian experience with the Ethical Code of the Competition Authority is quite encouraging. Moreover, a crucial element is also the human capital inside the public procurement authorities (de Rassenfosse et al., 2019 and Decarolis et al., 2020). But the same study by Arieli also shows how effective supervision is essential in preventing dishonest behavior and, in this respect, I certainly endorse Tátrai's lament about the need for a transparent and easily accessible list of criminal firms and individuals. Modern technologies can very easily solve the problems of easing the access to this list, if there is the willingness to collect and pool the data together. Moreover, all privacy concerns can be easily overcome through proper technologies as, in fact, there would be no need for the public procurer to be able to literally read off the list when the process should be automatized.

Conclusions – *Tünde Tátrai*

I do understand Decarolis's aversion to debarment as there is no denying that, in a general sense, combating corruption with legal instruments is not efficient. The rules I listed earlier as linked to corruption in the public procurement directives are not suitable for such purposes. Moreover, the so-called voluntary remedial measures achieve the exact opposite effect because the national authority or contracting authority lets the market operator return, provided that he apologizes and verifies having done everything possible to prevent such a situation (even corruption) in the future. Here, a *bona fide* approach fails to achieve the impact, which is also missed by Decarolis; that is, it does not change the attitude of the market operator. An administrative new procedural solution was created to resolve exclusion, which also cancels its impacts. This, however, does not mean that debarment would not have a restraining force.

Decarolis calls attention to modern technologies, yet it is undeniable that no matter what publicity is given to the data, it is not at all certain that we also provide transparency as I had earlier expounded in detail. A huge quantity of data does not necessarily mean that we obtain useful information. Rising resistance with respect to issues of data protection related to individuals results in not having any kind of public lists; instead, the managers concerned have to accept their own statements, which is a substantially poorer solution than building automated mechanisms and checking databases. There are, however, solutions whose social costs are lower and allocate social control not necessarily to expensive controlling organizations.

Picci (2007) suggests using IT technologies to publish the results of similar tenders across the country on user-friendly platforms so as to allow public procurement stakeholders to monitor contract characteristics across administrations. Picci (2007) also proposes a governance model of public works that relies on an internet-based "reputation system." "It allows for the routine production of statistics that are useful for monitoring purposes and it provides a coherent framework to limit rent-seeking and corruption."[4] This solution is in line with the significance of the role of society in combating public procurement corruption, also reinforced by OLAF in its study

"Identifying and Reducing Corruption in Public Procurement in the EU" (OLAF, 2013).

When Decarolis poses the question of the costs of combating corruption, he rightfully calls attention to the, often extreme, increase in costs caused by controlling mechanisms, organizations and obligations, and the endless procedures. This is supplemented by Kells (2011), who highlights the contradiction between different audit mechanisms. In relation to top-down monitoring recommended by Decarolis, I would call attention to different types of monitoring tools. I would highlight methods and solutions such as probity audits among the alternatives (see Beth, 2006), also taking into consideration the opinion of Shead (2001),[5] who writes about how to keep the bureaucrats honest. In his opinion, the use of probity audits and guidelines has flourished in the public sector across Australia.

> These guidelines tend to focus on competitive procurement processes and ignore broader factors applying to other processes in which probity audits are also used. Further, as there are no professional standards governing a probity audit, it is important that agencies have a clear understanding of their benefits and limitations and of the skills and experience required of a probity auditor before they commission one.
>
> (Shead, 2001)

What is particularly interesting in his opinion is that it is the organizations concerned in public procurement that know best what to audit, what are the weak points in the system. Following Decarolis's train of thought, in my view personalized monitoring solutions have a future, instead of the standard 3 in 1 government guidelines.

Conclusions – *Francesco Decarolis*

In this debate we have spanned a broad set of issues involving the legal and economic views on corruption in procurement. We discussed the EU rules and the tools currently available to combat corruption, we surveyed what the existing literature has to say about the efficacy of these tools and then we mentioned the problem of how to implement these tools in the absence of reliable data.

It is certainly a major source of frustration that, in an area subject to extensive requirements on transparency and data reporting, throughout Europe there is a generalized sense of inadequacy of the available data.

Tátrai's second document mentions a series of valuable projects that have tried either to address the problem of data collection or to use the existing data in the best possible way. In concluding her piece she stresses that, however, while most efforts have been focused on the phase of contract awarding, an equally salient moment in the life of the contract is its execution. In this regard, she correctly laments an even more systematic lack of high quality data. Indeed, I totally concur with both elements of this assessment.

First, corruption might well take place during the execution phase. Too little is known about whether this type of phenomenon materializes only after the contract-awarding phase or is also associated with corruption at the awarding stage. In the latter case, a completely honest awarding commission might select a firm that, nevertheless, ex post uses corruption to illicitly bolster its profits through price renegotiations, or extensions of the contract duration, or the delivery of a worse performance than what was originally promised.

The difficulty of monitoring and evaluating ex post performance makes corruption via actions taking place during the execution phase particularly appealing for the corrupted parties.

In particular, while in the awarding stage there is a clear player who has all the right incentives to expose any corrupt behavior – the competing firms not selected as winners of the tender – in the execution stage it is less obvious who will have an incentive to expose the malpractice, among those aware of it, or at least suspecting it.

Audit systems or denounces from final users of the good/service/infrastructure might play this role, but the time lag relative to the corrupt event will typically be substantial. In this respect, it is relevant to report that US procurement relies heavily on an additional tool, monetary incentives for whistleblowers. These have been claimed to be highly successful in encouraging the employees of federal contractors to denounce their employers for corruption episodes.[6]

Second, I concur that the data on ex post execution is typically of even inferior quality relative to the already despicable quality of the data existing for the awarding stage. While this might be justifiable for hard to measure quantities like the "quality" of a good/service/infrastructure, it cannot be justified for elements as simple as the final completion time and cost of the project. I would thus like to stress the need to begin by focusing on these simpler variables, to then aim at expanding the set of available measures to more refined ones.

Finally, I want to mention that, despite the best efforts to monitor both the awarding and the execution stages, we might be missing the elephant in the room: corruption in the early stages of the administrative (or political) decision to purchase a certain type of good/service/infrastructure.

Even if both awarding and execution stages are impeccable, the very existence of a public contract might be the result of initial corruption involving the choice of using public funds for this contract instead of something else. While cost–benefit analysis can be an important tool – maybe the only one I can think of – to make decisions sound and transparent, it is likely that corruption at this stage is, and will remain, larger economically and harder to combat than other forms of corruption.

Notes

1 Hunsaker (2009, p. 411).
2 For example Rose-Ackerman (2007).
3 See supra.
4 Picci (2007, p. 159).
5 Shead (2001, p. 66).
6 A well-known example in the case of the Department of Defense contracts is the program linked here: www.whistleblowersinternational.com/types-of-fraud/defense-contractor-military/.

References

Acconcia, A., Corsetti G., and Simonelli S. (2014). "Mafia and Public Spending: Evidence on the Fiscal Multiplier from a Quasi-experiment," *American Economic Review*, 104(7), 2185–2209.

Ades, A. and di Tella, R. (1997). "The New Economics of Corruption: A Survey and Some New Results," *Political Studies*, 45(3), 496–515.

Arieli, D. (2012). *The Honest Truth About Dishonesty: How We Lie to Everyone – Especially Ourselve*s, New York: Harper Collins.

Arozamena, L. and Weinschelbaum, F. (2009). "The Effect of Corruption on Bidding Behavior in First-price Auctions," *European Economic Review*, 53(6), 645–657.

Auriol, E. (2006). "Corruption in Procurement and Public Purchase," *International Journal of Industrial Organization*, 24(5), 867–885.

Auriol, E. and Søreide, T. (2017). "An Economic Analysis of Debarment," *International Review of Law and Economics*, 50, 36–49.

Baltrunaite, A. (2016). "Political Finance Reform and Public Procurement: Evidence from Lithuania." Working Paper, Institute for International Economic Studies, Stockholm University.

Becker, G. S., & Landes, W. M. (1974). *Essays in the Economics of Crime and Punishment. NBER Books.*

Beth, E. (2006). *Integrity in Public Procurement: Mapping out Good Practices.* Detailed outline of the report, OECD Symposium, Paris, November 30, 2006 www.oecd.org/governance/fightingcorruptioninthepublicsector/37864282.pdf.

Branzoli, N. and Decarolis, F. (2015). "Entry and Subcontracting in Public Procurement Auctions," *Management Science*, 61(12), 2945–2962.

Brogaard, J., Denes, M., and Duchin, R. (2015). "Political Connections, Incentives and Innovation: Evidence from Contract-level Data." Unpublished Working Paper, 2(05).

Burguet, R. and Che, Y. K. (2004). "Competitive Procurement with Corruption," *The RAND Journal of Economics*, 35(1), 50–68.

Burguet, R. and Perry, M. K. (2007). "Bribery and Favoritism by Auctioneers in Sealed-Bid Auctions," *The B.E. Journal of Theoretical Economics*, 7(1),

Celentani, M. and Ganuza, J.-J. (2002). "Corruption and Competition in Procurement," *European Economic Review*, 46(7), 1273–1303.

Chever, L. and Moore, J. (2012). "Negotiated Procedures Overrated-Evidence from France Questions the Commission's Approach in the Latest Procurement Reforms," *European Procurement & Public Private Partnership Law Review*, 7, 228–241.

Chever, L., Saussier, S., and Yvrande-Billon, A. (2017). "The Law of Small Numbers: Investigating the Benefits of Restricted Auctions for Public Procurement," *Applied Economics*, 49(42), 4241–4260.

Compte, O., Lambert-Mogiliansky, A., and Verdier, T. (2005). "Corruption and competition in procurement auctions," *Rand Journal of Economics*, 36(1), 1–15.

Conley, T. and Decarolis, F. (2016). "Detecting Bidders Groups in Collusive Auctions," *American Economic Journal: Microeconomics*, 8(2), 1–38.

Coviello, D. and Gagliarducci, S. (2017). "Tenure in Office and Public Procurement," *American Economic Journal: Economic Policy*, 9(3), 59–105.

Decarolis, F. and Giorgiantonio, C. (2020). "Corruption Red Flags in Public Procurement: New Evidence from Italian Calls for Tenders." Bank of Italy Discussion Papers (QEF).

Decarolis, F., Fisman, R., Pinotti, P., and Vannutelli, S. (2019). "Rules, Discretion, and Corruption in Procurement: Evidence from Italian Government Contracting." NBER Working Paper.

Decarolis, F., Giuffrida, L., Iossa, E., Mollisi, V., and Spagnolo, G. (2020). "Bureaucratic Competence and Procurement Outcomes." NBER Working Paper.

Decarolis, F., Pacini, R., and Spagnolo, G. (2016). "Past Performance and Procurement Outcomes." NBER Working Paper.

de Rassenfosse, G., Decarolis, F., Giuffrida, L., Iossa, E., Mollisi, V., Raiteri, E., and Spagnolo, G. (2019). "Buyers' Role in Innovation Procurement," CEPR Discussion Paper.

EXEP CR Report (2017). Contract registers – EXEP subgroup report 12.09.2017. http://ec.europa.eu/docsroom/documents/26421.

Di Tella, R. and Schargrodsky, E. (2003). "The Role of Wages and Auditing during a Crackdown on Corruption in the City of Buenos Aires," *The Journal of Law and Economics*, 46(1), 269–292.

Fenizia, A. (2018). "Breaking the Ties between the Mafia and the State: Evidence from Italian Municipalities." Working Paper.

Fisman, R. and Miguel, E. (2007). "Corruption, Norms, and Legal Enforcement: Evidence from UN Diplomatic Parking Tickets," *Journal of Political Economy*, 115(6), 1020–1048.

Galletta, S. (2016). "Law Enforcement, Municipal Budgets and Spillover Effects: Evidence from a Quasi-experiment in Italy." IdEP Economic Papers 1601, USI Università della Svizzera italiana.

Goldman, E., Rocholl, J., and So, J. (2013). Politically Connected Boards of Directors and the Allocation of Procurement Contracts," *Review of Finance*, 17(5), 1617–1648.

Greenwood, M. and Klotz, J. M. (2009). "The Fight against Corruption in Public Procurement: An Introduction to Best Practices," In R. H. García (ed.). *International Public Procurement: A Guide to Best Practice*. London: Global Law & Business pp. 57–74

Hunsaker, K. (2009). "Ethics in Public Procurement: Buying Public Trust," *Journal of Public Procurement*, 9(3/4), 411–418.

Kells, S. (2011). "Conflict between Independent Scrutinisers of Transport Megaprojects: Evidence from Australia," *European Journal of Transport and Infrastructure Research*, 11(1, January), 61–79. www.ejtir.tbm.tudelft.nl.

Koc, S. A. and Neilson, W. S. (2008). "Interim Bribery in Auctions," *Economics Letters*, 99(2), 238–241.

Lalive, R. and Schmutzler, A. (2011). "Auctions vs Negotiations in Public Procurement: Which Works Better?" ECON – Working Paper 209, Department of Economics, University of Zurich.

Lengwiler, Y. and Wolfstetter, E. (2010). "Auctions and Corruption: An Analysis of Bid Rigging by a Corrupt Auctioneer," *Journal of Economic Dynamics and Control*, 34(10), 1872–1892.

Menezes, F. M. and Monteiro, P. K. (2006). "Corruption and Auctions," *Journal of Mathematical Economics*, 42(1), 97–108.

Mironov, M. and Zhuravskaya, E. (2016). "Corruption in Procurement and the Political Cycle in Tunneling: Evidence from Financial Transactions Data," *American Economic Journal: Economic Policy*, 8(2), 287–321.

Montoya, E. (2016). *"Violence and Economic Disruption: Firm-Level Evidence from New Mexico."* PhD dissertation, UC Berkeley.

Muraközy, B. and Telegdy, Á. (2016). "Political Incentives and State Subsidy Allocation: Evidence from Hungarian Municipalities," *European Economic Review*, 89, 324–344.

OLAF (2013). "PWC-Ecorys: Identifying and Reducing Corruption in Public Procurement in the EU," (June) http://ec.europa.eu/anti_fraud/documents/anti-fraud-policy/research-and-studies/identifying_reducing_corruption_in_public_procurement_en.pdf.

Olken, B. A. (2007). "Monitoring Corruption: Evidence from a Field Experiment in Indonesia," *Journal of Political Economy*, 115(2), 200–248.

Olken, B. A. and Pande, R. (2012). "Corruption in Developing Countries," *Annual Review of Economics*, 4(1), 479–509.

Picci L. (2007). Reputation-based Governance of Public Works," in G. Piga and V. T. Khi (eds.), *The Economics of Public Procurement*. Chippenham and Eastbourne: GB. Antony Rowe Ltd, 159–182.

Rose-Ackerman , S. (ed.). (2007). *International Handbook on the Economics of Corruption*. Cheltenham: Edward Elgar.

Rozo, S. V. (2014). "Is Murder Bad for Business and Real Income? The Effects of Violent Crime on Economic Activity." Working Paper.

Schoenherr, D. (2018). "Political Connections and Allocative Distortions," *Journal of Finance*, 74(2), 543–586.

Shead, B. (2001). "Probity Auditing: Keeping the Bureaucrats Honest?" *Australian Journal of Public Administration*, 60(2, June), 66–70.

Szucs, F. (2017). "Discretion and Corruption in Public Procurement." Job Market Paper. Available at: https://economics.ceu.edu/sites/economics.ceu.edu/files/attachment/event/1135/szucsjmp.pdf.

8 Challenges in public procurement

Corruption and probity in public procurement

Marion Chabrost

Introduction

Corruption is defined by the World Bank as the abuse of entrusted power for private benefit. It can take many forms, one of which is a bidder's attempt to bribe a public authority in order to obtain a public procurement contract. Corruption is estimated to cost about 120 billion euros per year, representing 1 per cent of the European Union's GDP (European Commission, 2014). To put this figure into perspective, it represents slightly less than the annual budget of the EU in 2014, which amounted to 143 billion euros. Globally, corruption is estimated to cost about US$1.5 to US$2 trillion per year, roughly representing 2 per cent of global GDP (IMF, 2016). There are multiple purposes of bribes, but the major one appears to be for public procurement. Indeed, 57 per cent of known cases of corruption are related to public procurement (Figure 8.1).

Corruption in public procurement generates inefficiencies mainly due to a misallocation of the contract, higher price and/or lower quality, and a distortion of competition. In Europe, about 38 per cent of companies consider that corruption is a problem when doing business in their country (Figure 8.2). Whereas almost all Northern countries have figures below the EU average, corruption seems to be a significant issue in many European countries, including the more developed ones. For example, 52 per cent of French companies consider corruption to be a problem for doing business. As public procurement represents between 15 and 25 per cent of GDP in OECD countries, the stakes in fighting corruption are high. Also, the quality of public services depends on good practices in public procurement: the greater the extent of corruption, the more expensive and less efficient the public services are likely to be (Djankov et al., 2017).

As corruption is possible to the extent that a public authority can exert discretionary power, the limitation of this power in public procurement is perceived today as the most efficient way to overcome corruption. The European Directive for public procurement goes in this direction. However, the limitation of discretion in public has some costs and limitations, therefore

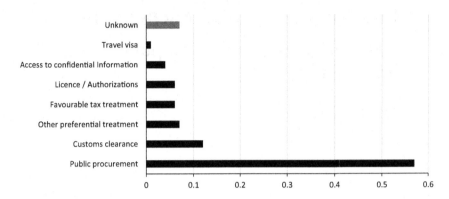

Figure 8.1 Purposes of bribes.
Source: OECD (2014).

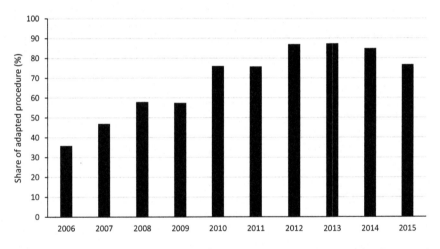

Figure 8.2 Share of adapted procedures for contract below the EU threshold in French
      municipalities (2006–2015).
Note: Share of adapted procedures over the total number of award notices at the
municipal level for contracts below the EU formal threshold.
Source: Chabrost and Saussier (2019).

relatively more discretionary power is given to public authorities. The next
section will be dedicated to the trade-off between efficiency and transparency
of public procurement. The regulation of public procurement in France is
a good illustration of this trade-off and is the subject of the third section.
Finally, we conclude with the development of digital technologies and the use
of open data as tools for increasing transparency.

Transparency and efficiency of public procurement

There are many procedures through which a good or a service can be awarded. Some procedures are rigid, restricting the discretionary power of public authorities in their choice of contractors. Others are more flexible, introducing more discretionary power for the public authority to select the preferred contractors, and potentially reducing competition. Such discretion might be introduced through award mechanisms that are based on negotiations instead of pure auctions (Bajari and Tadelis, 2001; Bajari et al., 2009; Herweg and Schmidt, 2017), through the use of imprecise criteria (Burguet and Che, 2004), or through restricted auctions (Chever et al., 2017; Coviello et al., 2017).

The economic literature suggests that buyers might deliberately choose to engage in award procedures that create room for public authorities' discretionary power for efficiency reasons. Discretion is defined as "the quality of having or showing discernment or good judgment" and the "ability to make responsible decisions" (Merriam-Webster). The primary reason for introducing discretion is that award procedures based on open auctions may lead to inefficient outcomes if the good or service to be procured is technically complex and/or barely contractible. In particular, discretion facilitates the dialogue between the parties to make the contracts as complete as possible (Goldberg, 1977; Bajari and Ye, 2001; Bajari et al. 2014). Using discretion to select the winning firm may also ease the implementation of relational contracts, thereby reducing the risk of ex post opportunistic behaviours (Spagnolo, 2012). As Coviello et al. (2017) show, discretion increases the probability that an incumbent is awarded the contract when renewed. Their results also suggest that incumbents are more likely to be renewed if they had better performance in the past than the average (in terms of delay). In addition, discretion could still be beneficial to the buyer in non-complex contracts, by reducing the cost and complexity related to the organization of the tender.

However, the economic literature also suggests that discretion associated with negotiation may be detrimentally used to favour a bidder during the award phase. The seminal paper of Burguet and Che (2004) illustrates manipulation power using scoring rules auctions, where the contracting authority may manipulate one dimension of qualitative criteria to favour one participant in the auction. The theory argues in favour of such a scoring rule, as it gives the buyer a larger set of choices between price and quality, potentially increasing the number of bidders, and makes collusion less sustainable. However, they show that with a high degree of manipulation power, corruption softens price competition and results in higher procurement costs. Indeed, one of the biggest issues of corruption in public procurement is that it increases costs.

Di Tella and Schargrodsky (2003) study the prices paid for basic inputs during a crackdown on corruption in the public hospitals of the city of Buenos Aires in Argentina, between 1996 and 1997. They find that detection of corruption decreases procurement costs by an average of 15 per cent. These findings were confirmed by Tran (2011), who obtained access to internal records of a bribe-paying firm in Indochina. He studied the impact of scoring and price-only auctions on corruption by taking advantage of two successive changes in the policy on award mechanisms. Whereas scoring auctions were found to increase the bribes and profits of bribe-paying firms, the implementation of price-only auctions reduced both the value of bribes and profits of those paying bribes. In Italy, Baltrunaite et al. (2018) show that tenders using discretion are more likely to select politically connected firms in more corrupt environments. In the same vein, Palguta and Pertold (2017) use public procurement data from Czech Republic. They observe that the possibility of pre-selecting participants to a tender under a particular threshold of contract value is likely to yield to a manipulation of procurement values so that the tender is below the threshold. They also observe that firms with a hidden owner are more likely to win the contract when the procurement value is manipulated. Finally, in a paper using data on almost 34,000 firms from the World Bank's Enterprise Surveys in 88 countries, Knack et al. (2017) found that in countries with more transparent procurement systems, where exceptions to open competition in tendering must be explicitly justified, firms report paying fewer and smaller kickbacks to officials.

An optimal award procedure should therefore be the result of a balance between the costs of corruption and the benefits of discretion. Bandiera et al. (2009) propose a distinction between active and passive waste in public procurement. On one side, active waste is defined as such that:

> Its presence entails direct or indirect benefit for the public decision maker. In other words, reducing waste would reduce the utility of the decision maker. The classical example is corruption in public procurement.

On the other side, passive waste is defined as such that:

> Its presence does not benefit the public decision maker. In other words, reducing waste would (weakly) increase the utility of the decision maker. [...] Another cause of passive waste, following Kelman [1990, 2005], is that excessive regulatory burden may make procurement cumbersome and increase the average price that the public body pays.

They exploit the procurement price differences among Italian public authorities for identical goods. The results indicate that most of the observed price difference between the buyers is due to passive rather than active waste. It is noteworthy that the goods under consideration in this study are standard and do not involve a high degree of contractual complexity.

To balance between passive and active waste, the EU sets a contract value threshold (hereafter the EU threshold) below which the Member States should determine the most suitable procedures and rules for awarding a contract, while complying with the fundamental principles of EU public procurement (equal treatment, non-discrimination, and transparency). A contract

Table 8.1 EU thresholds for public contracts from 2006 to 2015

Years	Supplies and services Euros	Public works Euros
2006–2007	210,000	5,270,000
2008–2009	206,000	5,150,000
2010–2011	193,000	4,485,000
2012–2013	200,000	5,000,000
2014–2015	207,000	5,186,000

Source: Commission Delegated Regulation (EU) 2017/2365 of 18 December 2017 amending Directive 2014/24/EU in respect of the application thresholds for the procedures for the award of contracts.

falls below the EU threshold if its estimated value is below the one set by the EU (Table 8.1). As soon as the value of the contract is high, the buyer shall not comply with national laws, but the EU laws instead. Therefore, there exist multiple award mechanisms which are adapted to the value and specificities of the goods and services to be contracted out (see Table 8.2 for a detailed presentation of the characteristics of each award mechanism).

An illustration of the trade-off between transparency and efficiency of public procurement: The case of France

Below the EU thresholds, national laws apply while still respecting the pillar principles set by the EU, namely, equal treatment, non-discrimination, and transparency. In France, public buyers may in this case use what is called an adapted procedure (*procédure adaptée*). Its main objective is to give a high degree of discretion and flexibility to the buyer to find out the most efficient way to procure goods and services involving low complexity. Indeed, projects that are more complex are usually more difficult to execute (Bajari et al., 2009; Chong et al., 2014). In this procedure,

> ways and means are freely chosen by the public buyer and should adapt to the nature and characteristics of the needs, the number or location of firms that are likely to participate to the tender, and to the circumstances of the procurement.

The buyer is, in particular, free to define the advertising and competitive processes that are the most proportionate to the purpose, value and circumstances of the purchase (see Table 8.3 for a detailed presentation of the characteristics of this procedure, as well as a comparison with the open auctions procedure).

The main benefits of this procedure are the possibility to directly negotiate, the possibility to adjust the deadlines to the constraints (nonexistence

Table 8.2 Decision matrix to support the choice of the procurement procedure

Procedures	Specific requirements for using the procedure	Stages	Minimum number of candidates	Level of competition	Workload for contracting authorities	Risk of complaints, remedies or irregularities	Incentive for innovative or tailored ideas/products
Open	None. It can be used for all purchases.	1. Selection and evaluation	None. All interested candidates can submit a tender.	HIGH Unlimited number of tenders.	HIGH All compliant tenders must be examined by the CA and this can delay the award. Resource intensive for both the CA and the candidates who have to prepare a complete tender.	LOW Decision made with a straightforward focus on the award. Limited transparency risks as an open, transparent, competitive procedure	LOW
Restricted	None. It can be used for all purchases.	1. Prequalification 2. Selection and evaluation	All interested candidates can submit an expression of interest. At least 5 pre-selected candidates can submit a tender	MEDIUM Limited number of candidates allowed to submit a tender.	MEDIUM Limited number of tenders to evaluate and therefore less resource intensive for the evaluation committee/CA.	MEDIUM Greater potential for collusion/ corruption due to the increased exercise of discretion by the CA.	LOW

Procedure	Conditions for use	Phases	Participation	Flexibility	Efficiency / administrative burden	Transparency and integrity	Complexity
Competitive procedure with negotiation	Fulfil one or more of the following criteria: An open or restricted procedure has attracted only irregular or unacceptable tenders. The needs of the CA cannot be met without the adaptation of available solutions. The subject matter includes design or innovative solutions.	1. Prequalification 2. Negotiation and evaluation	All interested candidates may request participation in response to a contract notice. At least 3 pre-selected candidates can submit a tender	Possibility to restrict participation only to market operators with high level of specialization. **MEDIUM**	Two-stage procedures might be longer in order to respect the required time limits **HIGH** The burden of proof for the circumstances allowing for the use of the procedure rests with the CA.	**MEDIUM** Greater potential for collusion/corruption due to the increased exercise of discretion by the CA.	**MEDIUM**
Competitive dialogue		1. Prequalification 2. Dialogue 3. Selection and evaluation		**MEDIUM** Limited number of candidates allowed to submit a tender. Possibility to restrict participation only to market operators with high level of specialization.	**HIGH** The CA is highly involved in the negotiation/dialogue with tenderers. Limited number of tenders to evaluate and therefore less resource intensive for the evaluation committee/CA. Two-stage or threestage procedures might be longer in order to respect the required time limits.	**HIGH** Greater potential for collusion/corruption due to the increased exercise of discretion by the CA. Transparency requirements are particularly challenging during the dialogue.	**HIGH**

(*continued*)

Table 8.2 Cont.

Procedures	Specific requirements for using the procedure	Stages	Minimum number of candidates	Level of competition	Workload for contracting authorities	Risk of complaints, remedies or irregularities	Incentive for innovative or tailored ideas/products
	The technical specifications cannot be established with sufficient precision by the CA with reference to defined standards or technical requirements. The contract cannot be awarded without prior negotiations due to specific risks or circumstances related to the nature, complexity, or legal and financial matters.						

Source: European Commission (2018).

Table 8.3 Main characteristics of the adapted and open auctions award procedures

	Adapted procedure (procédure adaptée)	*Open auction*
EU Threshold	Below.	Below or above.
Is negotiation possible?	Yes (but not mandatory), over all aspects.	Not possible on any aspect.
Publicity	- If the value of the contract <90,000€: mandatory, but publication is not. Free choice of publicity support. - If the value of the contract >90,000€, should be published in an official journal.	Should always be published in an official journal.
Consultation documents	Could be limited to the main characteristics of the awarding mechanism, to the condition of the negotiation, and to the selection criteria of the submitted tenders. The redaction of technical specifications is not mandatory, but recommended.	Very detailed and specific.
Submission deadline	Free choice.	Minimum of 52 days.
Proof of the firm's financial capabilities	Not mandatory. The participation of new firms (less than 3 years) is possible since they can provide a bank statement rather than a three-year balance sheet.	At least the turnover from the past three years.
Candidates' experience	Can be requested.	Cannot be requested.
Weighting of awarding criteria	Not mandatory.	Mandatory.
Restricted pool of candidates	Possible.	Not possible.
Awarding commission	Not mandatory.	Mandatory.
Immediate notification to the rejected participants	Not mandatory.	Mandatory.
Standstill[1]	Not mandatory.	Minimimum of 16 days.
Publication of the award notice	Not mandatory.	Mandatory.

Source: Legifrance, "Circulaire du 29 décembre 2009 relative au Guide de bonnes pratiques en matière de marchés publics", 2009, Direction des Affaires Juridiques, "Les marchés à procédure adaptée, 2015, EDT, Vade-Medum MAPA, 2010.

[1] The standstill is a suspensive deadline between the announcement date of the awarding notice and the signature of the contract. It allows for the rejected candidates to contest the ways the awarding process was conducted

of a minimal number of days to submit an offer), the possibility of not specifying the weights associated with selection criteria ex ante, the possibility to choose the most appropriate publicity support, a freedom of choice regarding the contracting formalism, and the possibility to directly contact the firms to submit an offer. Also, public buyers have the possibility to select the contractor based on his experience. It is noteworthy that, in the case of negotiation, the buyer has the possibility to restrict competition to a limited number of candidate firms. He is even advocated to do so since negotiating with too many candidates is a waste of time and thereby, carries a cost. It is estimated that it is difficult for a small public buyer to directly negotiate with more than two or three candidates. The restriction of competition to a pool of bidders should be notified in the call for tenders.

The flexibility offered by this procedure should lower the administrative burden of organizing a tender. It should result in lower ex ante procurement costs compared with the rigid open auctions procedure. The other ambition of this procedure is to facilitate the access of firms that are not able to participate in tenders above the formal thresholds, specifically new entrants and SMEs. Indeed, contracts above the formal threshold value require firms to supply a three-year balance sheet, a document that new entrants are not able to provide. On the other hand, the adapted procedure accepts a simple official bank statement. Additionally, new entrants and SMEs are often not used to formal procedures, which results in disproportionally high costs for them. Finally, it is recommended that the public buyer does not ask for an excessive number of documents, specifically from SMEs.

It is noteworthy that, under the formal thresholds, the authority is not compelled to use an adapted procedure. It has the possibility of using a formal one. In practice, below the European thresholds, French municipalities use both the adapted procedure and open auctions. Ultimately, below the European thresholds, French municipalities might decide to use a very flexible award procedure in terms of degree of discretion (the adapted procedure) or a formal one (an open auction). As the adapted procedure is considered less costly for simple contracts, we should only observe this type of procedure for projects with a value below the formal threshold.

Adapted procedure has been increasingly used in France. Whereas they represented less than 40 per cent of award procedures for contracts below the EU threshold in 2006, they represented almost 80 per cent of them in 2015. On average, adapted procedures represented approximately 70 per cent of calls for tenders in France between 2006 and 2015. This type of procedure had first been introduced in 2004, and has been increasingly used since (Figure 8.2). However, it appears that public buyers often opt for a formal procedure rather than an adapted procedure. The fear of legal risk is usually the primary reason indicated

Using the award notice of French municipalities, we assess the impact of an investigation into corruption, as defined by the opening of a judicial investigation, on procurement award mechanisms in municipalities. First, we compare the degree of discretionary power used in award procedures before and after an investigation is publicly raised in the local press. Corruption is more likely when a public authority uses an award procedure that allows for discretion. Second, we assess whether investigation of corruption triggers any change in the competitive environment (i.e., the number of participants to the tender) and in the location of winning firms (i.e., the choice of a local firm) when discretion is involved. All these potential effects of investigation are considered for both the investigated municipalities but also for the neighbouring municipalities, the latter not being under investigation.

We use two datasets. The first is a collection of information about public procurement contracts of French municipalities between 2006 and 2015. It includes every call for tenders in France (i.e., approximately 80,000 observations per year). We were able to collect award notices only for a subsample of contracts (i.e., for approximately 14,000 observations per year). When focusing only on municipalities, we end up with a sample of 64,304 observations, where each represents a contract.

The second dataset is a collection of publicly alleged or adjudicated cases of favouritism in public procurement that were published in the local press. In France, there is no institution that maintains a centralized and exhaustive registry of corruption cases to make such data public and easily accessible. So, to collect this information, we used an online platform collecting press articles from approximately 8,000 sources. We restricted our collection to cases that happened in France from 2005 to 2015. Through these press articles, we were able to collect the name of the investigated local official, the name of the public entity that he represents, and the date the official investigation has been opened. We were also able to track the cases over time and observe whether it was any judicial proceeding, and if this was the case, whether the defendant was found guilty. We eventually obtained 87 cases of favouritism (Figure 8.3). Almost all our collected cases were subject to an official investigation (81 per cent). Ninety-two per cent of cases that were investigated yielded to a lawsuit (for 8 per cent of them we have no information about whether the case was dropped or whether the trial is forthcoming). Then, of the cases that were brought before a court, the defendant was found guilty for 88 per cent of them. Interestingly, all sizes of municipalities are represented in our sample (Figure 8.4).

Suspicion of corruption could be triggered either by the denunciation from a third party or from auditing. It takes on a judicial dimension as soon as there is a formal complaint. Then a criminal investigation is opened by a criminal court and may yield to the custody and raid of the suspected entity. At the end of the investigation, the suspect is either prosecuted or the case is closed. The defendant incurs a penalty of up to two years of imprisonment and a fine of maximum 30,000 euros. Also, he may lose his citizen's privilege for up to five years. We consider a municipality to be investigated when an official investigation is opened (Figure 8.5). The reason is that the local press almost exclusively reports a corruption case once it is under inquiry.

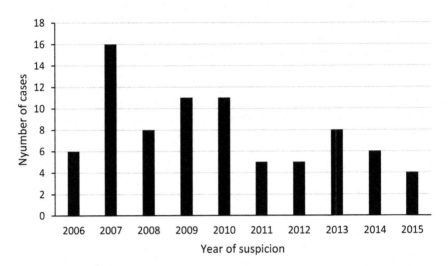

Figure 8.3 Distribution of cases of investigation in French municipalities (2006–2015).

Note: Those cases were collected using an online platform collecting press articles from about 8,000 sources. We collected publicly published alleged or judged cases of favouritism in public procurement. We brushed up the local press and restricted our collection to cases of favouritism at the municipal level.

Source: Chabrost and Saussier (2019).

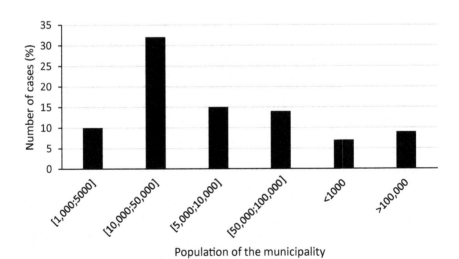

Figure 8.4 Distribution of the size of investigated municipalities (2006–2015).
Source: Chabrost and Saussier (2019).

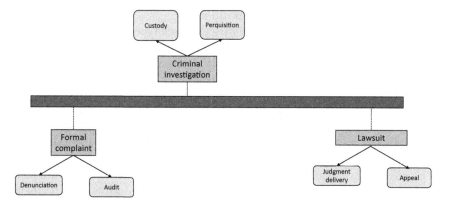

Figure 8.5 Chronology of legal proceedings in France.
Source: Chabrost and Saussier (2019).

Corruption is more likely when a public authority uses an award procedure that allows for discretion. According to the law, discretion may be used for contracts of value below the formal European thresholds using an adapted procedure. However, as discussed before, the use of such a mechanism is not mandatory, as the authority may decide to use a formal mechanism (i.e. an open auction). Therefore, we take advantage of this freedom of choice between an adapted and a formal procedure under the threshold to examine the impact of investigation of corruption on the degree of discretion chosen by a local contracting authority.

In a companion paper, Chabrost and Saussier (2019) use a differences-in-differences empirical strategy, which consists of a comparison of the outcomes of calls for tenders from a suspected municipality's (treatment group) with non-suspected ones (control group), before and after suspicion. They also apply the same strategy using the neighbours of suspected municipalities as the treatment group and non-neighbours as the control group.

Their results indicate that an investigated municipality does not react by opting for a more formal and rigid award mechanism (open auctions). As soon as one municipality is investigated for corruption, the probability of being effectively convicted is independent of its current choice of award procedure. Since the objective of the adapted procedure is to lighten the regulatory burden related to the organization of a tender, it might still be efficient for municipalities to go on with this procedure. However, their results indicate that neighbours of investigated municipalities do react as they are less likely to use an adapted procedure. They differentiate between neighbours of investigated municipalities that were eventually convicted and those that were found to be not guilty. Only neighbours of municipalities that are found guilty change their behaviour. This suggests that responsive neighbours to investigation might also be involved in the case under investigation, even though this conclusion is just a supposition.

In a second step, they assess the impact of such types of investigation over the outcome of the tenders, namely participation and localism. They observe that only investigated municipalities that are eventually found guilty attract more participants in their adapted procedures. The channel through which competition is fostered is not totally clear. It could either result from a change in the number of participants invited to the tender or it could be the consequence of firms more willing to participate in a tender in a municipality that is more likely to be under scrutiny. In addition, participation increases only for municipalities with an investigated neighbour that is eventually convicted. The possible explanations would be that either those municipalities are also corrupt, or that they just increase the number of invited firms to participate through fear of being unfairly suspected of corruption. Indeed, when using an adapted procedure, public buyers have the possibility to restrict competition. Another possibility is that firms are more likely to win the tender since those that were involved in the corruption case no longer participate in public procurements. Consequently, firms may be more willing to participate in the tender process.

Finally, they find that investigated municipalities select more distant (i.e. less local) bidders compared to other municipalities in adapted procedures. This effect is especially driven by municipalities that are eventually found guilty.

Two main conclusions are draw from this section. On the one hand, investigated municipalities do not react by opting for more formal and rigid award mechanisms. On the other hand, neighbours of investigated municipalities do react as they are less likely to use an adapted procedure where discretion is allowed. However, only neighbours of municipalities that are found guilty change their behaviour. Neighbouring municipalities may react for two reasons. First, if they are not corrupt and are just afraid that too much use of discretion would be misinterpreted, this would generate passive waste. Indeed, as the main objective of the adapted procedure is to provide the best value for money for low-value contracts, reducing their use by fear of being suspected is inefficient. Second, if the neighbour reacts because he is actually corrupt and potentially involved in the case under investigation, the change of behaviour would reduce active waste. In this case, knowing that investigations and prosecutions of corruption in public procurement are rare, means that investigations have a positive impact not only on the very few investigated municipalities but also on potentially corrupt neighbouring municipalities.

The use of open data and digital platforms

In the digital era, one purpose of public procurement is to increase its transparency and efficiency through the development of open data. By improving transparency and accountability, government performance, national competitiveness and social engagement, open data could be a powerful tool against

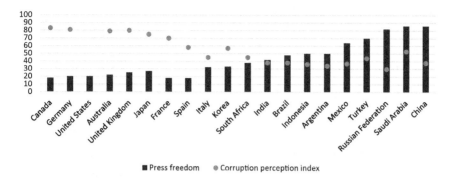

Figure 8.6 Press Freedom and Corruption Perception Index across G20 countries, 2016.

Note: the corruption perception index indicates the perceived level of public sector corruption in a given country. It ranges on a scale from 0 (high corruption) to 100 (low corruption). The freedom of the press score ranges from 0 (best) to 100 (worst) based on three categories (legal, politics, and economic environment).

Source: OECD (2016).

corruption (OECD, 2017). One expected consequence of the use of open data is to improve the transparency and accountability of governments. Since information is easier to collect and process, third parties (for example, citizens and NGOs) are therefore more able to monitor the decisions and expenditures of public buyers. When under more third-party scrutiny, a public buyer may be more likely to make better use of public funds (Spiller, 2008). Engaging in corrupt behaviour may be riskier due to this potentially higher level of scrutiny. Whistle-blowers have a key role in detecting misconduct in public procurement. A strong correlation between the freedom of the press and corruption levels exists since perceived corruption appears to be lower in countries with more press freedom (Figure 8.6). Transparency and accountability of public procurement may also be improved through more public disclosure of procurement agents' private interest. In the OECD countries, this level of disclosure is low, achieving an average of 20 per cent (Figure 8.7). In a few countries, amongst which France and Norway, there is no available information about it. The availability of such details is essential for detecting corrupt behaviours and the phenomenon of revolving doors (Barbosa and Straub, 2017). Having this type of information in France would constitute an important improvement in our analysis since we would be able to investigate the relationship between the use of an award procedure that allows for discretionary power and the connection between the investigated entity and private firms to whom the contract has been awarded.

We observe many inequalities in terms of public procurement data availability in OECD countries (Figure 8.8). Overall, data related to both

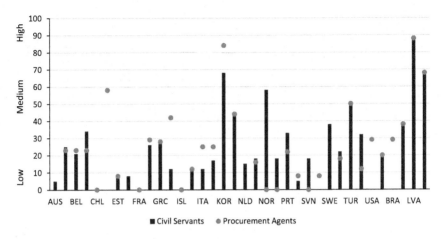

Figure 8.7 Level of disclosure and public availability of private interests, 2014
Source: OECD (2016).

	Pre-Tendering Phase					Tendering Phase		Post-Award Phase		
	Laws and Policies	General information for potential bidders	Selection and evaluation criteria	Contract award	Specific guidance on application procedure	Tender documents	Procurement plan of anticipated tenders	Justification for awarding contracts to selected contractor	Contract modifications	Tracking procurement spending
Argentina	•	•	•	•	•	•	•	□	O	O
Australia	•	□	□	•	□	□	•	◊	□	O
Brazil	•	•	•	•	◊	•	O	◊	•	•
Canada	•	•	◊	•	•	◊	O	◊	•	O
France	•	•	•	□	•	□	□	◊	•	◊
Germany	•	•	□	□	O	□	O	O	O	O
Italy	•	•	•	•	•	•	•	◊	•	◊
Japan	•	•	•	•	•	•	•	•	•	◊
Korea	•	•	•	•	•	•	•	•	•	•
Mexico	•	•	•	•	•	•	•	•	□	•
Spain	•	•	•	•	•	•	•	•	•	O
Turkey	•	•	•	•	•	•	◊	◊	◊	•
United Kingdom	•	•	O	•	•	O	•	□	O	O
United States	•	•	□	□	□	□	O	O	◊	□

• Always available
◊ Upon Request
□ Sometimes
O Not available

Figure 8.8 Public availability of procurement information at central level government, 2010.
Source: OECD (2016).

pre-tendering and tendering phases are always publicly available, except for Australia, France, Germany and the United States, where that essential information is not systematically provided (and sometimes not at all). More notable differences between the OECD countries appear for the availability of post-award phase data. It is noteworthy that Figure 8.8 indicates that in France, contract modifications are always disclosed. However, after an in-depth research and discussion with many procurement specialists and agencies, there is no publicly available information on contract amendments in France. Having this information would be particularly valuable since contract renegotiations, especially when purely opportunistic, represent one of the biggest issues associated with the awarding of public contracts.

One important issue is that even in the case where governments open the access to procurement data, they are often incomplete or require a high degree of processing. In France, procurement data are incomplete because they are not systematically reported (award notices), they do not cover all procurement processes (no data on contract renegotiations), and much crucial information is missing. On the latter point, data that would ensure transparency and accountability of procurement would be (i) the identity and bid value of all participants to the tender, (ii) the initial estimated value of the contract, (iii) the nature of negotiations if any, and (iv) details of what is in the adapted procedure. First, the identity of all participants to the tender would be useful to improve our analysis. Having this information would help to point out whether firms that are involved in the investigated corruptive scheme do also participate in the tenders of neighbouring municipalities that react to the investigation. This would also help to examine whether the pool of participants changes after an investigation is opened. Having the initial estimated value of the contract would also be an improvement in the sense that we would be able to assess whether the value threshold has been manipulated by the public buyer to use as an adapted procedure, and potentially for facilitating corruption. Finally, more transparency about how the adapted procedure takes place would greatly improve transparency. We do not have any public information whether there is a phase of negotiation and a restriction in the pool of bidders. Even though public procurement data are now accessible, they would need further improvement and more transparency to detect corruption and collusion in public procurement in France.

Conclusion

Detecting corruption in public procurement represents a huge waste of public funds. Increasing transparency of public procurement and reducing the discretion of the public authorities in charge of the procurement process are regular ways to contain corruption. However, this generates a trade-off between restricting discretion and having an efficient and a less burdensome procurement process for low complexity goods and services. Municipalities should not be reluctant to use a procedure associated with more discretion and more efficiency through fear of being unfairly suspected of corruption (third-party opportunism). Open and big data should discipline the municipalities. However, the data available to the public should be of good quality and the disclosed information should be accurate enough so that abnormal behaviour can be easily detected. However, the level of disclosure of the information should be a compromise between enough transparency for detecting suspicious behaviours and enough confidentiality for competition to be preserved and effective.

References

Bajari, P. and Tadelis, S., 2001. Incentives versus Transaction Costs: A Theory of Procurement Contracts. *The RAND Journal of Economics*, 32(3), pp. 387–407.

Bajari, P. and Ye, L., 2001. Competition versus Collusion in Procurement Auctions: Identification and Testing. *Working Paper, Stanford University, Department of Economics.*

Bajari, P., Houghton, S. and Tadelis, S., 2014. Bidding for Incomplete Contracts: An Empirical Analysis of Adaptation Costs. *The American Economic Review*, 104(4), pp. 1288–1319.

Bajari, P., McMillan, R. and Tadelis, S., 2009. Auctions versus Negotiations in Procurement: An Empirical Analysis. *Journal of Law, Economics, & Organization*, 25(2), pp. 372–399.

Baltrunaite, A., Giorgiantonio, C., Mocetti, S. and Orlando, T., 2018. Discretion and Supplier Selection in Public Procurement. *Temi di discussione (Economic Working Papers) 1178, Bank of Italy.*

Bandiera, O., Prat, A. and Valletti, T., 2009. Active and Passive Waste in Government Spending: Evidence from a Policy Experiment. *American Economic Review*, 99(4), pp. 1278–1308.

Barbosa, K. and Straub, S., 2017. The Value of Revolving Doors in Public Procurement. *TSE Working Paper*, Volume 17.

Burguet, R. and Che, Y.-K., 2004. Competitive Procurement with Corruption. *RAND Journal of Economics*, 35(1), pp. 50–68.

Chabrost, M. and Saussier, S., 2019. All for One and One for All! How Do Corruption Investigations Affect Municipalities' Public Procurement Choices? *Working Paper.*

Chever, L., Stéphane, S. and Yvrande-Billon, A., 2017. The Law of Small Numbers: Investigating the Benefits of Restricted Auctions for Public Procurement. *Applied Economics*, 49(42), pp. 1241–4260.

Chong, E., Staropoli, C. and Yvrande-Billon, A., 2014. Auction versus Negotiation in Public Procurement: Looking for Empirical Evidence. In: *The Manufacturing Markets, Legal, Political and Economic Dynamics.* Cambridge: Cambridge University Press, pp. 120–142.

Coviello, D., Guglielmo, A. and Spagnolo, G., 2017. The Effect of Discretion on Procurement Performance. *Management Science*, 64(2), pp. 715–738.

Di Tella, R. and Schargrodsky, E., 2003. The Role of Wages and Auditing during a Crackdown on Corruption in the City of Buenos Aires. *The Journal of Law & Economics*, 46(1), pp. 269–292.

Djankov, S., Ghossein, T., Islam, A. M. and Saliola, F., 2017. *Public Procurement Regulation and Road Quality*. Washington, DC: World Bank.

European Commission, 2014. *EU Anti-corruption Report*. Available at: https://ec.europa.eu/home-affairs/what-we-do/policies/organized-crime-and-human-trafficking/corruption/anti-corruption-report_en.

European Commission, 2018. *Public Procurement Guidance for Practitioners*. Available at: https://ec.europa.eu/regional_policy/en/information/publications/guidelines/2018/public-procurement-guidance-for-practitioners-2018.

Goldberg, V. P., 1977. Competitive Bidding and the Production of Precontract Information. *Bell Journal of Economics*, 8(1), pp. 250–261.

Herweg, F. and Schmidt, K. M., 2017. Auctions versus Negotiations: The Effects of Inefficient Renegotiation. *The RAND Journal of Economics*, 48(3), pp. 647–672.

IMF, 2016. *Corruption: Costs and Mitigating Strategies*. Washington, DC: International Monetary Fund.

Kelman, S., 1990. *Procurement and Public Management: The Fear of Discretion and the Quality of Government Performance*. Washington, DC: AEI Press.

Kelman, S., 2005. *Unleashing Change: A Study of Organizational Renewal in Government*. Washington, DC: Brookings Institution Press/Ash Center.

Knack, S., Biletska, N. and Kacker, K., 2017. Deterring Kickbacks and Encouraging Entry in Public Procurement Markets: Evidence from Firm Surveys in 88 Developing Countries. *SSRN Scholarly Paper ID 2985503, Social Science Research Network, Rochester, NY.*

OECD, 2014. *OECD Foreign Bribery Report – An Analysis of the Crime of Bribery*. Paris: OECD.

OECD, 2016. *Preventing Corruption in Public Procurement*. Paris: OECD.

OECD, 2017. *Compendium of Good Practices on the Use of Open Data for Anticorruption*. Paris: OECD.

Palguta, J. and Pertold, F., 2017. Manipulation of Procurement Contracts: Evidence from the Introduction of Discretionary Thresholds. *American Economic Journal: Economic Policy*, 9(2), pp. 293–315.

Spagnolo, G., 2012. Reputation, Competition, and Entry in Procurement. *International Journal of Industrial Organization*, 30(3), pp. 291–296.

Spiller, P., 2008. An Institutional Theory of Public Contracts: Regulatory Implications. *Working Paper. National Bureau of Economics, Cambridge, MA.*

Tran, A., 2011. Which Regulations Reduce Corruption? Evidence from the Internal Records of a Bribe-paying Firm. *Mimeo. School of Public & Environmental Affairs.*

9 Municipal procurement of social care

Opportunistic behavior opportunities

Niels Uenk, Jan Telgen and Madelon Wind

Introduction

As in other developed economies there is a huge strain on government budgets for health and social care in the Netherlands. The expenditure rises much faster than the economy in light of the aging population. The Netherlands faces these challenges of reducing the growth in expenditure of social care even more than other developed countries. The expenditure on long-term health and social care in the Netherlands is the highest of the OECD countries, and the expenditure is annually growing at a higher pace than the Dutch economy (OECD, 2017), which is not sustainable in the long term. Therefore, a major reform was implemented in 2015 in the Netherlands. Part of that reform was the transfer of the responsibility for social care from the central government to the local governments, a total of 393 municipalities in 2015. None of these municipalities had any experience in buying these specific social care services: they were all new to this line of public procurement. These municipalities were starting from the same starting point (completely blank) and had to commission these social care services under the exact same conditions. Noteworthy, the municipalities had extensive discretionary room for maneuver to organize social care services. This constitutes a unique research setting: a live experiment with hundreds of organizations buying the same services at the same time. These municipalities chose a wide range of different approaches for outsourcing social care services. We observed extensive variations in multiple aspects of outsourcing: the procurement procedures used to contract care providers, the fundamental commissioning models used for social care services, reimbursement methods for social care, as well as many details (contract duration, prices, etc.). In this chapter we present the findings of an extensive research project analyzing the municipal procurement of each of the 393 Dutch municipalities' adult social care services.

Context of study

Social care services

We define social care services as those services aimed at supporting individuals with needs arising from old age or a mental and/or physical impairment in their self-reliance and to participate in society. This includes services such as home care, household support, respite care, and sheltered homes. Up until 2015, social care services in the Netherlands were coordinated centrally through the *Algemene Wet Bijzondere Ziektekosten* (Exceptional Medical Expenses Act) or AWBZ. The AWBZ constituted a mandatory insurance scheme for social care for the entire Dutch population. The AWBZ was administered by health care insurers that, in practice, delegated responsibilities to 42 different regions. Having introduced a purchaser–provider split early on, the provision of social care services was completely outsourced: in each of the 42 regions the largest regional health care insurer in that region managed the procurement of social care services according to a nationally standardized system of services and procurement policies. At the start of the millennium the expenditure for social care services grew rapidly in the Netherlands, especially after a Dutch court ruling put an end to allowing waiting lists – a consequence of a former cost containment policy to procure limited capacity. Partly as a response to the rising costs, the Netherlands started to dismantle the AWBZ, decentralizing social care to the Dutch municipalities. Home support (home care) services were decentralized in 2007 with the introduction of the *Wet Maatschappelijke Ondersteuning* (Social Support Act) or 'Wmo'. The AWBZ was completely dismantled in 2015, and additional types of social care services were added to the scope of the extended 'Wmo 2015'.

Social care service reforms in the Netherlands

Moving away from a central standardized system of intervention (i.e., service) definitions, tariff structures, and procurement strategies, starting in 2015 each of the 393 Dutch municipalities became individually responsible to contract social care service providers. Under the Wmo 2015 municipalities have to organize social care for citizens who need support because of a handicap, mental disorder, or those with age-related needs. The Wmo 2015 defines the conditions and basic rights for social care for citizens without prescribing a detailed system of services or contracting regulations. This provides considerable discretion for municipalities to organize social care in the way they see fit. The former central standardized system was abandoned, providing municipalities the opportunity to devise their own system of outsourced services and responsibilities, service specifications, reimbursement methods, contracts, and the mechanisms to award these contracts. In short, municipalities have complete freedom in choosing such strategic commissioning choices, where the term commissioning signifies the more strategic choices in outsourcing – in line with Murray (2009). These choices determine the manner in which municipalities try to achieve their outsourcing goals (e.g. contracting high quality social care services for fair prices), and also affect financial and quality incentives for care providers. The specific goals that municipalities in the Netherlands generally aim to achieve with outsourcing social care services relate to the intentions of the decentralizations of social care. The Dutch government aimed to achieve different – coherent – goals with decentralizing social care. Social care services are organized by the government body closest to citizens, aiming for social care that is better tailored to the individual client's needs and demands. A related goal is improving the coordination and collaboration among care providers – achieving better integrated social care. These improvements are also expected to reduce expenditure on social care. In the first year alone, the budget for the decentralized social care services was cut by 11 percent to 32 percent, depending on specific types of care (Rijksoverheid, 2014). Municipalities therefore have an urgent need to transform the provision of social care services. Simply copying the pre-2015 approach to commissioning social care is not a viable option in the long run: the goal of organizing long-term care more tailored to citizen's individual needs and demands would not be met. And with severe budget cuts, municipalities would exceed their budgets.

Commissioning models and their incentives

In this research we identify how municipalities shaped their relationships with private care providers for the provision of social care services. We distinguish four different commissioning models, where a commissioning model is an archetype approach of municipalities in shaping its relationships with care providers for the provision of supplies or services – in this case social care services. The commissioning model constitutes a combination of fundamental choices in the coordination and organization of social care services. These choices concern, for example, which organizations are contracted, the scope of contracts with care providers, how social care service provision is reimbursed, and which competitive mechanisms are introduced. The combination of these choices defines the responsibilities, incentives, opportunities, and risks for contracted care providers in the provision of social care services. The combination of these choices also determines which opportunities and incentives a care provider has for opportunistic behavior, and who suffers the consequences. Theoretically, with 393 commissioning municipalities, there are 393 different combinations of these choices or, when considering that municipalities buy different types of social care services, even more. However, when accepting some degree of variation within commissioning models, we have identified four archetypical commissioning models used by Dutch municipalities.

Before discussing the four commissioning models, we first introduce certain considerations that are relevant when studying commissioning models. First, we introduce the notion of *supplier opportunism*, and we briefly discuss supply management literature with respect to supplier opportunism. Two other considerations we introduce are the *monopsony market* and the *Dutch reform goals*: achieving more tailored, integrated care, achieving innovation, improving cost efficiency, and considering continuity of care for existing clients. These considerations are relevant when analyzing the opportunities each model inhibits for care providers to behave opportunistically.

We then present the findings of our empiric research – identifying the commissioning models. Based on inductive reasoning we analyze the opportunities for opportunistic behavior of contracted care providers in each of the commissioning models. Here we distinguish three perspectives: the client perspective, the commissioning municipality perspective, and the care provider perspective. Each of these stakeholders may be affected by care provider opportunism, where, in the third perspective, opportunistic behavior of one care provider may affect other care providers.

Three considerations for public procurement of social care services

Supplier opportunism

Opportunistic behavior from suppliers in a buyer–supplier relationship is theorized in agency theory. Agency theory addresses under which contractual arrangements the relationship between a Principal (here the municipality as buyer) and Agent (the contracted care provider) operates most efficiently (Eisenhardt, 1989; Tate et al., 2010). Agency theory is concerned with solving measurement and motivation problems that occur when Principals and Agents have differing goals and desires, and it is economically or otherwise infeasible for the Principal to verify the Agent's performance (Eisenhardt, 1989). An especially interesting context for studying principal–agent problems is the service triad. Where in common buyer–supplier relations the buyer also receives the supplies or services, in a service triad a third party (the end-customer) receives the services (Li & Choi, 2009). As the buyer does not directly experience quality of service delivery, he needs to take measures in order to ensure that the behavior of the supplier and the services delivered are appropriate (Van Der Valk & Van Iwaarden, 2011). In their seminal work Li and Choi (2009) are the first to address specific issues in service triads, focusing on shifting relationship structures over time, incorporating the 'structural hole' concept from Social Network Theory (Burt, 1992), and emphasizing the benefits of being in a bridge position as a buyer between customer and supplier. One of the underlying assumptions of agency theory is that agents (suppliers) act out of self-interest. Where the agent's behavior cannot be efficiently monitored, the agent has an opportunity to put in less effort than agreed, known as 'moral hazard'. Suppliers then behave opportunistically to maximize their utility at the expense of the Principal. Li and Choi (2009) propose the buyer in a service triad should intervene in order to prevent losing the 'bridge position' altogether, meaning the buyer remains investing in relational ties with the end-customer as recipient of the services. Municipalities buying social care services on behalf of their citizens is a typical example of a service triad. Based on agency theory, municipalities are advised to take action to prevent opportunistic behavior by contracted care providers. In this research we analyze different relational configurations between municipality and contracted care providers (the commissioning models). Through inductive reasoning we identify the possibilities for opportunistic behavior by contracted care providers.

Monopsony market

The 393 Dutch municipalities together form the only buying body of social care services related to the Wmo 2015. In a monopsony – also known as a buyer's monopoly – there is one buyer, and the commissioning choices of this buyer determine the corresponding market characteristics and structure. To illustrate: consider a municipality that would only buy services from large, countrywide operating organizations. Small care providers that are completely dependent for their business on this municipality will either need to merge with others or they will disappear if they are not contracted. The Dutch municipalities together are the single buyer of many social care services, and their choice in commissioning may have a strong impact on the resulting market structure.

Dutch reform goals

The 2015 reform of social care services in the Netherlands was aimed at bringing a more tailored approach to social care services. One of the fundamental starting points of decentralizing social care to municipalities was the conviction that the lowest government body is best suited to arrange a system of social care tailored to the individual needs of clients – fitting the local infrastructure and local cultural differences. Municipalities in the Netherlands have a wide scope of social responsibility, such as social care and support for the elderly and youth care, debt relief, support for children with special needs in school, labor reintegration, and the administration of social security benefits. Another goal of the decentralization of social care, related to tailoring social care services to the needs of individual clients, was to improve the integrated provision of social care and support in families with multiple needs. Finally, the government also intended to put a halt to the unsustainable growth of the costs of social care services that the Netherlands had witnessed. These goals call for new approaches to the provision of social care services, or in other words, innovation. And this, in turn, calls for new approaches to commissioning social care services. A stronger focus on cost-effectiveness, together with incentives for innovation, are necessary to achieve these reform goals. There was consensus that these new goals would not be achieved by simply copying the manner in which social care services was organized and commissioned prior to 2015. Finally, a radical reform of social care services may have a strong impact on current clients. They may lose their professional social care service provider and be confronted with new services and rules. The Wmo 2015 has provisions that force the municipalities to consider continuity of care for existing clients.

The different commissioning models each inhibit different risks for opportunistic behavior of contracted care providers. Depending on the commissioning model, care provider opportunism may affect the municipality (financially), the recipient of social care (clients in this research), and other care providers. A care provider may be affected by opportunistic behavior of another care provider especially when the former is in a subcontractor relationship with the latter care provider. Furthermore, care provider opportunism may obstruct achieving the goals of the Dutch reform (decentralizing), which, can be argued, harms society in general. We describe each commissioning model, and then discuss the opportunities for care provider opportunism, where we highlight the perspectives mentioned before.

Findings: Commissioning models and opportunities for care provider opportunism

The 'AWBZ model'

The AWBZ model is named after the AWBZ which, up until 2015, regulated social care services in the Netherlands. The AWBZ model closely resembles the former approach to contracting social care services. In the AWBZ model, municipalities only contract the incumbent care providers. Municipalities typically only invite the incumbent care providers for contract negotiations or they only allow proposals from the incumbent care providers. While care providers that participate in the procurement procedure may be required to submit a proposal specifying quality and prices for different social care services, there is no actual competition over contracts: each of the incumbent care providers is contracted. The AWBZ model is characterized by the use of contracts with annual budget allocations. The municipality contracts a limited number of care providers, and the municipality agrees an annual budget with each contracted care provider. Care providers need to account for the use of the budget. Therefore, the contract specifies a range of different care services. While the AWBZ system had over 200 different social care services (referred to as 'NZa codes' after the Nederlandse Zorgautoriteit ('Dutch Care Authority'), which defined and managed this set of social care services), the municipalities adopting the AWBZ model typically contract for a reduced number – up to 50 services. The other services are not included in the scope of the Wmo 2015 or were hardly ever used. For each of these services, the municipality agrees on a tariff on a fee-for-service reimbursement basis with each of the care providers. The tariffs are negotiated in the procurement procedure, or follow on from the formal care provider proposal.

Care providers account for the spending of their budget by invoicing municipalities the amount of services provided to clients against their associated agreed tariff. The client's care entitlement determines the services the care provider should provide on a weekly basis. The care entitlement of a client in the AWBZ model is specified in terms of inputs per week: for example, a client is entitled to four hours of 'specialized personal assistance for people with psychogeriatric impediment'. Under a fee-for-service reimbursement of social care services, the fixed budget contract actually is an annual maximum production agreement: the care provider can provide social care services up to the agreed budget. As the 2015 decentralization of social care came with strong budget cuts, municipalities could not completely copy the 2014 contracts of incumbent care providers. To reduce social care expenditure, municipalities typically aimed to lower the service tariffs and reduce budgets compared to the 2014 contracts.

Opportunities for opportunism in the AWBZ model

Clients: In the AWBZ model, clients at first sight come off easy. The model is a continuation of existing policy and practice, and for clients already receiving social care, little or nothing changes. Clients can keep their current care provider, and more importantly their current caregiver(s), and the exact same care service entitlement. This continuity of care – a client keeping the same caregiver – is generally considered an important quality across different types of health care such as primary care and mental health care, although continuity may have different definitions in different types of care (Adeoye, Brutus, & Sarfraz, 2014). Continuity of care has several dimensions: informational, management, and relational continuity (Haggerty et al., 2003). In social care especially the relational continuity is emphasized as clients build up a trusting relationship with their caregiver.

Municipality: Municipalities run a serious risk in this model. First of all, fee-for-service reimbursement of social and health care services is associated with a perverse incentive to over-produce care services. Fee-for-service reimbursement rewards volume (Miller, 2009) and is now widely recognized as perhaps the single biggest obstacle to improving health care delivery (Porter & Kaplan, 2016). Incentives for efficient, innovative, and value-based provision lack in fee-for-service reimbursement. The fee-for-service reimbursement facilitates supplier-induced demand (SID): the overconsumption of medical services that is generated by the economic interest of providers (Sørensen & Grytten, 1999). The fact that SID is not just a theoretical supply concept is evidenced by van Noort et al. (2017), demonstrating how supply factors explain 17 to 23 percent of variation in the number of home care clients per inhabitant in the Netherlands. The budget allocation should, in theory, limit the extent of SID. However, if budgets are too tight, care providers typically respond by maintaining a waiting list for care services. Waiting lists for social care services are considered undesirable, and under the AWBZ even considered illegal (Schut & van den Berg, 2010), as it means people in need cannot access social care and support in a timely manner. Waiting lists therefore become a means for care providers to put pressure on local politicians to increase their budget. Furthermore, maintaining the former approach to commissioning social care services while the goals of the reform are to promote more tailored care, better integration of different types of social care services, and reduce expenditure, does not seem a sensible approach for the longer term.

Care providers: The AWBZ model typically maintains the status quo among care providers. Those care providers that are new and have not been contracted in previous years do not get an opportunity for a direct contract with the municipality. Their only option is to subcontract with the care providers that are directly contracted by the municipality. This puts the former group in a vulnerable position, as the contracted care providers are in a powerful position. While the municipality is publicly held accountable for their commissioning approach – and exploitation of care providers would not be publicly accepted – the conditions under which care providers are subcontracted are far less visible to both the municipality and the public in general. O'Flynn et al. (2014) refer to this risk as the 'squeezing out of smaller providers' and the subsequent loss of social capital. Squeezing out smaller providers can relate both to the contract conditions (e.g. tariffs) a subcontractor may be forced to accept, and the volume of clients of the subcontractor that is controlled by the main contractor.

Population-based commissioning

In the model of population-based commissioning, a municipality contracts care one main contractor per district of the municipality for certain types of social care. A more generalized version of this commissioning model for health and social care is discussed in literature (Billings & De Weger, 2015) and various government-commissioned reports and working papers; see, for example, O'Flynn et al. (2014) and Addicott (2014) under the heading of a 'prime contractor', 'prime provider' or 'lead provider' model. The number of districts – and therefore the number of distinct main contractors – varies between one and four in the municipalities applying this model. A 'one-district' municipality consequently contracts one care provider for certain types of social care for the entire municipal population. The main contractor is responsible for all social care service provisions of the agreed type within its district. Given the procurement approach up until 2014, reflected in the AWBZ model, the market of social care services is typically far less concentrated at the moment a municipality introduces the population-based commissioning.

Throughout 2014 there were no regions or municipalities with private care providers with sufficient capacity to independently provide all social care services for entire districts or municipalities. As a consequence, organizational and market adjustment is necessary, which may take shape in different ways:

1. The main contractor is an alliance or other kind of formal collaboration between several existing (usually incumbent) social care providers;
2. The main contractor takes over personnel of other social care providers who therefore disappear from the local market;
3. The main contractor sub-contracts other care providers to meet the required capacity and quality criteria; or
4. A combination of these.

The main contractor is financed through condition-adjusted capitation (Miller, 2009): the care provider receives one lump sum budget per annum that is based on characteristics of the population for which the care provider is responsible. While the budget may be determined by estimating the expected number of clients within the population and their cumulative social care service demand, payment does not depend on actual delivery of social care as in fee-for-service reimbursement. Rather, the contract between municipality and main contracted care provider specifies quality criteria, procedures, protocols, and desired performance outcomes. Municipalities use performance outcomes related to social care provision such as the minimum level of client satisfaction, average time between intake and start of social care service provision, and the absence of waiting lists. Outcomes relating to aspects other than client service provision may be specified as well, for example a sufficient level of sub-contractor satisfaction (where the main contractor works with sub-contractors). The scope of the contract may vary in the different types of social care included. Furthermore, the contract scope may vary in terms of additional activities such as client case management, and even organizing the access and scrutiny process for clients that request social care services. While many municipalities have municipal or independent 'social community teams' as the gateway to social care, some municipalities in the population-based commissioning model integrate this activity in the contract of the main contractor.

Opportunities for opportunism in population-based commissioning

Clients: The main contractor typically receives an annual fixed lump sum budget. Where other models – with fee-for-service reimbursement – have a perverse incentive of overproduction, the incentive is the opposite in the population-based commissioning model. From a purely financial point of view, the main contractor has an incentive to provide as few services as possible. Consequently, clients are at risk of care provider opportunism, in the form of financially driven underproduction. The risk is even greater when the main contractor is responsible for the gateway to social care. The main contractor has a financial incentive to refuse social care (arguing the client is not entitled to care), or to 'upcode' the client in such a way that their care is outside the scope of the main contractor contract and therefore his budget. Furthermore, when a municipality adopts the population-based commissioning model, there is no choice among care providers for a client. Consequently, for many existing clients this model forces them to switch to the main contractor, losing their current caregiver – meaning at the very least that the 'relational continuity of care' is lost.

Municipality: When contracting main contractors, a municipality in fact creates an oligopoly or even a monopoly position for the main contractors. These markets do not function well as competition is absent. Furthermore there is vender lock-in or a 'hostage situation' for the municipality: the municipality becomes over-reliant on this one main contractor. This presents challenges if the main contractor fails or chooses to exit the contract (O'Flynn et al., 2014). The care provider may start to exploit its power position, demanding a higher budget under the threat of waiting lists. Subsequently, it becomes much more difficult to switch a contract to a different care provider. And even if the municipality decides to contract a new main contractor, this would involve substantial transaction costs. The risk of opportunistic behavior by the main contractor in this model is further magnified by the fact that the municipality puts itself at a more distant position from the care provider and client. Contrary to the suggestion of maintaining close relational ties with end-customers as a buyer in a service triad ('maintaining a state of bridge decay rather than allowing bridge transfer' (Li & Choi, 2009) in service triad literature), the municipality positions itself as far as possible from its care-receiving citizens. This magnifies the risk of opportunistic behavior by the main contractor, because of the weak information position of the municipality.

Care providers: Any model where care providers depend on their competitors to be able to provide care in a region or municipality, puts these care providers in a very vulnerable position. We have already discussed the opportunities for the contracted care providers to behave opportunistically because the contracted care provider controls both the volume and the conditions under which it subcontracts. In the population-based commissioning model, these risks are magnified compared to the AWBZ model – since there is only one main contractor. As a consequence, every other care provider than the main contractor relies on being subcontracted by the latter.

Catalogue model

The catalogue model centers around a catalogue of different social care services, for which the municipality contracts care providers. This catalogue of services may resemble the old set of 'NZa codes', although municipalities in the catalogue model have typically reduced the amount of different services even further compared to municipalities in the AWBZ model. A more fundamental difference between the AWBZ model and the catalogue model is the absence of contracts with a fixed budget allocation in the catalogue model. The catalogue model is characterized by the use of standardized framework agreements with a wide variety of care providers. The municipality contracts care providers for the services in the catalogue, with standardized terms and conditions, and allows clients the freedom to choose a contracted care provider. As the framework agreements do not include a budget agreement, the care provider depends on individual clients choosing, or staying with, their organization for the provision of social care services. There is no necessity for municipalities to limit the number of different care providers in catalogue model framework agreements. In the catalogue model, there is no requirement that each contracted care provider is capable of delivering every service in the catalogue. Care providers can be contracted for every service or a subset of the services in the catalogue. This lowers the threshold for smaller or specialized care providers to be contracted. In the absence of ex ante competition, municipalities contract each of the *interested* care providers that meet their standardized quality and suitability criteria. This results in framework agreements with a few dozens of contracted care providers across the different social care services in smaller municipalities contracting on their own, to over two hundred contracted care providers in the biggest municipalities or municipal procurement collaborations.

Another fundamental element in the catalogue model is the role of case managers in the assessment of citizens' entitlements to social care, and monitoring social care outcomes. In the catalogue model, municipalities use case managers who are independent of the contracted care providers. Upon a citizen's request for social care services, the case manager assesses the citizen's need for support and discusses with the citizen opportunities for informal care and support. If there is a need for formal social care, the case manager assigns the appropriate services from the catalogue, and the citizen – becoming client – can choose from the care providers contracted for the service(s). The case manager has a pivotal role in the catalogue model. Often these case managers are organized in social community teams. Case managers may be municipal staff or sourced from organizations that are not contracted for providing formal social care services.

With respect to the reimbursement of social care services there are two different municipal approaches in the catalogue model. On the one hand, municipalities contract the social care services in the catalogue with a fee-for-service reimbursement. For each service there is a standardized tariff. This tariff corresponds to, for example, one hour of ambulatory personal assistance, a part-day (four hours) of day care, or a day (24 hours) of respite care. The formal care entitlement of a client specifies one or multiple services and the duration per period, for example 'two hours of household support per week'. On the other hand, other municipalities contract social care services in the catalogue with an outcome-based bundled payment. Each service is then associated with certain outcomes. These outcomes are either specified upfront in the contract, or specified by the case manager tailored to the needs of the individual client upon formalizing the care entitlement. These outcomes are specified at the individual or family level: 'the client opens and reads his mail', 'the client is able to cope with his disability', 'the client pays his bills timely', 'the client has a clean house and clean clothes', etc. The care entitlement of a client thus does not specify the production of services, rather the relevant outcomes that a care provider needs to accomplish permanently (e.g. the client can cope with his disability and is mentally stable) or periodically (e.g. the client has a clean house – every week the house is cleaned).

Opportunities for opportunism in the catalogue model

Clients: Opportunities for supplier opportunism in the catalogue model depend on the type of reimbursement. With fee-for-service reimbursement, there is a perverse incentive for care providers to over-produce services (supplier-induced demand). Depending on the attitude of clients toward receiving social care, this can either be perceived positively (clients who prefer more social care services) or negatively (clients who do not want more support than is strictly necessary). Therefore the risk is 'neutral'. With outcome-based bundled payments, there is a financial incentive for care providers to achieve outcomes with as little effort as possible – which may lead to underproduction. Clients are free to switch care providers – and in the Dutch context there are more than enough alternative care providers contracted in this model for most types of care: this limits the risk. The catalogue model offers clients extensive freedom of choice among care providers, and secures relational continuity of care.

Municipality: Many of the opportunities for care provider opportunism diminish in the catalogue model. Through the case managers that are independent of care providers that provide social care services, the municipality maintains a pivotal position in the social care service triad. The municipality does not allow the bridge position to be taken over by the care providers, a state referred to as 'permanent bridge decay' in service triad literature (Li & Choi, 2009). The municipality can monitor care provider behavior and performance and observe client perceptions of service quality. This strongly reduces opportunities for opportunistic behavior of care providers. However, monitoring care providers is a bigger challenge in the catalogue model, since there are typically many more contracted care providers compared to the other models. If contract management is not set up thoroughly, and monitoring care provider performance is not done rigorously, this in turn increases opportunities for opportunism. Furthermore, there are risks associated with the type of reimbursement. As discussed before, with fee-for-service reimbursement there is a perverse incentive for overproduction, which would lead to overspending on social care by the municipality. With outcome-based bundled payment there is an incentive for underperformance, leading to reduced service quality, but then it is mostly the clients who suffer the consequences.

Care providers: Since every care provider that meets the quality criteria qualifies for a contract, the opportunism risks associated with subcontracting are absent in the catalogue model. The catalogue model does not affect the market of social care service providers, rather, it provides opportunities to enter the market for new care providers.

Client auction model

In the *client auction model*, or henceforth the *auction model*, the municipality organizes an auction for every (new) client entitled to social care services: care providers have to offer a proposal and 'bid' for every client. There are several stages, from contracting to provision of social care in this model.

First, the municipality sets up an electronic marketplace. Access to this marketplace is restricted: only invited or admitted care providers are granted access to the marketplace by the municipality, and can participate in auctions. The municipality only admits care providers to the marketplace that meet the municipalities' suitability criteria and quality criteria, and that accept the terms and conditions of service provision and the auction system. The procedure that the municipalities use to allow access to the electronic marketplace closely resembles the procurement procedure leading to framework agreements in the catalogue model. In both models, the procedure is characterized as an 'authorization procedure' aiming to verify the organizations' suitability for service provision. The procedure leads to a (framework) agreement that specifies the conditions for care service provision without actually providing a guarantee for production. A successful proposal by care providers allows 'access' to the framework agreement or electronic marketplace, and the *possibility* of being selected for provision of social care. Actually being selected to provide social care services to clients requires another step.

The process of care entitlement and client selection of a care provider differs markedly between the catalogue model and the auction model. In the auction model, municipalities use case managers who are independent of the contracted care providers similar to the catalogue model. Upon a citizen's request for social care services, the case manager assesses the citizen's need for support and discusses with the citizen opportunities for informal care and support. If there is a need for formal social care, the case manager in the auction model writes an anonymous description of the client's impairment, social support needs, and relevant aspects of his or her situation. This *case description* is then put up for auction in the electronic marketplace, where admitted care providers can see the client description. The care providers are then allowed to write a proposal for the provision of social care to this client, based on the anonymous description. In the proposal, the care provider must describe both the care plan: the type of social care services and activities, what goals and results to work on, as well as the price. It is expected that multiple care providers would put in a proposal for a client, such that the client – together with the municipal case manager – can select the proposal that best fits his preferences. The client decides, together with the case manager, where the latter should ensure a cost-effective proposal is selected.

Opportunities for opportunism in the client auction model

Clients: The auction model facilitates social care services tailored to the individual needs and situation of the client. Additionally, clients are involved in the selection of the care provider, emphasizing their preference. The basis for making this choice extends beyond the characteristics of the care provider itself (as in other models), as there is a choice in the care provider approach for their specific situation. This model also allows relational continuity of care, assuming the current care provider participates in the (re)auction of the client. Of course, there is a risk that care providers may have opportunities not to deliver the social care as promised in the offer. This risk depends on the level of detail used in the proposal.

Municipality: A weakness of the auction model lies in the fact that care providers have to make a proposal for social care for a client who they have not actually met themselves. The care provider has to rely on the description of the client and the context provided to them by the municipality. Omissions or inaccuracies in the client case description may provide opportunities for the care provider that 'wins' the auction to renegotiate their proposal – to their own benefit – when care provision has started. Especially with clients with multiple needs or more complex problems, the care provider may argue it was not possible to foresee the extent of support the client needed based on the case description. While this may be the honest opinion of a bona fide care provider, opportunistic care providers may try to renegotiate the care entitlement out of a financial incentive, not because the client needs more expensive care but purely for their own financial gain.

Care providers: Similar to the catalogue model, no care providers are forced to subcontract in the auction model. Every care provider has equal opportunities to win client auctions, and small or specialized care providers can actually cherry-pick those clients who best fit their profile. The auction model may therefore actually be favorable to small and specialized care providers.

Discussion and conclusion

In this research we analyzed municipal procurement of social care services, identifying four archetypical approaches to commission these services. We then analyzed for each of these models the opportunities that contracted care providers have to behave opportunistically. Opportunistic behavior from contracted care providers may affect the clients receiving care, the municipality as commissioner and financer of social care, and competing care providers. When clients are affected by care provider opportunism, they are confronted with a *skimping* care provider, not putting in the efforts and delivering the quality of services according to contractual agreements (Sørensen & Grytten, 1999). In an extreme situation, a care provider – when managing the gateway to social care – could actually refuse social care to a citizen – also known as shirking (Sørensen & Grytten, 1999). Opportunism at the cost of the municipality as the buyer of care services relates to SID, following perverse incentives in the reimbursement method of social care services. The care provider provides a higher volume of services than the clients actually need, at the expense of the municipality. Finally, opportunism at the cost of other care providers occurs in main contractor–subcontractor relationships between care providers. The care provider in a subcontractor position is vulnerable, and may be squeezed out by the main contractor (O'Flynn et al., 2014).

Through inductive reasoning, we find that clients are most at risk of suffering the consequences of care provider opportunism in both population-based commissioning and the catalogue model with outcome-based bundled payment reimbursement – although in the latter model, the municipality has ample opportunities to monitor care provider performance and behavior, which may mitigate the risk. Municipalities are most at risk of care provider opportunism in the AWBZ model, population-based commissioning, the catalogue model with fee-for-service reimbursement, and – to a minor extent – the client auction model when client case descriptions allow discussion after allocating a client to a care provider. Again, the risk with respect to the catalogue model may be mitigated through properly organizing the client's case management, which is fundamental to the catalogue model. Finally, subcontracted care providers face the highest risk of being squeezed out by a primary contracted care provider in both the AWBZ model and the population-based commissioning model.

This study focuses on opportunities for care providers to behave opportunistically. There is no model where each of the stakeholders is completely protected against care provider opportunism. In a service triad, the buyer, by definition, has a weak information position as it is not the recipient of the service delivery. Important to note is that the fact that there is an opportunity for opportunistic behavior evidently does not mean care providers necessarily make use of this opportunity. Some of the discussed behavior can also be explained by the intrinsic motivation of care providers. Consider, for example, a fee-for-service reimbursed system of social care. There is a financial incentive to provide more care services than strictly necessary, and if indeed overproduction is observed, this may be attributed to the opportunity and incentive for opportunistic behavior. However, the care provider in this situation may in fact simply be motivated by his intrinsic belief that he is doing the client a favor by supporting and caring as much as possible. Even then it is important to recognize that the same behavior (providing more care services than the client may actually need), driven by intrinsic rather than opportunistic motivation, is not penalized but actually rewarded. This illustrates that the incentives and opportunities for overproduction in commissioning models do not exclusively relate to opportunism, and are very important for public social care commissioners to be aware of.

A final remark: this research studies commissioning models only through the lens of the risks for undesirable care provider behavior. It does not mean that the models with stronger risks, such as the AWBZ model and population-based commissioning, are models to avoid in general. Models such as population-based commissioning may, to a great extent, facilitate the achievement of the reform goals (cost-efficient, tailored, and integrated provision of social care services). Municipalities and public bodies commissioning social services in general should make a holistic analysis of their policy goals, and choose the commissioning model that best fits their goals. This study contributes by highlighting the risks with respect to opportunism in each of the models.

References

Addicott, R. (2014). *Commissioning and contracting for integrated care*. London: The King's Fund, (November), 1–62.

Adeoye, S., Brutus, V., & Sarfraz, S. (2014). Long-term continuity care: Unanticipated consequences, viable solutions. *The Journal of Medical Practice Management: MPM*, *30*(2), 104–109.

Billings, J., & De Weger, E. (2015). Contracting for integrated health and social care: A critical review of four models. *Journal of Integrated Care*, *23*, 153–175.

Burt, R. S. (1992). *Structural holes: The social structure of competition*. Cambridge, MA: Harvard University Press.

Eisenhardt, K. M. (1989). Agency theory: An assessment and review. *Academy of Management Review*, *14*(1), 57–74.

Haggerty, J. L., Reid, R. J., Freeman, G. K., Starfield, B. H., Adair, C. E., & McKendry, R. (2003). Continuity of care: A multidisciplinary review. *BMJ: British Medical Journal*, *327*(7425), 1219–1221.

Li, M., & Choi, T. Y. (2009). Triads in services outsourcing: Bridge, bridge decay and bridge transfer. *Journal of Supply Chain Management*, *45*(3), 27–39.

Miller, H. D. (2009). From volume to value: Better ways to pay for health care. *Health Affairs*, *28*(5), 1418–1428.

Murray, J. G. (2009). Towards a common understanding of the differences between purchasing, procurement and commissioning in the UK public sector. *Journal of Purchasing and Supply Management*, *15*(3), 198–202.

OECD. (2017). *OECD health statistics 2017*.

O'Flynn, J., Dickinson, H., O'Sullivan, S., Gallet, W., Currie, K., Pettit, M., Pagan, A., & Robinson, T. (2014). Prime Provider Model. An opportunity for better public service delivery? Social Policy Working Paper no. 18. University of Melbourne and Brotherhood of St. Laurence, Published Report.

Porter, M. E., & Kaplan, R. S. (2016). How to pay for health care. *Harvard Business Review*, (August), 1–27.

Rijksoverheid. (2014). Meicirculaire gemeentefonds.

Schut, F. T., & van den Berg, B. (2010). Sustainability of comprehensive universal long-term care insurance in the Netherlands. *Social Policy and Administration*, *44*(4), 411–435.

Sørensen, R. J., & Grytten, J. (1999). Competition and supplier-induced demand in a health care system with fixed fees. *Health Economics, 8*(6), 497–508.

Tate, W. L., Ellram, L. M., Bals, L., Hartmann, E., & van der Valk, W. (2010). An Agency Theory perspective on the purchase of marketing services. *Industrial Marketing Management, 39*(5), 806–819.

Van Der Valk, W., & Van Iwaarden, J. (2011). Monitoring in service triads consisting of buyers, subcontractors and end customers. *Journal of Purchasing and Supply Management, 17*(3), 198–206.

van Noort, O., Schotanus, F., van de Klundert, J., & Telgen, J. (2017). Explaining regional variation in home care use by demand and supply variables. *Health Policy, 122*(2), 140–146.

Part IV

Public procurement and international trade agreements

CETA, TTIP and beyond

From the publication of the Wealth of Nations by Adam Smith in 1776, the idea that free trade among different nations could improve overall welfare has been widely accepted. Notwithstanding this, history testifies that most of those that feared to be hurt by foreign competition tried to influence politics to obtain protection against products coming from abroad. This led to the creation of different kinds of barriers to trade, such as tariffs and quotas, but also to a corresponding huge body of international law devoted to lighten the ties of these "protective" trade instruments.

International Trade Agreements started to be negotiated after World War II, with the common goal of reducing trade barriers among participants and enhancing economic gains deriving from international trade. At that time, public procurement was excluded from this framework, being first introduced in 1981, following the increase of its international dimension. After almost 40 years, the question of if and how these agreements are effective and able to produce positive impacts on overall volumes traded has still to be fully answered.

In the debate presented in this chapter both Yukins and Fazekas try to highlight the main challenges and barriers of the international agreements on public procurement. Yukins reviews some of the major procurement-related trade agreements together with the legal measures used to implement effective trade agreements and discusses their potential benefits. He then proposes a three-layer approach for the understanding of trade agreements, posing questions on the effective capacity of existing trade agreements to: (i) allow "better value" buying; (ii) be legally enforceable; (iii) transferring best practices. Fazekas on his end tries to identify, reviewing theory and empirics, the mechanisms expected to deliver transparent and non-discriminatory behaviors, to improve tendering practices and to provide effective remedies. He also discusses the effective motivation of governments to engage in efficiency enhancing trade practices and in monitoring and enforcing activities.

The two concluding contributions deepen some of the existing international agreements. Grier carefully describes the WTO agreement on Government Procurement (GPA) and reasons on similarities and differences with Regional Trade Agreements (RTAs) negotiated by the US and by the EU with other countries, drawing the conclusion that the prospects for expansion of the international procurement arena seems to depend more on RTAs than the GPA, even though the latter will continue to act as a template for those agreements.

The chapter by Cernat and Kutlina-Dimitrova focuses instead on international openness, trying to look beyond direct cross-border procurement and including in the measurement also commercial presence procurement and value-added indirect international procurement. This approach suggests a greater EU international openness and an important role for TTIP negotiations.

10 Public procurement and international trade agreements – CETA, TTIP and beyond

Colloquium

Christopher R. Yukins and Mihály Fazekas

Opening remarks – *Christopher Yukins*

International agreements

This chapter will assess the effectiveness of trade agreements which address public procurement markets, focusing especially on the international trade agreements between North American and European nations, and with a special emphasis on legal measures that shape those agreements' effectiveness. The chapter will assume that "effectiveness" of trade agreements should be assessed as other elements of public procurement are measured, that is, whether they result in better outcomes for the men, women and children who depend on the goods and services being purchased through their public procurement systems. Measuring effectiveness in this way is admittedly less elegant than a purely economic measure of markets opened; at the same time, though, this more holistic approach may better capture the diverse policy interests at play in public procurement.

Major trade agreements regarding public procurement

While there are literally hundreds of trade agreements which address procurement (Anderson et al., 2015) a few bear special mention when assessing European and North American public markets: the plurilateral Agreement on Government Procurement (GPA), which has effectively opened the non-defence markets of most industrialized nations; the EU–Canada Comprehensive Economic and Trade Agreement (CETA), which is an important example of a market-opening agreement launched despite a rising tide of protectionism; and the United States' reciprocal defence procurement agreements with its military allies, bilateral arrangements which open critical defence markets and which have been largely overlooked in policy discussions.

The World Trade Organization's GPA is the leading international agreement to open public procurement markets. It is a plurilateral agreement, which means that certain WTO members have separately agreed to join the

GPA. The Member States of the EU participate as a bloc, and the United States, Canada and many other industrialized nations are also parties to the GPA[1] (WTO GPA). The parties agree among themselves, in a complex plurilateral arrangement, to open their procurement markets, generally for specified procurements above certain monetary thresholds. Besides agreeing to afford non-discrimination and national treatment to vendors from other GPA parties, the parties agree to follow certain minimum standards for procurement – standards intended to mitigate "non-tariff barriers to trade", such as discriminatory technical standards that may in practice block foreign vendors (Yukins & Schooner, 2007).

Canada's recent agreement with the European Union, CETA, was built on earlier trade agreements (including the GPA) but also included new provisions on procurement, such as a commitment by Canada to match European practice by publishing procurements at all levels of Canadian government (national, provincial and local).[2] CETA stands as a counterpoint to the EU's long-standing effort to persuade other nations, including China and the United States, to afford more access to their public procurement markets.[3] CETA thus stands in marked contrast to emerging protectionist efforts in the United States under the Trump administration (Bowsher et al., 2018). More subtly, CETA shows that because international agreements involving procurement tend to advance in parallel, incrementally, when one nation (such as the United States) bogs down in protectionism for domestic political reasons (Yukins, 2019), other nations can continue to offer new approaches for opening public procurement markets.

While the GPA and CETA focus on non-defence procurement,[4] the United States' reciprocal defence procurement agreements (between the U.S. Department of Defense and its counterpart ministries of defence) generally open trade in defence materiel and related services (Yukins, 2018).[5] Although these reciprocal agreements open defence markets, unlike the GPA and CETA, the reciprocal defence agreements do not give vendors that suffer discrimination the right to challenge (or "protest"). But the U.S. Defense Department's regulations carefully implement the reciprocal agreements,[6] and those regulations' market-opening measures are fully recognized in bid challenges brought by vendors in U.S. forums.[7] Thus, though the reciprocal agreements may not themselves create legal protections, the U.S. implementing regulations do.

Legal challenges, barriers and benefits

The legal effectiveness of these trade agreements turns, for the most part, on whether vendors and nations that face discrimination in transnational procurement trade can effect change, through legal challenges or otherwise. In the United States, as noted, the reciprocal defence procurement agreements' trade guarantees have been enforced through challenges based on violations of the agreements' implementing regulations. On the other hand, the leading

U.S. federal bid challenge forums (the Government Accountability Office and the U.S. Court of Federal Claims) have hesitated to enforce other trade agreements – those not carefully implemented by U.S. statutes and regulations – on the agreements' own terms.[8] There are other statutory barriers to enforcement in the U.S. system, even if the trade agreements explicitly contemplate allowing vendors to challenge discrimination (Yukins, 2017). Finally, although trade agreements typically allow nations to resolve discriminatory trade barriers through intergovernmental dispute mechanisms,[9] those intergovernmental mechanisms are almost never used, probably because the stakes in any given procurement are too low to warrant a government-to-government challenge.

Another way to erase barriers is through ongoing intergovernmental discussions, such as the working programs established by the GPA parties to address lingering trade barriers under the GPA.[10] These intergovernmental efforts, like the model procurement law published by the United Nations Commission on International Trade Law (UNCITRAL),[11] help frame what is in fact an international movement toward convergence in procurement rules. The converging rules – the fact that the legal rules which define procurement systems look ever more alike – may not snuff out trade barriers as they emerge, but the common rules do make the trade barriers more glaringly obvious and offer a backdrop, or set of best practices, against which to assess protectionism.

Conclusion

From a legal perspective, assessing the effectiveness of trade agreements means thinking in layers. The base layer is conceptual: the trade agreements should be measured not merely in terms of the dollars, euros or yen opened to competition, but more broadly in terms of whether the agreements further the goals of procurement by allowing public buyers to buy better goods and services – whether they facilitate best value purchasing, in the vernacular.

The second layer is a tactical one, in the marketplace itself: are trade agreements making it possible for vendors to challenge barriers to procurement trade? The U.S. experience there is mixed: judicial and administrative forums have balked when asked to enforce agreements directly, but have sustained vendor challenges when the underlying agreements have been fully implemented in national law. At the same time, the dispute processes for intergovernmental challenges have gone almost completely unused. The lesson, it seems, is to "domesticate" the international agreements in national rules, and to depend on vendors to press those rules.

The third layer is a more global one, which looks to international agreements' role in framing a rapidly converging set of procurement rules around the world. Trade agreements help define best practices in procurement rules, and because those agreements evolve in parallel around the world, they continue to advance even when protectionism and isolationism may overwhelm an individual nation. The agreements do more than merely open markets: they are effective because they chart a durable path toward better procurement systems.

Opening remarks – *Mihály Fazekas*

Trade in government contracts has received scant but somewhat increasing academic attention in recent years (Georgopoulos et al., 2017), while trade agreements including public procurement clauses have grown steadily.[12] Nevertheless, there is no systematic review of empirical evidence informed by elaborate theory to date that provides for the main motivation of this memo. Hence, the main question we seek to explore is the following: Under which conditions do trade agreements in public procurement produce the intended positive impacts?

In order to begin to systematically answer this question, I will set out comprehensive theoretical arguments for why public procurement trade agreements would or would not produce their intended consequences, while I will also offer a review of empirical findings pertaining to some key elements of the theory. Crucially, any trade agreement's success is predicated on the existence of a buyer who is looking for a better deal, a lower price or higher quality, as well as on the existence of a seller who is willing and able to provide those better products. Both capacity and willingness to engage in efficiency enhancing procurement trade are needed. It is the latter, the genuine desire of the buyer to procure more efficiently, which sets public procurement trade aside from private to private trade (Fazekas & Skuhrovec, 2016). In addition, governments who are parties to public procurement trade agreements are expected to monitor whether they themselves fulfil their treaty obligations, which further curtails motivations for genuinely engaging in efficiency enhancing trade rather than cheating the rules.

The style of this memo is discursive, briefly engaging with a wide range of arguments rather than getting into great depth in any of them. The intent is to spark debate and inspire further research.

The promises

By and large, most trade agreements in public procurement, like the WTO's Government Procurement Agreement,[13] attempt to open up national public procurement regimes by pushing for more transparency, non-discrimination of foreign suppliers, setting minimum standards for procedural rules (e.g. time limits), and strengthening review procedures (WTO, 2015). All these required changes upon accession, are to apply strictly to a subset of procurement procedures as defined by minimum contract values, a taxonomy of buyers included in the agreement, and a list of sectors opened up.

All the procurement trade agreement-induced reforms are expected to drive up the country's public procurement exports in sectors where it has comparative advantage, and enhance domestic public procurement efficiency through greater openness to foreign competition and better governance, while imposing some costs (e.g. some domestic suppliers going bankrupt due to stronger foreign competition) (Gourdon & Messent, 2017). Given that any export gain is dependent on the trading bloc's existing members' greater domestic efficiency through greater openness to foreign competition, I will focus on the impact channels expected to bring about this latter improvement.

- **Transparency**: Greater transparency is expected to lower transactions costs which is likely to have been prohibitively expensive for foreign firms to start with (e.g. tender advertisement on the buyer's physical notice board) (Hoekman, 2015). Lower transactions costs can increase the pool of companies submitting a bid and also confer lower bidding costs to those who would have bid under the previous transparency regime. If transparency reform is coupled with the introduction or improvement of the country's e-procurement system, benefits may increase further (Fazekas & Blum, 2020). More bidders and lower bidding costs for existing market participants both are likely to contribute toward lower prices and higher quality.
- **Non-discrimination**: Eliminating discrimination of foreign bidders in supplier qualification, technical specification, bid assessment, and payments – explicit (e.g. prohibition for any foreign company to bid) or implicit (e.g. specifying tendering terms favouring a domestic supplier) – increases the pool of potential bidding companies (Anderson et al., 2011). More bidders are likely to drive prices down and quality up.
- **Tendering procedures**: Improving the design of tendering procedures such as better time limits (e.g. length of advertisement period) is expected to confer benefits both to market entrants and incumbents, hence increasing the pool of potential bidders as well as lowering bidding costs to all of those already in the market (Fazekas & Kocsis, 2020). These are likely to lower prices and increase quality.
- **Remedies procedures**: Setting up or improving the functioning of a remedies body dedicated to public procurement may entail setting more appropriate time limits for challenging decisions or making sure that the design of the body limits favouritism toward any particular company. More effective remedies procedures may discipline buyers and increase trust in the impartiality of public procurement in the country increasing the pool of companies bidding, hence likely improving process and quality (Thai, 2009, Chapter 33).

The doubts

Against this wide range of expected and desired positive impacts, two principal doubts can be raised, that of lacking motivations of governments to engage in efficiency enhancing trade, and that of governments' and international organizations' weak monitoring and enforcement of trade enhancing rules in public procurement. I will discuss each of these fundamental challenges to the benefits of trade in public procurement.

First, motivations to engage in efficiency enhancing trade are weakened both by political and bureaucratic considerations. Many, if not most, governments around the globe – but also their individual ministries, agencies and subnational units – are driven by particularistic considerations which means that they are weakly bound by formal, written rules requiring the equal treatment of all citizens (Mungiu-Pippidi, 2015; North et al., 2009; Rothstein & Varraich, 2017). Corruption is widespread in public procurement in developed as well as developing countries (Fazekas & Kocsis, 2020; OECD, 2007). But pork-barrel politics as well as inclination of local politicians to use public procurement for local economic development purposes are also supposedly widespread. Under any of these circumstances, governments and their various organs will not be motivated to exploit efficiency gains from trade if it harms their particularistic, local, favoured suppliers. If foreign suppliers are willing to assimilate to such local circumstances by, for example, bribing officials, donating to electoral campaigns or employing local subcontractors, incentives may be aligned with trade still.

Bureaucratic considerations may also curtail motivations of public bodies to engage in efficiency enhancing procurement trade. In a typical public procurement setting, budgets are allocated at the beginning of the year from which procurement plans set out what should be bought for which value. As long as trade lowers prices, it represents a challenge to public bureaucracies facing fixed budgets and schedules of contracts, which simply have to be allocated. As returning a part of the budget to the treasury is undesirable, lower procurement prices may lead to unnecessary spending. However, if improved competition due to procurement trade leads to higher quality for the same price, it may well be in the interests of even the most inflexible bureaucracy.

Second, governments are expected to monitor themselves in the implementation of international procurement trade norms while international bodies such as the WTO or the Court of Justice of the EU are supposed to monitor and enforce rules too (Fazekas & Tóth, 2017). If a government lacks the genuine motivation for pursuing efficiency enhancing trade in procurement while also lacking sufficient separation of powers, which is often the landmark of particularistic governance regimes, then self-monitoring and rule enforcement are likely to be largely ineffective. As for international bodies, most of their monitoring and enforcement efforts fall on legal norms as enshrined by parliaments without any significant systematic understanding of implementation. This is highly troubling as avoiding the genuine implementation of trade rules is the easiest at the local level where tendering terms are being drafted and bidders evaluated.

Against the background of all these concerns, one further consideration should be brought into the picture, potentially saving the day. In circumstances where there is no reasonable local supplier capable of delivering a minimally acceptable quality and price, even the most corrupt government might opt for a foreign company, as long as the procured products have sufficient salience or electoral visibility. In this set-up, trade may truly increase efficiency, contributing to the public good, without hurting domestic power groups.

The unknowns and the failures

Underlining the difficulty of monitoring and enforcement of policy implementation, there is little reliable data on trade in public procurement (Messerlin, 2015), even in the European Union, which has one of the deepest procurement trade regimes globally (Cernat & Kutlina-Dimitrova, 2015). However, what little and only partially reliable data shows is that the extent of direct cross-border trade is marginal (Kutlina-Dimitrova & Lakatos, 2014). The gap between total trade openness and public procurement data openness is large, 56.6 per cent versus 5.9 per cent in the EU in 2009–2014; while EU institutions located in the very same Member States, but arguably having considerably less home bias, procure over 55 per cent from abroad (Fazekas & Skuhrovec, 2016). However, how much indirect procurement trade there is, is a lot harder to know; for one, company cross-boarded ownership is hard to track, let alone imported goods sold by domestic suppliers (European Commission, 2017).

Response to Mihály Fazekas – *Christopher Yukins*

Two important things happened after I submitted the initial essay that opened this chapter. First, Mihály Fazekas submitted an essay (above) which posited that, while cross-border procurement trade may not grow *directly* through prime contracts, cross-border procurement trade has grown indirectly through supply chains and indirect investments, driven by competitive pressures to fill unseen market gaps (and to avoid more nationalistic barriers to entry at the direct contracting level).

Mihály Fazekas' observations are certainly borne out in transatlantic defence markets, in which the leading prime contractors are typically highly "national" corporations that draw on transnational subcontractors and suppliers.

Although (as the essay that opened this chapter noted) the transatlantic defence market is framed by much more comprehensive free trade agreements (reciprocal defence procurement agreements between the United States and its allies), the pattern of defence trade described here – more limited direct contracting across borders, and intensive indirect cross-border procurement – corroborates Dr. Fazekas' astute observations, which we will return to again below.

The second important thing that happened was the United States' publication of the proposed text of the U.S.–Mexico–Canada Agreement (USMCA), which would replace the North American Free Trade Agreement (NAFTA).

Although the USMCA was born out of perhaps the most raucous and aggressive international trade negotiations in modern times, led by a pugilistic U.S. president willing to disrupt international markets in order to secure his political future, the government procurement provisions in chapter 13 of the USMCA ultimately turned out to be remarkably similar to earlier free trade agreements involving procurement.

A number of observers have pointed out[14] that the broader USMCA drew largely from the draft Trans-Pacific Partnership (TPP) agreement from which President Trump loudly withdrew in early 2017. A close examination of the legal texts of the USMCA's chapter 13 and the TPP's chapter 15 (the government procurement chapters) confirms the striking similarities between the draft USMCA and the draft TPP agreement. The draft TPP provisions were, in turn, drawn from the World Trade Organization's Government Procurement Agreement.[15] Indeed (and remarkably) by lodging an explicit reservation to Article 13.2 of the agreement, Canada did not even join chapter 13 of the USMCA,[16] probably because the new USMCA would have largely duplicated Canada's existing arrangement with the United States under the GPA.

Thus, although the USMCA is supposed to define an open, integrated market across Canada, the United States and Mexico under one agreement, trade across the region in *procurement* markets instead would be defined by bilateral agreements between Mexico and the United States (under the USMCA), between Canada and the United States under the WTO GPA, and between Canada and Mexico under the recent Comprehensive and Progressive Agreement for Trans-Pacific Partnership (CPTPP).[17]

In sum, despite loud promises by President Trump to improve upon NAFTA, and despite obvious gaps in the prior NAFTA regime regarding procurement,[18] the USMCA – the Trump administration's leading achievement in trade – reflects little real change regarding procurement. This may carry a subtle lesson for future trade negotiations: if the most explosive negotiations in modern times yielded almost no changes regarding procurement, future trade agreements may follow the same gentle, upward trajectory in their approach to procurement. Trade agreements regarding procurement may, in other words, be relatively stable and predictable.

That, in turn, returns us to my opening essay in this chapter, which argued that trade agreements regarding procurements can be understood (as per Figure 10.1 below) in three "layers":

Taking these together, this model asks (1) whether a trade agreement opens the door to allow purchasers to buy better-value goods and services from abroad, (2) whether that "open door" is legally enforceable, and if so (3) whether the agreement, by thus allowing challenges to obstructive practices, in effect facilitates harmonization across best practices between nations.

This model, coupled with Dr. Fazekas' empirical observation that procurement markets appear to advance most rapidly when they grow *indirectly*, suggests a hopeful future for cross-border procurement. If the agreements

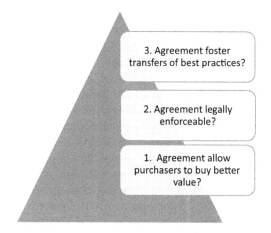

Figure 10.1 Three "layers" of trade agreements regarding procurements.

that facilitate cross-border procurement trade are now relatively stable and predictable, and those agreements focus first on facilitating *direct* procurement (prime contracts), in time those agreements – if enforceable – may be able to fill the remaining gaps in *direct* procurement (the gaps between "fortresses" in the transatlantic market described above, for example) and help meld best practices across borders.

Response to Christopher Yukins – *Mihály Fazekas*

Failed aspirations and potential for progress

As Christopher Yukins eloquently put forward, barriers to trade in public procurement start with the weaknesses of statutory instruments and ineffective channels for legal redress. Main international legal norms are often inadequately implemented in national legislation, hence do not facilitate discriminated bidders' legal challenge, while intergovernmental dispute resolution fora are barely used in spite of their clear legal standing.

These problems should hardly come as a surprise given the lack of political and bureaucratic motivations of governments to enforce and make use of procurement trade agreements. In a world of cosy relations between suppliers and politicians who depend on them for their campaign finances (Fazekas et al., 2018) and fixed annual agency budgets, there are relatively few public officials who are genuinely interested in efficiency enhancing trade in public procurement while also having the power to make the necessary purchasing decisions. In the absence of effective monitoring, external actors will not be able to lend additional incentives to domestic purchasers either.

While the results of procurement trade agreements in general have been weak, for example a paltry 5.9 per cent of procurement was genuinely cross-border in the EU in 2009–2014, selected examples show how much is possible to achieve if some of the above barriers are overcome. For example, building on the work of Fazekas and Skuhrovec (2016), comparing EU institutions' own purchases with similar purchases made by national buyers in their host countries (e.g. the EU's CEDEFOP institution and comparable Greek buyers) shows how much is possible. After carefully matching contracts awarded by EU institutions across EU Member States by contract value, main sector (2-digit CPV code), and year of contract award, while also removing consultancy and educational services which might be fundamentally differently specified by EU institutions (e.g. pan-European research studies), we see that the gap between within-EU Member States' and EU institutions' procurement trade narrows to 35 percentage points (6.5 per cent versus 41.5 per cent share of foreign suppliers) with the gap being very small in some Member States such as Greece, France, or the UK (Figure 10.2). This shows that it is indeed

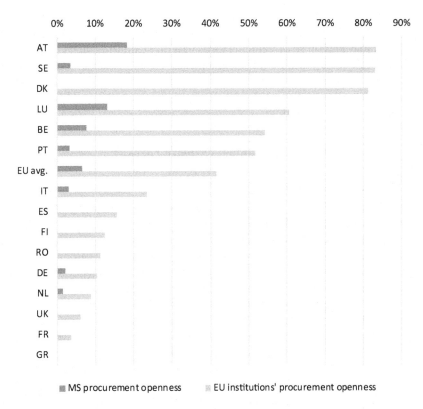

Figure 10.2 Share of foreign registered suppliers by Member States and EU institutions residing in them, Member States with EU institutions awarding at least 50 contracts in 2009–2014, TED, goods, works and non-consulting services.

conceivable that in many works and goods sectors demands are local, while on average, the home-bias free level of trade would be closer to 30 per cent rather than the current 5–6 per cent in Europe (if one accepts EU institutions' standard purchases as a valid benchmark).

Trade in government contracts: Where it works

Given the constraints outlined above, including lack of effective legal challenge and weak incentives and monitoring, it is most likely that procurement trade agreements will advance through necessity and through the back door only. First, a careful look at the contracts awarded to non-local suppliers in the EU and extensive anecdotal evidence suggests that trade actually takes place where domestic supply markets are very weak or non-existent. This would lead to the idea that procurement trade can advance incrementally, filling a patchwork of gaps in the supply. Such trade is facilitated by trade agreements but, assuming real and strong public demand for such niche markets, it is questionable how much added value they represent.

Nevertheless, thanks to broader trade liberalization achievements, namely facilitating business-to-business trade in goods and services and liberalizing foreign direct investment and foreign ownership of domestic enterprises, procurement trade might advance indirectly, potentially amounting to a greater share of domestic procurement than the headline figures suggest. Second, procurement trade can take place through subcontracting and long supply chains. If international trade is extensively underpinning government suppliers' products then maybe the low prevalence of direct procurement trade is not a cause for concern. At the same time, the need for a domestic supplier to contract the government foreign suppliers that are only acting as subcontractors may impose unnecessary transactions costs the size of which we have no estimate. Third, a look at the ownership network of government suppliers in the EU lifts cross-border procurement penetration from 1.7 per cent to 21.9 per cent in 2009 to 2015 according to DG GROW figures (European Commission, 2017).

Conclusions – *Christopher Yukins*

Direct procurements with foreign prime contractors show remarkably low market penetration

As the European Commission noted in a 2017 report, *Measurement of Impact of Cross-Border Penetration in Public Procurement*, at page 27, European domestic procurement markets consistently accommodate *indirect* contracting, through domestically based affiliates of foreign-based vendors – more quickly than those markets accommodate *direct* procurement from foreign vendors. (Across seven years, for example, the Commission report found that 3 per cent of contracts by value went to direct procurement from foreign vendors, and 20.4 per cent for indirect.) There is a parallel pattern in the defence market: as Jeffrey Bialos and his co-authors noted in their landmark study on transatlantic defence trade, *Fortresses and Icebergs*: while prime contractors are typically national "fortresses", their subcontractors and suppliers readily penetrate markets internationally. This echoes the Commission report's finding, at page 16, that market penetration is consistently higher in private markets than in public markets.

Free trade agreements, a growing and overlapping body of regional and bilateral arrangements, tend to focus on barriers to direct procurement, through prime contracts awarded to foreign vendors

Although the recent U.S.–Mexico–Canada Agreement reflected deeply contentious negotiations – Canada departed entirely from the procurement chapter, for example – the USMCA, which drew on the troubled Trans-Pacific Partnership and the WTO Government Procurement Agreement, reflected a stable pattern in international trade agreements: a focus first on barriers to *direct* contracting.

The issue, then, is whether – and how – foreign trade agreements can close these persistent gaps between direct and indirect procurement, and between public and private market penetration. Some open questions:

- Are these persistent gaps a cause for concern? Do they reflect inefficient public procurement markets? If contracting entities cannot purchase best value, does that result in a loss in public welfare? What of the offsetting gains in domestic welfare?
- What causes these gaps – why are there such persistent obstacles?
- Can changes to trade rules really affect market penetration?
- Should trade agreements be more narrowly focused on key obstacles to penetration, such as fostering methods of procurement that facilitate cross-border procurement trade, e.g., competitive dialogue (see Commission report, at page 69).
- Should trade agreements be postured to make regulatory cooperation easier, for example to reduce barriers in technical standards?
- As we sort out the role of trade agreements, how will they be structured – multilaterally, plurilaterally or bilaterally? What effects are the major trading parties, including the U.S., the EU and China, having on trade agreements involving procurement?
- As the international agreements change, should those negotiating them change? Should economists, trade or procurement specialists, or lawyers be negotiating them?

Should we focus more on the collateral impacts of protectionism in procurement – on the broader impact that protectionism can have on supply chains and national economies?

Conclusions – *Mihály Fazekas*

What next?

Given the arguments put forward so far regarding the effectiveness of trade agreements in public procurement and what can be done, where should scarce political and financial capital be invested? We started off by identifying distinct mechanisms which are expected to deliver the desirable impacts of trade in government contracts: fostering transparency, enforcing non-discrimination, improving tendering practices, and guaranteeing effective remedies. In the face of weak motivations of domestic actors and the lack of international monitoring and enforcement capacity, which impact mechanism should be further facilitated to get any tangible result?

First, let us reiterate that a lot of progress in international procurement trade has been a linchpin to globalized supplier markets and product standards as well as increasingly liberalized FDI flows among major economies (e.g. ease with which subsidiaries are set up in a foreign country). By implication, trade facilitation shall capitalize on the efficiency gains of procuring standardized goods and services supplied by a wide variety of international companies rather than only a national (preferred) supplier. Defining technical standards that facilitate international competition is a question of political will and it often goes against the interests of domestic suppliers who may have contributed to political campaigns or spent big money on lobbying (Fazekas et al., 2018). Still, making it easier to procure using standardized specifications or technologically open-ended functionalities can enable those on the buyer side who happen to have the right motivations and decision-making powers.

Second, successes of trade in government contracts frequently build on well-functioning, open, and efficient public procurement tenders. Electronic procurement such as e-submissions, wide advertisement, and fair scoring criteria are all hallmarks of open trade. For example, building on the comparison of national purchasers and EU institutions tapping into the same supplier markets we evoked already (Fazekas & Skuhrovec, 2016), marked differences in tendering practices arise. Looking at some key indicators of market openness developed by Fazekas & Kocsis (2020), a clear pattern arises: EU institutions are more likely to use open procedure types than their matched national counterparts (88 per cent versus 85 per cent), while they are also more likely to advertise for a sufficiently long period (83 per cent versus 74 per cent of contracts fall in the long, competition facilitating advertisement period category), moreover they are also more likely to use objective, easily verifiable quantitative criteria for prices and quality (75 per cent versus 46 per cent of contracts falling in the open, market-entry facilitating assessment criteria category). By implication, facilitating the spread of good practices in the use of these and further procurement methods, techniques, and approaches is likely to advance procurement trade, very much in line with the observations of Professor Yukins.

Does it pay?

Making the case for such subtle reforms as opposed to highly visible legislative changes is likely to be challenging. Hence, understanding and monitoring tangible gains in prices and quality is of paramount importance. However, there is no simple, one-sentence description of what positive impacts may look like. Drawing on the closest evidence to date, the few rigorous impact evaluations looking at the impact of opening up within country procurement trade in large, diverse countries have yielded mixed results. Lewis-Faupel et al. (2016) found that e-procurement in India and Indonesia increased the share of non-local bidders which resulted in higher quality but not in lower prices, while more recently Blum et al. (2018) found a similar increase in non-local suppliers but with a strong impact on lowering prices (price reduction of 5–14 per cent). None of these studies could estimate the longer-term impacts on technology transfer or dynamic employment impacts, potentially underestimating the benefits of opening up to trade. Nevertheless, it is possible to make a case for a less high profile, but more tailored, trade facilitation approach whose impact is carefully monitored based on these studies.

Notes

1 See World Trade Organization, *Agreement on Government Procurement*, www.wto. org/english/tratop_e/gproc_e/gp_gpa_e.htm.
2 CETA Art. 19.6, www.international.gc.ca/trade-commerce/trade-agreements-accords-commerciaux/agr-acc/ceta-aecg/text-texte/19.aspx?lang=eng.
3 European Commission, *Public Procurement*, http://ec.europa.eu/trade/policy/accessing-markets/public-procurement/.
4 For example, while CETA covers certain procurement by Canada's Department of National Defence, per chapter 19 and annex 19–2, the goods covered by CETA under annex 19–4 do not appear to include weapons systems.
5 See U.S. Department of Defense, *Reciprocal Defense Procurement and Acquisition Policy Memoranda of Understanding*, www.acq.osd.mil/dpap/cpic/ic/reciprocal_procurement_memoranda_of_understanding.html; see also Christopher R. Yukins, European Commission Proposes Expanding the European Defence Fund – A Major Potential Barrier to Transatlantic Defense Procurement, *60 Government Contractor, para. 196* (June 27, 2018), https://papers.ssrn.com/sol3/papers.cfm?abstract_id=3204844.
6 Defense Federal Acquisition Regulation Supplement 225.872 et seq., 48 Code Fed. Regulations 225.872 et seq.
7 See, for example, *Seabeam Instruments, Inc.*, Comp. Gen. B-247853, 92-2 CPD, para. 30 (GAO, July 20, 1992).
8 See, for example, *Per Aarsleff A/S v. United States*, 829 F.3d 1303 (Fed. Cir. 2016); *Per Aarsleff als*, Comp. Gen. B-410782 (GAO, February 18, 2015).
9 See, for example, WTO, *Agreement on Government Procurement – Dispute Mechanisms*, www.wto.org/english/tratop_e/gproc_e/disput_e.htm.
10 See, for example, WTO, *Agreement on Government Procurement – Work Programmes*, www.wto.org/english/tratop_e/gproc_e/gpa_wk_prog_e.htm.

11 UNCITRAL, *Model Law on Public Procurement* (2011), www.uncitral.org/uncitral/en/uncitral_texts/procurement_infrastructure/2011Model.html.
12 See www.wto.org/english/tratop_e/gproc_e/memobs_e.htm.
13 See www.wto.org/english/docs_e/legal_e/rev-gpr-94_01_e.htm.
14 See, for example, Michael Collins, New Trade Deal with Canada, Mexico Borrows Heavily from Pact that Trump Abandoned, *USA Today*, October 3, 2018, www.usatoday.com/story/news/politics/2018/10/03/usmca-new-trade-deal-canada-borrows-pact-trump-abandoned/1498224002/.
15 See, for example, Jedrzej Gorski, The Impact of the TPP on Opening Government Procurement to International Competition in the Asia-Pacific Region, *8*(2) *Trade Law & Development*, 66 (2016), www.tradelawdevelopment.com/index.php/tld/article/viewFile/274/266.
16 See https://ustr.gov/sites/default/files/files/agreements/FTA/USMCA/13%20Government%20Procurement.pdf.
17 See, for example, Government of Canada, *Summary Backgrounder: United States – Mexico – Canada Agreement,* http://international.gc.ca/trade-commerce/trade-agreements-accords-commerciaux/agr-acc/usmca-aeumc/summary-sommaire.aspx?lang=eng.
18 See, for example, Christopher R. Yukins, International Trade Agreements and U.S. Procurement Law (co-author with Allen B. Green) (chapter in forthcoming volume, *American Bar Association*, 2018).

References

Anderson, R. D., Müller, A. C., & Pelletier, P. (2015). *Regional Trade Agreements and Procurement Rules: Facilitators or Hindrances*, EUI Working Paper RSCAS 2015/81, available at https://papers.ssrn.com/sol3/papers.cfm?abstract_id=2707219.
Anderson, R. D., Pelletier, P., Osei-Lah, K., & Müller, A. C. (2011). *Assessing the Value of Future Accessions to the WTO Agreement on Government Procurement (GPA): Some New Data Sources, Provisional Estimates, and an Evaluative Framework for Individual WTO Members Considering Accession*, Staff Working Paper No. ERSD-2011–15. Geneva, Switzerland.
Blum, J. R., Siddique, I., Fazekas, M., & Samaddar, S. (2018). *Evaluating the Impact of Introducing E-procurement in Bangladesh. Policy Note.* Unpublished manuscript. Washington, DC.
Bowsher, M., Sundstrand, A., & Yukins, C. L. (2018). *Tale of Three Regulatory Regimes – Dynamic, Distracted and Dysfunctional: Sweden, the United Kingdom and the United States*, 2017 Government Contracts Year in Review Conference Briefs International 2-1, available at https://papers.ssrn.com/sol3/papers.cfm?abstract_id=3135805.
Cernat, L., & Kutlina-Dimitrova, Z. (2015). *International Public Procurement: From Scant Facts to Hard Data*, Working Paper No. RSCAS PP 2015/08. Florence.
European Commission (2017). *Measurement of Impact of Cross-border Penetration in Public Procurement.* Brussels: European Commission.
Fazekas, M., & Blum, J. R. (2020). *Improving Public Procurement Outcomes: Review of Tools and the State of Evidence Base* (under review). Washington, DC.
Fazekas, M., & Kocsis, G. (2020). Uncovering High-Level Corruption: Cross-National Corruption Proxies Using Government Contracting Data. *British Journal of Political Science, 50*(4), 155–164.

Fazekas, M., & Skuhrovec, J. (2016). Universalistic Rules–Particularistic Implementation: The EU's Single Market for Government Purchases. In *OECD Integrity Forum*. Paris: OECD.

Fazekas, M., & Tóth, B. (2017). *The Effectiveness of the European Union in Safeguarding Competition in Public Procurement Markets*, Working Paper series No. GTI-WP/2017:04. Budapest.

Fazekas, M., Ferrali, R., & Wachs, J. (2018). *Institutional Quality, Campaign Contributions, and Favouritism in US Federal Government Contracting*, Working Paper series No. GTI-WP/2018:01. Budapest.

Georgopoulos, A., Hoekman, B., & Mavroidis, P. C. (Eds.). (2017). *The Internationalization of Government Procurement Regulation*. Oxford: Oxford University Press.

Gourdon, J., & Messent, J. (2017). *How Government Procurement Measures can Affect Trade*, OECD Trade Policy Papers No. 199. Paris.

Hoekman, B. (2015). *International Cooperation on Public Procurement Regulation*, Working Paper No. RSCAS 2015/88. Florence.

Kutlina-Dimitrova, Z., & Lakatos, C. (2014). Determinants of Direct Cross-border Public Procurement in EU Member States. *Review of World Economics, 152*, 501–528.

Lewis-Faupel, S., Neggers, Y., Olken, B. A., & Pande, R. (2016). Can Electronic Procurement Improve Infrastructure Provision? Evidence from Public Works in India and Indonesia. *American Economic Journal: Economic Policy, 8*(3), 258–283.

Messerlin, P. (2015). *How Open are Public Procurement Markets?* Working Paper No. RSCAS 2015/89. Florence.

Mungiu-Pippidi, A. (2015). *The Quest for Good Governance. How Societies Develop Control of Corruption*. Cambridge: Cambridge University Press.

North, D. C., Wallis, J. J., & Weingast, B. R. (2009). *Violence and Social Orders. A Conceptual Framework for Interpreting Recorded Human History*. Cambridge: Cambridge University Press.

OECD (2007). *Integrity in Public Procurement. Good Practice from A to Z*. Paris: OECD.

Rothstein, B., & Varraich, A. (2017). *Making Sense of Corruption*. Cambridge: Cambridge University Press. http://doi.org/DOI: 10.1017/9781316681596.

Thai, K. V. (2009). International Public Procurement: Concepts and Practices. In K. V Thai (Ed.), *International Handbook of Public Procurement* (pp. 2–24). London: CRC Press.

WTO. *Checklist of Issues for Provision of Information Relating to Accession to the Revised Agreement on Government Procurement*. Geneva, Switzerland: World Trade Organization.

Yukins, C. R. (2017). The Trump Administration's Policy Options in International Procurement, *Government Contracts Year in Review Briefs 3*, available at https://papers.ssrn.com/sol3/papers.cfm?abstract_id=2925953.

Yukins, C. R. (2018). European Commission Proposes Expanding the European Defence Fund – A Major Potential Barrier to Transatlantic Defense Procurement, *60 Government Contractor, para. 196* (June 27), available at https://papers.ssrn.com/sol3/papers.cfm?abstract_id=3204844.

Yukins, C. R. (2019). Trump Executive Order Calls for More Aggressive Use of the Buy American Act – An Order Likely to Have More Political than Practical Effect, *61 Government Contractor, para. 219* (July 31), available at https://ssrn.com/abstract=3432377.

Yukins, C. R. & Schooner, S. L. (2007). Incrementalism: Eroding the Impediments to a Global Public Procurement Market, *Georgetown Journal of International Law, 38*, 529, available at http://papers.ssrn.com/sol3/papers.cfm?abstract_id=1002446.

11 Growing significance of regional trade agreements in opening public procurement

Jean Heilman Grier

Introduction

When the international trading system was establishment following World War II, government procurement was excluded. Nearly 35 years later, in 1981, the first international procurement agreement was implemented. Since then, a growing number of countries have exchanged access to their procurement markets under international agreements or are in negotiations to open their procurement to foreign suppliers.

The Agreement on Government Procurement (GPA) under the World Trade Organization (WTO) has attracted 48 members and serves as a model for other trade agreements with procurement commitments. While the membership in the GPA is expanding, its slow growth is primarily fueled by countries that agree to seek accession as part of their terms for becoming WTO members. Meanwhile, many WTO members are bypassing the GPA in favor of undertaking procurement commitments in regional trade agreements (RTAs), both bilateral and multi-party. Even GPA parties are expanding their bilateral commitments in RTAs rather than in the GPA.

This chapter compares the role of the GPA and RTAs in opening public procurement markets. It is divided into two sections. It begins with an overview of the treatment of government procurement in the multilateral trading system and the development of the GPA as a plurilateral agreement. It then examines the factors behind the expansion of the GPA and its prospects for continued growth, given that it now includes all developed countries.

The second section examines the role of RTAs in expanding international procurement commitments, focusing on agreements negotiated by the United States (US) and the European Union (EU), as well as the Comprehensive and Progressive Trans-Pacific Partnership (CPTPP). It also considers several other key agreements as well as negotiations that may expand procurement commitments.

The US played an active role in negotiating a number of RTAs with substantial procurement commitments from the 1980s through 2016. It was instrumental in negotiating Canada's opening of the procurement of its provinces under a bilateral agreement that led to the incorporation of that coverage in the GPA. The US also championed the negotiation of two major regional agreements, one of which it signed but did not implement. Its trade agenda changed under President Donald Trump who, at the beginning of his presidency, took a pivotal action when he withdrew the US from a comprehensive 12-country Asia-Pacific agreement in favor of bilateral agreements and abandoned the leadership role that the US had long held in the international trading system. The remaining 11 parties implemented the CPTPP, which is the largest RTA with substantial procurement commitments and is expected to draw more parties.

In contrast to the US, the EU is pursuing an ambitious trade agenda that includes negotiating RTAs with GPA partners, especially Canada and Japan, which expanded significantly commitments they have taken under the GPA. Asian countries are also actively negotiating RTAs, including the Regional Comprehensive Economic Partnership, which includes China.

The chapter concludes that, with constraints on broadening GPA membership and the proliferation of RTAs that open public procurement, RTAs likely offer the greater potential of leading the expansion of international procurement commitments. The GPA will, however, continue to serve as the template for other agreements.

Government procurement in the multilateral system

This section begins with a brief overview of the treatment of government procurement in the development of the international trading system, from its exclusion for more than three decades to incorporation of procurement commitments in plurilateral agreements that provide access to procurement markets only for the signatories. It then examines the plurilateral agreements, including the factors in their expansion and the prospects for adding new members.

Exclusion of government procurement from multilateral trade agreements

When the international trading system was organized following World War II with the negotiation of the General Agreement on Tariffs and Trade (GATT), the US proposed bringing government procurement under the same obligations as other trade measures. However, GATT signatories were not ready to abandon or restrain their "buy local" policies and practices. As a consequence, they excluded government procurement of goods from the GATT's national treatment obligations (Blank & Marceau, 1996). GATT Article III:8(a) states:

> The provisions of this Article shall not apply to laws, regulations or requirements governing the procurement by governmental agencies of products purchased for governmental purposes and not with a view to

commercial resale or with a view to use in the production of goods for commercial sale.

Nearly five decades later, when international rules on the trade in services were negotiated, the government procurement of services was similarly excluded from the national treatment, most-favored-nation and market access obligations of the WTO's General Agreement on Trade in Services (GATS) under Article XIII:1.

GATT Code on Government Procurement

Negotiations to bring government procurement under international trading rules began in the 1970s in the Organisation for Economic Cooperation and Development (OECD), and subsequently moved to the Tokyo Round of Multilateral Trade Negotiations. They culminated in the first international agreement to apply to government procurement, the GATT Code on Government Procurement (GATT Code), which entered into force on January 1, 1981. It was established as a plurilateral agreement because not all GATT members were ready to open up their procurement. Only 21 signatories implemented the Code (Blank & Marceau, 1996).

Rather than applying the existing GATT rules to procurement as the US had proposed more than three decades earlier, special rules tailored to procurement were developed. They required Code members to provide non-discriminatory treatment to the goods and suppliers of the other parties and to apply procurement procedures that ensured transparency, non-discrimination and fairness in the procurement process. The scope of the GATT Code was limited to the procurement of goods by the central government entities listed by each signatory. The Code's basic structure has served as the template for subsequent agreements with procurement commitments (see appendix, Architecture of International Procurement Agreements). It was amended in 1988 and remained in effect for 15 years (Blank & Marceau, 1996; Grier, 2016g).

WTO Government Procurement Agreement

The parties to the GATT Code undertook negotiations to extend the scope and coverage of the Code in parallel with the Uruguay Round of Multinational Trade Negotiations (Uruguay Round), which was launched in 1986 in Punta del Este, Uruguay. The procurement negotiations concluded with the signing of the WTO Agreement on Government Procurement (GPA) in Marrakesh, Morocco on April 15, 1994, the same day the Agreement Establishing the World Trade Organization was signed. Like the GATT Code, which it replaced, the GPA is a plurilateral agreement (Grier, 2016g).

The GPA entered into force on January 1, 1996 for Canada, the EU (and its 15 Member States: Austria, Belgium, Denmark, Finland, France, Germany,

Greece, Ireland, Italy, Luxemburg, the Netherlands, Portugal, Spain, Sweden and the United Kingdom), Israel, Japan, Norway, Switzerland and the US, and on January 1, 1997 for the Republic of Korea (Korea), which had not been a party to the GATT Code. Subsequently, four other GATT Code signatories joined the GPA through its accession process: the Netherlands with respect to Aruba (Aruba) in 1996; and Hong Kong China, Liechtenstein and Singapore in 1997. The scope of the GPA extended beyond the GATT Code's coverage of procurement of goods by central government entities to include procurement by sub-central government entities and other entities, such as utilities and government enterprises, as well as procurement of services and construction services (Grier, 2016g). With the expansion of procurement, the GPA parties incorporated a number of reciprocity conditions in their coverage schedules (Grier, 2019f).

Under a built-in mandate in Article XXIV:7(b) of the 1994 GPA, its parties commenced negotiations in 1997 with the aim of improving the Agreement and achieving "the greatest possible extension of its coverage among all Parties on the basis of mutual reciprocity." In December 2006, the parties reached a provisional agreement on a revision of the GPA text, with the exception of its Final Provisions, and excluding new market access commitments. After another five years of negotiations, they concluded the revision of the GPA at the end of 2011 and adopted a "Decision on the Outcomes of the Negotiations under Article XXIV:7 of the Agreement on Government Procurement" in March 2012 (Grier, 2016g).

The revised GPA entered into force on April 6, 2014 with the ratification by two-thirds of the 15 parties: Canada, the EU, Hong Kong China, Iceland, Israel, Liechtenstein, Norway, Singapore, Chinese Taipei and the US. Later in 2014, Japan and Aruba also ratified it, followed by Armenia in 2015 and Korea in 2016. Only Switzerland has not yet ratified the revised agreement and continues to apply the 1994 GPA. When it completes its ratification, the 1994 GPA will cease to have effect (Grier, 2016g).

The 2012 revision improved the GPA but did not alter its fundamental obligations or the rights of the parties under it. The rewrite of its text clarified obligations, removed ambiguities, redundancies and outdated provisions, and adopted a structure that reflects the procurement process and facilitates its use. The updated provisions also incorporated modern procurement practices, in particular relating to the use of electronic means in the conduct of procurement. The revision also expanded the procurement the parties covered under the GPA. Following the revision, the WTO Secretariat estimated that the parties annually open procurement worth approximately US$1.7 trillion under the Agreement (Grier, 2016g, 2017e).[1]

The revised GPA in Article XX:7 calls for new negotiations three years after its entry into force to "progressively" reduce and eliminate discriminatory measures and achieve "the greatest possible extension of its coverage among all Parties on the basis of mutual reciprocity." The WTO Committee on Government Procurement, which oversees the implementation of the

GPA, has not yet commenced a new round of negotiations. It indicated in its 2018 annual report that "when it is considered useful and timely to do so," it will initiate new negotiations (WTO, 2018b).

The GPA's current membership is comprised of 20 parties, covering the procurement of 48 WTO members:

> Armenia; Australia; Canada; the EU and its 28 Member States (Austria, Belgium, Bulgaria, Croatia, Czech Republic, Cyprus, Denmark, Estonia, Finland, France, Germany, Greece, Hungary, Ireland, Italy, Latvia, Lithuania, Luxembourg, Malta, the Netherlands, Poland, Portugal, Romania, Slovak Republic, Slovenia, Spain, Sweden and the UK); Hong Kong, China; Iceland; Israel; Japan; Korea; Liechtenstein; Moldova; Montenegro; Aruba; New Zealand; Norway; Singapore; Switzerland; Chinese Taipei; Ukraine; and the US.
>
> (WTO, 2019a)

Expansion of GPA membership

The GPA in Article XXII:2 allows any WTO member to accede to the Agreement on terms agreed between it and the parties. The GPA accession process is based on negotiations on the procurement that the acceding country will cover under the Agreement and a determination that its procurement system conforms with the GPA.

Since the GPA entered into force in January 1996, its membership has more than doubled, growing from 22 WTO members to 48 members. It now constitutes slightly less than one-third of all WTO members. Three factors underlie that 25-member expansion: EU enlargement added 13 Member States;[2] seven countries acceded to the GPA on their own initiative, most within the first two years of the GPA's implementation;[3] and five countries joined the GPA to fulfill commitments made in their accessions to the WTO (Grier, 2018a).[4]

Since the WTO's establishment in 1995, two-thirds (24) of the countries or economies that have acceded to that multilateral institution have committed to seek GPA membership as part of their protocols of accession. Of the 24, nine have become GPA parties (Grier, 2018a);[5] six are actively engaged in GPA accession negotiations: China submitted its seventh offer in 2019 (Grier, 2019i);[6] Kazakhstan, Kyrgyz Republic; North Macedonia; Russian Federation; and Tajikistan. Eight members have not begun the accession process or progressed beyond initial steps (Afghanistan, Albania, Georgia, Jordan, Mongolia, Oman, Saudi Arabia and Seychelles) or have withdrawn their application for accession (Panama in 2013) (Grier, 2018a).

Of the 12 countries that joined the WTO since 1995 without a commitment to seek GPA accession, several indicated that they might consider joining at a later date (e.g., Vietnam, Cambodia and Cape Verde), but expressed reservations (Grier, 2018a). Vietnam offers a compelling perspective. In its

WTO accession negotiations, several members encouraged it to join the GPA. It responded that it wanted "to focus its limited resources on the implementation of the multilateral agreements [and] would consider" joining the GPA after its WTO accession (WTO, 2006). Although it became a WTO member in 2007 and an observer to the GPA in 2012, it has not sought accession. Instead, it has agreed to open its government procurement in two trade agreements: the CPTPP and a bilateral RTA with the EU.

In joining the WTO, the Lao People's Democratic Republic commented that a decision on whether to join the GPA "would depend on the capacity of governmental agencies to manage the terms and conditions of the Agreement" (WTO, 2012). Tonga observed that the GPA "had not been drawn up with the situation of very small developing countries, such as Tonga, in mind." It pointed out that few, if any, of its government contracts would be covered under GPA thresholds and its large contracts were often subject to aid organizations' procurement rules (WTO, 2005). Many of the developing or least-developed countries currently engaged in negotiations to join the WTO will likely be pressed by current WTO members to make commitments to seek GPA membership.

Following its decision to leave the European Union (Brexit), the United Kingdom, in June 2018, applied for membership in the GPA "in its own right." On February 27, 2019, the parties approved the UK's accession to the GPA, noting that it would be covered by the GPA as an EU Member State until its withdrawal from the EU or the expiration of any transition period during which it is treated as an EU member. The Committee directed the UK to update its GPA schedules by proposing rectifications of its entity lists within three months of becoming a party in its own right (WTO, 2019e; Grier, 2018j). With its exit from the EU on January 31, 2020, the UK is no longer an EU Member State but will continue to be covered under the GPA as an EU Member State until the end of the transition period (WTO, 2020).

Before WTO members apply for GPA accession, they generally seek observer status. The Agreement in Article XXI:4 provides that any WTO member may participate as an observer by submitting a written notice to the Committee. Observers may participate in relevant Committee discussions and obtain access to the Committee's working documents. Even though becoming an observer imposes no obligations, only 33 WTO members, and one country in negotiations to accede to the WTO (Belarus), have observer status, and approximately one-half of them have GPA accession commitments. The observers, with the year they gained that status in parentheses, are:

Afghanistan (2017); Albania (2001); Argentina (1997); Bahrain (2008); Belarus (2018); Brazil (2017); Cameroon (2001); Chile (1997); China (2002); Colombia (1996); Costa Rica (2015); Ecuador (2019); Georgia (1999); India (2010); Indonesia (2012); Jordan (2000); Kazakhstan (2016); Kyrgyz Republic (1999); Malaysia (2012); Mongolia (1999); North Macedonia (2013); Oman (2001); Pakistan (2015); Panama (1997);

Paraguay (2019); Philippines (2019); Russian Federation (2013); Saudi Arabia (2007); Seychelles (2015); Sri Lanka (2003); Tajikistan (2014); Thailand (2015); Turkey (1996); United Kingdom (2020); and Vietnam (2012).

(WTO, 2019a; Grier, 2018e)

The GPA includes no members from Africa or Latin America. Eight Latin American countries are observers, but none have sought GPA member-ship even though they are parties to numerous RTAs with procurement commitments. Only two African countries (Cameroon and the Seychelles) are GPA observers, with the Seychelles undertaking a commitment to seek GPA membership when it joined the WTO in 2015. Seven GPA parties are from Asia: Australia, Hong Kong China, Japan, Korea, New Zealand, Singapore and Chinese Taipei (Grier, 2018a).

The GPA membership includes all developed countries and all but four (Chile, Colombia, Mexico and Turkey) of the 37 OECD members (Grier, 2018a; OECD, 2019). Among the G20, a grouping of "the world's largest advanced and emerging economies" that represent two-thirds of the world's population, 85 percent of global gross domestic product and more than 75 percent of global trade, only half are GPA parties. In addition to China and Russia, which are engaged in GPA accession negotiations, the other G20 countries that are not GPA members are: Argentina, Brazil, India, Indonesia, Mexico, Saudi Arabia, South Africa and Turkey (G20, 2019).

For the foreseeable future, expansion of GPA membership appears likely to depend on fulfillment of WTO members' obligations to pursue accession to the Agreement and persuading countries that are seeking to join the WTO to make a GPA commitment. Since all developed countries are GPA parties, the Agreement's advancement rests on accessions by developing and least-developed countries. A challenge for GPA parties is how to attract long-term WTO members to join the plurilateral agreement.

Prospects for multilateral procurement commitments under the WTO

Prospects for multilateral commitments on procurement under the WTO appear bleak for the foreseeable future. A modest attempt to develop an agreement focused on procurement transparency was rejected by the WTO membership; and a built-in mandate for an agreement on procurement in ser-vices has seen little progress in more than two decades.

Over 15 years ago, the WTO members jettisoned a very modest pro-posal to negotiate a multilateral agreement that would have imposed only transparency-related rules on the procurement of all WTO members. That effort began in 1996 when the WTO's First Ministerial Conference set up a multilateral Working Group on Transparency in Government Procurement to conduct a study on transparency in government procurement practices and develop elements for an agreement. Five years later, the organization's Fourth

Ministerial Conference agreed that negotiations on a multilateral agreement on transparency in procurement would take place after the next ministerial conference, based on a decision at that Conference on modalities of negotiations (WTO, 2019b; Grier, 2016g).

Even though the negotiations were to be limited to transparency aspects of procurement and would not have restricted the application of domestic preferences nor required the opening of procurement to foreign suppliers, WTO members could not reach a consensus to launch negotiations when the ministers met in 2003. As a consequence, the WTO General Council determined that the issue would not be included in the Doha Development Work Program and no work on the issue would be undertaken in the WTO during the Doha Round of trade negotiations. Since that decision, the Working Group on Transparency in Government Procurement has been inactive. In a proposal for reforming the WTO, the EU recommended elimination of idle WTO committees, such as the procurement working group (Grier, 2016g, 2018g).

Another effort to develop multilateral procurement commitments under the WTO remains alive but with few prospects of success. The GATS in Article XIII:2 provides a mandate for multilateral negotiations on government procurement of services, which were to commence within two years after the GATS entered into force in 1995. A Working Party on GATS Rules, established to undertake work related to the procurement mandate, *inter alia*, has done little more than gather information and study issues related to the procurement of services. Only a few WTO members have expressed interest in undertaking commitments on procurement of services (Grier, 2016g).

Regional trade agreements

Overview

Since the conclusion of the Uruguay Round and the establishment of the WTO in 1995, the multilateral trading system "has not produced a broad set of new trade liberalization agreements," with the exception of several limited scope agreements, such as the Trade Facilitation Agreement (Williams, 2018). As a consequence of the lack of advancement of trade commitments in the multilateral arena, WTO members have turned increasingly to negotiations of regional trade agreements to develop new trade rules and expand trade commitments. For this discussion, the term "RTA" follows its use in the WTO as "any reciprocal trade agreement between two or more partners, not necessarily belonging to the same region." It includes both bilateral and multiparty agreements. Such agreements are often referred to as free trade agreements (FTAs). Those terms are used interchangeably in the following discussion (WTO, 2019d).

RTAs constitute one of the exemptions from the core WTO principle of non-discrimination among members. In order for an RTA to be authorized under the WTO, it must meet certain requirements. In particular, in accordance with GATT Article XIV:8(b) and GATS Article V:1, it must cover "substantially all the trade" between its parties.

RTAs "have risen in number and reach over the years, including a notable increase in large plurilateral agreements under negotiation" (WTO, 2019d). The US Congressional Research Service found that since 1990 the number of RTAs grew sixfold from fewer than 50 to nearly 300. All WTO members are a party to at least one RTA and, as of 2014, each member had an average of 11 RTA partners. Of RTAs notified to the WTO between 2000 and 2014, 46 percent include commitments on government procurement (Williams, 2018).

This part examines the role of RTAs and certain bilateral agreements in opening procurement markets. It focuses on agreements negotiated by the US and the EU, as well as other key agreements that expand, or have the potential of expanding, procurement commitments among two or more economies outside of the GPA.

US trade agreements

The US discussion is divided into two sections. It first examines the US's negotiation of FTAs and two bilateral agreements with substantive procurement obligations, covering the 1980s through 2016. It also considers two major agreements that the US championed: it ultimately withdrew from one and did not complete the other. The discussion then turns to the negotiation of trade agreements by the Trump administration between 2017 and 2019.

US trade agreements and negotiations (1980s to 2016)

Beginning in the 1980s, the US negotiated 15 FTAs with 20 countries, "for numerous economic, political, and strategic reasons" (Williams, 2018). It included substantial government procurement obligations as a core element of its FTAs, with the exception of an FTA with Jordan. That Agreement only committed the parties to enter negotiations on Jordan's accession to the GPA, based on its July 12, 2000 application (Grier, 2017e).

The US negotiated its first two FTAs with GATT Code partners. A 1985 FTA with Israel represented a modest beginning for procurement commitments, with a mere seven paragraphs devoted to procurement. The two countries went beyond their GATT Code commitments with the application of a lower threshold (US$50,000). Israel opened procurement of its Ministry of Defense, which it did not cover under the Code (nor does it cover under the GPA), and relaxed its GATT Code offset requirements, except for defense procurement. The FTA does not include any procedural obligations (Grier, 2017e).

The US entered its second FTA with Canada, also a GATT Code signatory. That agreement set a precedent of including a separate government procurement chapter in a broader trade agreement. The two countries reaffirmed their rights and obligations under the Code and added several expanded procedural obligations to those in the Code, in particular, bid challenges procedures. They also broadened their procurement commitments by applying a lower threshold (US$25,000) than under the Code to their federal government procurement (Grier, 2013).

The Canada FTA was superseded in 1995 by the North American Free Trade Agreement (NAFTA), which applied to Canada, Mexico and the US. NAFTA could not incorporate the GATT Code since Mexico was not a signatory. As a consequence, NAFTA included a procurement chapter with detailed principles and procedures, following the basic structure of the Code. It was the first US agreement to open procurement of services and government enterprises (Grier, 2013).

Beginning in 2000, the US negotiated several FTAs with its Latin American neighbors: Chile, Colombia, Panama, Peru and six Central American countries (Costa Rica, Dominican Republic, El Salvador, Guatemala, Honduras and Nicaragua); none have joined the GPA. In Asia, the US expanded its access to foreign procurement through FTAs with Australia, Korea and Singapore, all GPA parties. Those agreements included lower thresholds than in the GPA but, in the case of the Korea FTA, a more limited scope as it only applies to central government procurement. In the Middle East and North Africa, the US entered FTAs with Bahrain, Morocco and Oman, which are not in the GPA. All the FTAs have similar government procurement chapters patterned after the NAFTA chapter but incorporating a number of provisions from the revision of the GPA, which was under negotiation at the same time as the FTAs. Agreements with GPA parties largely incorporated GPA provisions. The US implemented the last of those FTAs, with Colombia, Korea and Panama, in 2012 (Grier, 2017e).

In addition to the FTAs, the US negotiated two agreements with the EU and Canada, which were limited to procurement commitments. The first, the 1995 US–EU Exchange of Letters followed the signing of the GPA in 1994 and gave the EU access to more procurement than the US offered under the GPA. It is the only agreement in which the US undertook commitments to open the procurement of: (i) the Massachusetts Port Authority; (ii) two states not covered by the GPA (North Dakota and West Virginia), the procurement not covered under the GPA by a state that it lists in the GPA (Illinois); and (iii) seven cities: Boston, Chicago, Dallas, Detroit, Indianapolis, Nashville and San Antonio. The EU arrangement is limited to a requirement that the covered city or state allow EU suppliers to participate in its procurement on the same basis as domestic suppliers only if it invites tenders from out-of-city or out-of-state suppliers, respectively. The EU assumed no obligations under that agreement (Woolcock & Grier, 2015).

The second procurement-only agreement, the 2010 US–Canada Agreement on Government Procurement, demonstrated the "effective negotiating muscle of GPA parties outside of the venue of the WTO" (Dawar, 2017, 116). Canada and the US exchanged, for the first-time, permanent and reciprocal commitments under the GPA with respect to provincial, territorial and state procurement. The US had withheld the states that it covers under the GPA from Canada because it had not offered coverage of its provinces (USTR, 2010).

The impetus for the 2010 agreement was enactment of the American Recovery and Reinvestment Act of 2009 (ARRA), which required the use of US-made iron, steel and manufactured goods in public projects funded by the legislation, unless the project was covered by a trade agreement or another exception applied. As Canada did not cover any sub-central entities under the NAFTA or the GPA, it had to comply with the Buy American requirements. In negotiations to address Canada's concerns with lack of access to the infrastructure projects funded by ARRA, the US agreed to not apply the legislation's Buy American requirement to Canadian goods and suppliers in several ARRA-funded programs in exchange for access to the procurement of Canada's provinces. Canada opened its provincial procurement for the first time and agreed to bind that coverage under the GPA. It also offered the US temporary access to provincial and municipal construction projects. The US gave Canada access to the procurement of the 37 states that it covers under the GPA (Grier, 2014a).

Under President Barack Obama, the US pursued negotiations of two major regional FTAs, the Trans-Pacific Partnership (TPP) with Asia-Pacific countries and the Transatlantic Trade and Investment Partnership (TTIP) with the EU. Those FTAs "would have nearly doubled the share of US trade occurring with FTA partners" (Williams, 2018). In February 2016, the US and 11 other countries signed the TPP agreement. The other TPP signatories were Australia, Brunei Darussalam (Brunei), Canada, Chile, Japan, Malaysia, Mexico, New Zealand, Peru, Singapore and Vietnam. Under that agreement, the US offered its GPA coverage, adding one small entity (Denali Commission) but excluding coverage of any states or other sub-central entities. However, it committed to take up expansion of procurement, including sub-central procurement, three years after the TPP entered into force (Grier, 2016f). The TPP agreement had not been approved by the Congress before the end of the Obama administration.

The second major agreement pursued by the Obama administration was the TTIP. In July 2013, the US and the EU commenced negotiations of the TTIP in order to expand trade and investment. One of their shared goals was to obtain "substantially improved access to government procurement opportunities at all levels of government on the basis of national treatment" (USTR, 2013). The EU considered expansion of public procurement among its top TTIP priorities. In particular, it wanted access to sub-central entities that the US does not cover under the GPA and the exclusion of EU firms from US application of Buy American requirements, in particular those that require use of US-produced iron, steel and manufactured products in highway, transit and railway projects funded by the US Department of Transportation (Woolcock & Grier, 2015).[7]

After more than three years of negotiations, the two sides were unable to reach agreement before the Obama administration ended. One of the obstacles to concluding the negotiations was the US's unwillingness to open procurement beyond its GPA obligations. President Trump did not resume those negotiations; instead, he is pursuing a new agreement with the EU. In giving mandates to the European Commission for the new negotiations, the EU Member States clarified that their 2013 TTIP negotiating objectives "must be considered obsolete and no longer relevant" (Council of the EU, 2019).

Negotiations of trade agreements (2017 to 2019)

At the beginning of his presidency in January 2017, President Trump withdrew the US from the TPP and expressed his intent to negotiate FTAs on a bilateral rather than a multi-party basis (White House, 2017; Grier, 2017a). The withdrawal from the TPP marked a departure from US leadership in the development of ambitious trade agreements. As of 2019, the Trump administration had negotiated a modest revision of an FTA with Korea,[8] a new agreement to replace NAFTA and a limited agreement with Japan.

In May 2017, the administration informed Congress of its intention to renegotiate NAFTA under the requirements of the Bipartisan Congressional Trade Priorities and Accountability Act of 2015, often referred to as "Trade Promotion Authority" (TPA). The legislation provides for a streamlined consideration of trade agreements by the Congress and an "up or down" vote without amendments, provided the administration complies with certain transparency and consultation requirements (Fergusson & Davis, 2018). The negotiations began in August 2017 and concluded with the signing of the United States–Mexico–Canada Agreement (USMCA) on November 30, 2018, as a replacement of NAFTA. The administration referred to it as "a 21st century, high-standard agreement" that would be a model for future trade agreements (USTR, 2018b).

Before the USMCA was implemented, the three countries amended it. The Protocol of Amendment, signed on December 10, 2019, incorporated revisions that addressed concerns of members of the U.S. House of Representatives with the original Agreement. The changes affected USMCA provisions relating to state-to-state dispute settlement, labor, environment, intellectual property and rules of origin (USTR, 2019e; Grier, 2019k). Following completion of their domestic approval procedures, the parties agreed to implement the USMCA on July 1, 2020.

During the negotiations, the US had proposed capping its NAFTA partners' access to US procurement at the monetary level of the combined procurement that they opened to the US. That would have drastically altered the approach that the US had used successfully for more than 35 years to negotiate trade agreements. In prior negotiations, the US had sought reciprocal procurement opportunities but not a "dollar-for-dollar match" (Grier, 2017d).

Both Canada and Mexico rejected the US capping proposal. Canada did not undertake any procurement commitments in the USMCA; its exclusion from the procurement chapter is a "first" for a US FTA. The US and Canada will only be able to participate in one another's procurement markets under the GPA. The new Agreement does not expand existing procurement commitments as Mexico and the US will roll over their NAFTA commitments, with one exception. The US adds an exclusion, not found in NAFTA, that limits purchases of textiles and apparel by the Transportation Security Administration in the Department of Homeland Security to US suppliers, in accordance with the so-called "Kissell Amendment" in ARRA. That exclusion will align the USMCA with other FTAs that exclude that procurement (Grier, 2018h).

Under the USMCA, the US replicates its NAFTA coverage of 52 federal entities, in contrast to the 85 entities that it covers under the GPA, and six government enterprises. Mexico covers the same 23 federal entities and 36 government enterprises as in NAFTA. The USMCA allows Mexico to continue to set aside procurement for Mexican suppliers. Its federal entities may set aside annually procurement contracts up to $2.328 billion, subject to an adjustment for cumulative inflation. Within that amount, the total value of contracts set aside by Petróleos Mexicanos (PEMEX) and Comisión Federal de Electricidad (CFE) (Federal Electricity Commission) may not exceed $466 million each year. NAFTA had also allowed permanent set-asides: $1.2 billion for all entities, except PEMEX and CFE, which were allowed to set aside $300 million annually (Grier, 2018h).

The USMCA's government procurement text improves the outdated NAFTA text, closely following the TPP's procurement chapter but drawing several additional provisions from the GPA. That was consistent with an earlier agreement among the NAFTA parties. In the negotiations of the TPP, Canada, Mexico and the US had agreed, in a side letter, to replace the procedures that apply to NAFTA procurement with the TPP's procurement procedures (Grier, 2016a, 2018h).

The US International Trade Commission (ITC), an independent, quasi-judicial federal agency, concluded that the USMCA would likely have a "moderate" impact on the US economy and that its procurement provisions would have "little impact on US firms and taxpayers." It recognized, however, that US suppliers' loss of their access to Canadian procurement under NAFTA, in particular its lower thresholds (US$25,000 for goods and US$80,317 for services), in contrast to higher GPA thresholds "could negatively affect some US firms" (USITC, 2019; Grier, 2019d). In the TPP negotiations, Canada and the US had reached a side agreement to raise their NAFTA thresholds to the higher thresholds in the TPP, which were aligned with their GPA thresholds (Grier, 2016a).[9]

On October 16, 2018, the US Trade Representative (USTR) notified Congress of the Trump administration's intent to negotiate trade agreements with the EU, Japan and the UK (USTR, 2018c). Subsequently, it published separate but similar negotiating objectives for each of the three sets of negotiations to comply with TPA requirements. The notifications indicated that the US is seeking comprehensive agreements with all three trading partners (USTR, 2018d, 2019b, 2019c).

The US's objectives include government procurement as an element of the proposed agreements. Its procurement objectives "mirror" US goals for the renegotiation of NAFTA: the US seeks increased procurement opportunities and reciprocity for US goods, services and suppliers. At the same time, it carves a wide swath of US procurement from the negotiations by excluding state and local government procurement and maintaining a number of exclusions. They include small business set-asides, which apply to almost a quarter of federal procurement, as well as Buy American requirements attached to federal funding for state and local projects (USTR, 2018d, 2019b, 2019c; Grier, 2019b, 2019e).

The US and the UK began preparation for negotiations of an FTA in July 2017 with the establishment of a Trade and Investment Working Group, which met periodically (USTR, 2019a).

In contrast to the broad US objectives for negotiations with the EU, which include agriculture, the EU Member States have approved two narrow negotiating mandates, on industrial goods and conformity assessment, and expressly excluded agriculture (Council of the EU, 2019). Based on a preliminary agreement reached in July 2018 between the presidents of the US and the European Commission, the two sides began talks in May 2019 in an effort to determine the scope of the talks (European Commission, 2018d). Any agreement that is reached is not likely to include procurement since the US objectives exclude procurement of primary interest to the EU, as illustrated in the TTIP negotiations (Grier, 2019b).

In the fall of 2019, the US and Japan concluded a mini trade package that includes two agreements, one on agricultural and industrial tariffs and the other on digital trade. On October 7, 2019, they signed them. Under the US–Japan Trade Agreement, Japan will provide greater market access for US agricultural products by eliminating or lowering tariffs on $7.2 billion of US food and agricultural products. For its part, the US will eliminate or reduce tariffs on agricultural imports from Japan valued at $40 million and on certain industrial goods from Japan such as machine tools, turbines, bicycles and musical instruments. The US–Japan Digital Trade Agreement prohibits duties on digital products distributed electronically, such as e-books and music, and data localization requirements that restrict where data can be stored and processed. It also commits the parties to ensure that data can be transferred across borders by all suppliers, to protect against forced disclosure of proprietary computer source code and algorithms, and to permit the use of electronic authentication and electronic signatures (USTR, 2019d; Grier, 2019h).

Comprehensive and Progressive Agreement for Trans-Pacific Partnership

After the US withdrew from the TPP, the 11 remaining signatories, on March 8, 2018, signed a slightly slimmed-down version of the agreement, renamed the Comprehensive and Progressive Agreement for the Trans-Pacific Partnership (CPTPP, 2018). The CPTPP incorporated the TPP with the exception of 22 provisions that it suspended but did not revoke. Two are government procurement provisions. One clarifies that in setting conditions for participation in a procurement, a procuring entity could promote compliance with labor laws in the territory in which the good is produced or the service is performed. A second suspended provision removes a deadline (three years after entry into force) for commencing negotiations to expand procurement covered by the Agreement (Grier, 2018c).

The CPTPP entered into force on December 30, 2018 after ratification by six signatories: Australia, Canada, Japan, Mexico, New Zealand and Singapore. Vietnam's ratification followed in January 2019. The Agreement has yet to be ratified by Brunei, Chile, Malaysia and Peru. With its implementation, the CPTPP is open to accession by any State or separate customs territory that is a member of Asia-Pacific Economic Cooperation and any State or separate customs territory with the agreement of the parties. Several countries, including the UK, have expressed interest in the Agreement (Grier, 2019a; UK DIT, 2018).

All CPTPP signatories, with the exception of Malaysia and Vietnam, have undertaken procurement commitments under either the GPA (Australia, Canada, Japan, New Zealand and Singapore) or RTAs. For example, Australia, Canada, Chile, Mexico, Peru and Singapore entered FTAs with the US. The CPTPP builds on the participants' existing commitments, adding coverage in some cases but offering less in other instances. In the following discussion, key elements of CPTPP coverage are considered in relation to commitments under the GPA and FTAs with the US (Grier, 2016d).

The CPTPP parties apply a broad array of thresholds, with GPA thresholds most frequently used. Only Brunei covers all goods purchased by its Ministry of Defence, in contrast to the use of positive lists by the other parties to specify their commitments for defense entities. Australia excludes the procurement of blood and blood-related products, including plasma-derived products, in its agreements. It also excludes the procurement of motor vehicles by its central government from the CPTPP and the US FTA; its similar exclusion under the GPA expired on January 1, 2019 (Grier, 2016d, 2018i).

With regard to the coverage of services, the CPTPP does not apply a uniform approach. Five signatories (Australia, Chile, Mexico, New Zealand and Peru) cover all services except those explicitly excluded; Brunei opens all services; and the others (Canada, Japan, Malaysia, Singapore and Vietnam) list the services that they open. Peru offered three services that it excluded from its US FTA: architectural services; engineering and design services; and engineering services during the construction and installation phase. The parties open all construction services, except those excluded. In addition, in contrast to the GPA, which does not cover build–operate–transfer (BOT) contracts and public works concessions, the CPTPP includes such coverage, except for parties opting out of it (Malaysia, Mexico and Vietnam). Japan also covers procurement under its private finance initiative, a type of public–private partnership (PPP), as it does under the GPA (Grier, 2016d).

Of the CPTPP participants, Canada added the greatest number of new entities, in comparison to its existing commitments under the GPA and NAFTA: 12 entities, including PPP Canada Inc., Canada Development Investment Corp. and Canada Lands Co., Ltd., as well as several bridge and pilotage authorities and museums. Australia offers three more federal entities under the CPTPP than the GPA and lists the same government enterprises under both agreements, but slightly fewer than under its 2005 FTA with the US (Grier, 2016d, 2018i).

Japan added 12 other entities (the third category of coverage) to its GPA coverage, primarily railway companies, as well as three entities related to Japan Post. While Japan did not carry into the CPTPP all of the other entities that it covers under the GPA, it added three that are not listed in the GPA: JKA, Management Organization for Postal Savings and Postal Life Insurance and the Open University of Japan Foundation. New Zealand's coverage includes only ten of the 19 entities in the other entities category that it covers under the GPA; it withholds all of those entities from Mexico (Grier, 2016f).

Singapore added ten authorities, boards, councils and its Civil Service University to its GPA entity coverage, but it excluded two GPA-listed universities (Nanyang Technological University and National University of Singapore). Chile listed three ministries in the CPTPP that are not included in its US FTA. Peru covers 32 central government entities in the regional RTA, in contrast to 67 entities in the US–Peru FTA. It omits from the CPTPP 31 universities that it listed in its US FTA (Grier, 2016f).

Only five signatories (Australia, Canada, Chile, Japan and Peru) cover sub-central government entities under the CPTPP and in doing so closely follow their GPA or FTA commitments. Japan added one designated city, Kumamoto-shi, to its GPA coverage. Several Australian states and territories list more entities under the CPTPP than under the GPA. Malaysia, Mexico, New Zealand and Vietnam do not cover any sub-central entities. Brunei and Singapore have none (Grier, 2016d, 2018i).

Six parties (Australia, Brunei, Canada, Chile, Peru and Vietnam) exclude preferences and other procurement measures that benefit small and medium-sized businesses (SMEs). Australia also takes a reservation in the GPA that is not found in the CPTPP or the US FTA: in order to protect sensitive government information, its procuring entities may use technical specifications "that may affect or limit the storage, hosting or processing of such information" outside its territory. Chile takes two exclusions: preferences that benefit micro, small and medium-sized enterprises and the procurement of storage and hosting of government data and related services (Grier, 2016d, 2016f, 2018i).

Brunei is the only CPTPP party to cover the procurement of all goods, services and construction services, with few exclusions. It also negotiated limited transitional measures. It may apply higher thresholds for procurement of goods and services for four years after it implements the Agreement. It may also delay implementation of several provisions of the Agreement for three years, including the requirement to publish a notice of the award of a contract. Finally, it was allowed five years to establish an impartial domestic review authority (Grier, 2015d).

Mexico replicates its NAFTA coverage, including its permanent offsets and set-asides, as well as the transitional measures that it applied under NAFTA between 1994 and 2002. For the first nine years after it implements the CPTPP, Mexico may set aside for its suppliers: (i) specified percentages, beginning at 50 percent and declining to 30 percent in Year 9, of the total value of contracts for goods, services and construction services procured by PEMEX and CFE, as well as construction services procured by entities other than PEMEX and CFE; and (ii) US$1.34 billion of its total procurement, which may be allocated by all entities, except PEMEX and CFE. In addition, for eight years after it implements the CPTPP, it may exclude procurement by the Ministry of Health, Mexican Social Security Institute, Institute for Social Security and Services for Government Employee, and Ministry of National Defense of drugs that are not currently patented in Mexico or whose Mexican patents have expired (Grier, 2016e).

The CPTPP allows Malaysia and Vietnam to apply a number of transitional and other special measures to facilitate opening their government procurement for the first time. These measures demonstrate the ability of an RTA to provide more extensive and tailored measures for developing countries than are available under the GPA, which may make RTAs more attractive than GPA accession (Grier, 2018a).

Under the CPTPP, Malaysia has made relatively modest government procurement commitments. When it ratifies the CPTPP, it will open the procurement of 24 ministries and the Prime Minister's Department, limited to listed divisions, departments, agencies, institutes and other governmental units. Its central government coverage is generally comparable to that of other parties but its offer of only four other entities is much more limited (Grier, 2015c).

Malaysia's special measures, particularly with respect to construction, are aimed primarily at protecting its Bumiputera, ethnic Malays that comprise a majority of its population. Malaysia reserves the right to accord Bumiputera status to eligible companies and to apply set-asides and price preferences under its Bumiputera policy, as specified in the Agreement. It will be permitted to set aside annually, for Bumiputera, 30 percent of the total value of its procurement of the construction services that it covers under the CPTPP (Grier, 2015c).

The CPTPP permits Malaysia to apply price preferences, ranging from 1.25 percent to 10 percent, with the higher preferences applied to the lower-valued procurement, for three categories of Bumiputera: (i) Bumiputera suppliers that provide goods and services originating from any CPTPP party in procurement between RMB500,000 and RMB15 million in value, with the preferences ranging from 7 percent for the lowest-valued procurement to 2.5 percent for the highest-valued; (ii) Bumiputera suppliers that provide goods and services originating from non-CPTPP countries in procurement valued between RMB500,000 and RMB15 million, with preferences ranging from 3.25 percent to 1.25 percent; these preferences must also be applied to other Malaysian suppliers and CPTPP suppliers that offer goods and services from any CPTPP party; and (iii) Bumiputera manufacturers for goods valued between RMB10 million and RMB100 million with preferences ranging from 3 percent to 10 percent (Grier, 2015c).

In addition, Malaysia will be permitted to apply several transitional measures. First, it may apply high thresholds to all of its covered procurement during transitional periods that range from seven years to 20 years. Over the longest period (20 years), Malaysia will reduce a high starting threshold of 63 million SDRs for construction services to 14,000,000 SDRs. Its permanent threshold will be the highest threshold applied by the central government entities of any CPTPP party. Second, for the first 25 years after Malaysia implements the CPTPP, it may exempt "procurement funded by an economic stimulus package in response to a severe nationwide economic crisis." Finally, it will be permitted to apply offsets for 12 years after it implements the Agreement to procurement with a value of more than RM50 million, which is conducted by its Prime Minister's Department and 16 of its 24 listed ministries. For the first four years, it may apply offsets up to 60 percent of the value of the contract; that level will drop to 40 percent during the next four years, and to 20 percent during the final four years of the offset period (Grier, 2015c).

Vietnam's procurement commitments under the CPTPP are described below in a comparison of its coverage of procurement under an RTA negotiated with the EU, the only other agreement in which it has agreed to open its procurement.

EU RTAs

The EU "lead[s] in the pursuit and formation of RTAs with a total of 59 partners" (Williams, 2018). It negotiated ambitious public procurement commitments in several recently completed RTAs with Canada, Japan and Singapore, which significantly expanded their GPA-covered procurement. The EU negotiated an RTA with Vietnam that opens slightly more Vietnamese procurement than the CPTPP. The EU's RTA with Mexico exceeds its commitments under NAFTA and the CPTPP with its coverage of procurement by Mexican states. The RTAs are examined in the following sections.

EU–Canada Comprehensive Economic and Trade Agreement

In September 2017, the EU and Canada implemented the Comprehensive Economic and Trade Agreement (CETA) (EU–Canada CETA, 2017a, 2017b; Grier, 2017c). Both added to the procurement that they exchanged under the GPA (EU–Canada CETA, 2017b). Under the agreement, Canada gave the EU access to 20 central government entities that it does not cover under the GPA; the EU provided Canada with access to the nearly 200 central government entities of the Member States that it withholds under the GPA (EU–Canada CETA, 2017b; Grier, 2014c).

With regard to sub-central entities, Canada offered "first-time coverage" of the so-called "MASH sector," comprised of municipalities, municipal organizations, school boards and publicly funded academic, health and social service entities. Only the Yukon does not cover that sector. For its part, the EU accords Canada access to procurement of all regional or local contracting authorities and all contracting authorities (bodies governed by public law as defined by the EU procurement directive), coverage that it withholds under the GPA. Canada also reduced the threshold for the goods and services purchased by its sub-central entities from 355,000 SDRs under the GPA to 200,000 SDRs, matching the EU's threshold (EU–Canada CETA, 2017b; Grier, 2014c).

Canada also substantially expanded its coverage of other entities, from its ten GPA-listed entities to include all Crown corporations at the federal level and most Crown corporations at the provincial level, as well as corporations controlled by municipalities. It also covered mass transit procurement in all provinces with certain restrictions. In purchases of mass transit vehicles, Ontario and Quebec may require the successful bidder to provide up to 25 per-cent local content. In addition, Quebec may require final assembly in Canada (EU–Canada CETA, 2017b; Grier, 2014c).

The EU reciprocated Canada's opening of its Crown corporations and other entities with access to most of the utility sectors that it withholds under the GPA, namely: drinking water; electricity; transport by urban railways, automated systems, tramway, trolley bus, bus or cable; and transport by railways. The EU also provides Canada with access to utilities providing gas or heat. The only sectors that the EU continues to withhold from Canada are airports and mari-time or inland ports (EU–Canada CETA, 2017b; Grier, 2014c).

Unlike under the GPA, the EU provides Canada with access to its works concessions. In turn, Canada covers a form of BOT contracts awarded by most of its entities: contracts that

> involve, as complete or partial consideration, any grant to the supplier of the construction service, for a specified period of time, of temporary ownership or a right to control and operate the civil or building work resulting from such contract, and demand payment for the use of such work for the duration of the contract.
>
> (EU–Canada CETA, 2017b)

Finally, both the EU and Canada expand on the services that they cover under the GPA (EU–Canada CETA, 2017b; Grier, 2014c).

EU–Japan Economic Partnership Agreement

On February 1, 2019, the EU and Japan implemented the EU–Japan Economic Partnership Agreement (EPA) (European Commission, 2019a). In response to Japan's opening of procurement that it does not cover under the GPA, the EU gave it access to procurement that it withholds under the plurilateral agreement. That includes 13 central government entities of Member States. However, the EU did not provide Japan with the full access to its Member States' entities as it did for Canada under CETA (EU–Japan EPA, 2019; Grier, 2018b).

Under the EPA, Japan significantly extended sub-central coverage beyond its GPA commitments. It gave the EU access to procurement by: (i) all local independent administrative agencies that are subject to its Local Independent Administrative Agency Act (No. 47 of 2003), detailing the coverage with a list of 87 entities (51 universities and colleges, 25 hospitals or medical centers and 11 technical or industrial research centers); (ii) 48 "core cities," cities with a population of approximately 300,000; and (iii) Kumamoto-shi, a designated city that it added in the CPTPP. For the core cities, the RTA only applies to the procurement that is conducted under open tendering and excludes purchases of construction services. It also limits their obligation to treating EU suppliers no less favorably than locally established suppliers, including with respect to access to any review procedures. The agreement also allows the cities to encourage SMEs' participation in procurement. The EU responds to Japan's subcentral coverage by providing access to local administrative units with a population between 200,000 and 499,999, also limited to non-discrimination obligations. To match Japan's new commitments, the EU covers hospitals and universities that are governed by public law and provides an extensive indicative list of the entities. Japan also covers the production, transport and distribution of electricity by 28 prefectures and cities, reversing an exclusion in the GPA (EU–Japan EPA, 2019; Grier, 2018b).

With respect to other entities, Japan opened the procurement of six entities that it does not cover under the GPA, including the Information Technology Promotion Agency and Pharmaceutical and Medical Devices Agency. It also withdrew its GPA exclusion of procurement of goods and services related to the operational safety of transportation and opened that procurement by its sub-central entities and five railway-related entities (Hokkaido Railway Company, Japan Freight Railway Company, Japan Railway Construction Transport and Technology Agency, Shikoku Railway Company and Tokyo Metro Co., Ltd). For its part, the EU allows Japanese suppliers to participate in the procurement of railway equipment and rolling stock by procuring entities that are covered by the EU utilities directive and provide or operate railway networks, procurement that it excluded under the GPA. The commitments for both parties relating to railway procurement became effective in February 2020, one year after the EPA entered into force (EU–Japan EPA, 2019; Grier, 2018b).

Both Japan and the EU open more services under the EPA than under the GPA. Japan offers an additional 21 categories of services purchased by its central government entities, including telecommunications-related services, insurance and pension fund services, supply services, advertising and photography services, and translation and interpretation services. It also added 11 services purchased by its sub-central entities, including beverage-serving services, leasing or rental services and various management consulting services. The EU provides Japan with access to five new categories of services procured by its central government entities, including telecommunications-related services and photographic and packaging services. It also opens seven categories of services procured by its sub-central entities, including management consulting services. The EU also covers two categories of services (hotel and restaurant services and beverage-serving services) that are limited to a national treatment regime and to purchases above €750,000 by central and sub-central entities and €1 million by other entities. It also opens real estate services purchased by all covered entities (EU–Japan EPA, 2019; Grier, 2018b).

EU–Singapore Free Trade Agreement

In October 2018, the EU and Singapore signed the European Union–Singapore Free Trade Agreement (EUSFTA). The EUSFTA entered into force on November 21, 2019 upon completion of domestic approval procedures by both parties (EU–Singapore FTA, 2019a; Singapore MTI, 2019). In the EUSFTA's procurement chapter, the parties extend their commitments beyond the GPA in four areas: central government coverage; utilities and other entities; public–private partnerships; and services. They expand upon their GPA coverage of central government entities in different ways. As with Canada under CETA, the EU gives Singapore access to the nearly 200 central government entities of Member States that it withholds under the GPA. For its part, Singapore significantly reduces the goods and services threshold applied by its central government entities from its GPA threshold of 130,000 SDRs to 50,000 SDRs (EU–Singapore FTA, 2019b; Grier, 2019c).

In the second area of expansion, Singapore has more than doubled its coverage of other entities from 23 under the GPA to 57 entities. The EU provides Singapore with access to all utilities, including its railways sector, which it withholds under the GPA. PPP coverage represents the third area of expanded commitments. The text of the EUSFTA's Government Procurement Chapter applies to various contractual arrangements such as BOT contracts. The EU provides Singapore with access to its works concessions, which it does not provide under the GPA (EU–Singapore FTA, 2019b; Grier, 2019c).

Singapore adds a number of service categories that it does not cover under the GPA, including computer services and telecommunications services. That coverage will open up services that the EU covers under the GPA only on a reciprocal basis. As a consequence, Singapore firms will gain access to EU services that include computer-related services, telecommunications services, land transport services, maintenance and repair services, sewage and refuse disposal, and architecture and engineering services (Singapore MTI, 2019; Grier, 2019c).

EU–Vietnam Free Trade Agreement

In December 2015, the EU and Vietnam concluded the EU–Vietnam Free Trade Agreement (European Commission, 2016). It is expected to be ratified in 2020. A comparison of Vietnam's procurement commitments under the EU FTA and the CPTPP, which were negotiated at about the same time, shows that Vietnam will provide the EU with access to slightly more procurement and be subject to more stringent transitional measures than under the CPTPP (Grier, 2016c).

The two agreements differ with respect to most thresholds. For the goods and services purchased by central government entities, both agreements set Vietnam's permanent threshold at 130,000 SDRs. To reach it, the CPTPP allows a 25-year transition period, while the EU FTA limits the transition period to 15 years. They also differ in the level of the initial transitional thresholds: the CPTPP sets it at 2 million SDRs, in contrast to 1.5 million SDRs in the EU FTA. For construction services thresholds applied by central government entities, both agreements set a 15-year transition period with different thresholds: the CPTPP begins with a threshold of 65.2 million SDRs and ends at 8.5 million SDRs, while the EU FTA threshold moves from 40 million SDRs to 5 million SDRs (Grier, 2016c).

Vietnam's coverage of entities differs slightly between the two pacts. While it lists one more central government entity (Ministry of Public Security) under the CPTPP than under the EU bilateral, it adds four more entities to the EU agreement in the "other covered entities" category: two state-owned enterprises (Vietnam Electricity and Vietnam Railways) and two universities (Vietnam National University, Hanoi and Vietnam National University, Ho Chi Minh City). While Vietnam does not offer any sub-central coverage under the CPTPP, it will open procurement of two Vietnamese cities (Hanoi and Ho Chi Minh City) to the EU (Grier, 2016c).

Vietnam offers slightly broader coverage of services under the CPTPP, including data network, electronic message and information services. In both agreements, Vietnam excludes preferences for SMEs. Its broad exclusion of SME preferences under the CPTPP (any procurement involving any form of preference to benefit SMEs) contrasts with a much narrower EU FTA exclusion, which applies only to procurement of goods and services whose value is estimated at 260,000 SDRs or less and may not be applied to SMEs with more than 500 permanent full-time employees (Grier, 2016c).

Both trade deals permit Vietnam to delay implementation of several obligations. They exempt Vietnam from dispute settlement challenges relating to its procurement obligations for five years. The CPTPP also gives Vietnam three years to establish a domestic review system. In delaying implementation of other provisions, the EU pact sets a 10-year limit, while implementation under the CPTPP is postponed until Vietnam's e-procurement system is operational, except for a seven-year limit on a reduced tendering period requirement (Grier, 2016c).

Vietnam is allowed under both agreements to apply offsets, for 18 years under the EU agreement and 25 years under the CPTPP. While they apply the same offset percentages, 40 percent for the first ten years and 30 percent for the remainder of the offset period, they differ in the application. Under the EU agreement, the percentages apply to the value of a contract, but, under the CPTPP, to the total value of covered procurement (Grier, 2016c).

The EU tailors its entity coverage to Vietnam's coverage, particularly with regard to sub-central entities and utilities. It only offers "cities-regions," such as the regions of Brussels and Berlin, to Vietnam. The EU also limits its coverage of public bodies at the sub-central level to those providing health services or higher education services or those carrying out research activities. To match Vietnam's coverage of utilities, the EU offered utilities engaged in the transport or distribution of electricity and railway services (Grier, 2016c).

The EU FTA and CPTPP will apply essentially the same procurement rules since both are modeled after the GPA. The EU FTA incorporates several GPA provisions that are not in the CPTPP, such as provisions for electronic auctions (Grier, 2016c).

EU–Mexico Trade Agreement

In April 2018, the EU and Mexico reached an agreement in principle on a new trade pact, which modernizes their 1997 Global Agreement. The agreement in principle captured the results of the negotiations to that date (European Commission, 2018b).

Two years later, on April 28, 2020, the EU and Mexico concluded negotiations of "the last outstanding element" of their new trade agreement. The missing element was "the exact scope" of the opening of their public procurement markets (European Commission, 2020; Grier, 2020). Of particular note, Mexico committed – for the first time in any trade agreement – to open the procurement of half of its states (14 when the agreement is signed and two more states within two years of signature) (Grier, 2020). Under the new agreement, Mexico will open more procurement to EU suppliers than it has to other trading partners. The EU is offering Mexican suppliers "reciprocal access" to the European procurement market, including its utilities market (Grier, 2018d).

Another area of expansion of procurement commitments in the new agreement relates to PPPs. The EU will provide Mexican companies with access to its works concessions in exchange for participation in Mexico's PPPs. Mexico covers PPP projects undertaken by its central government and other entities, but not sub-central entities. Such projects are not subject to obligations in the Agreement relating to notices and domestic review procedures (Grier, 2020). Under the USMCA and the CPTPP, Mexico excluded BOT contracts and public works concessions contracts (Grier, 2016b, 2018d).

The text of the procurement chapter will include "new generation disciplines" that are equivalent to those in the GPA. It will also permit environmental and social considerations to be taken into account during the procurement process, provided they are non-discriminatory and are linked to the subject matter of the procurement. Mexico also agreed to publish all of its public tenders on a single procurement website (Grier, 2018d).

EU–Mercosur Agreement

On June 28, 2019, the EU reached an agreement in principle on a new trade arrangement with the four founding members of Mercosur, a South American bloc: Argentina, Brazil, Paraguay and Uruguay. (Venezuela did not participate in the negotiations as its membership in Mercosur was suspended in 2016.) On government procurement, the EU and Mercosur countries agreed to modern procurement disciplines based on the revised GPA. Their market access commitments will be limited to the federal and central government level based on reciprocity. The Mercosur countries will be allowed to apply transitional measures in order to comply with the procurement rules and adapt to EU thresholds (European Commission, 2019c; Grier, 2017b, 2019g).

EU RTA negotiations

In Latin America, the EU is also engaged in negotiations with Chile to modernize the 2002 EU–Chile Association Agreement. The EU's 2017 negotiating mandate included seeking "significantly enhanced mutual access to public procurement markets at all administrative levels (national, regional and local authorities), as well as by [state-owned enterprises] and undertakings with special or exclusive rights operating in the public utilities sectors" (Council of the EU, 2018). The EU also wants to align existing rules and disciplines with the revised GPA and add new provisions, such as "avoiding local content or local production requirements" (Council of the EU, 2018). Chile and the EU held their fourth round of negotiations in April 2019 (European Commission, 2019b).

In addition, the EU is seeking greater engagement with countries in Southeast Asia. Its trade and investment agreements with Singapore are the first it has concluded with a member of the Association of Southeast Asian Nations (ASEAN) and represent an important step toward the EU's ultimate goal of a trade and investment agreement with ASEAN. It launched negotiations with ASEAN in 2007 but they stalled in 2009; the two sides are working on a possible resumption. The EU has also initiated bilateral talks with other ASEAN members: Malaysia (2010), Thailand (2013), the Philippines (2015) and Indonesia (2016). It has negotiated or is in the process of negotiating RTAs with all the CPTPP parties (European Commission, 2018a). In June 2018, the EU launched separate FTA negotiations with Australia and New Zealand (European Commission, 2018c). Based on its RTAs with other GPA partners, it could be expected to seek an expansion of their GPA coverage, in exchange for procurement that it does not open to them under the GPA (Grier, 2015b, 2018i).

Regional Comprehensive Economic Partnership

The Regional Comprehensive Economic Partnership (RCEP) is under negotiation between the ten members of ASEAN (Brunei, Cambodia, Indonesia, LAO PDR, Malaysia, Myanmar, Philippines, Singapore, Thailand and Vietnam) and its six FTA partners. The "plus six" group is comprised of Australia, China, India, Japan, Korea and New Zealand. Seven RCEP participants are also signatories of the CPTPP: Australia, Brunei, Japan, Malaysia, New Zealand, Singapore and Vietnam. The RCEP negotiations aim "to achieve a modern, comprehensive, high-quality, and mutually beneficial economic partnership agreement among the ASEAN Member States and ASEAN's FTA partners" (ASEAN, 2018; Grier, 2018a).

When the RCEP negotiations were launched in 2012, they did not include government procurement. However, in 2017, a chapter on procurement was added, albeit with narrower aims than many RTAs. Its focus is "on provisions to promote transparency of laws, regulations and procedures, and develop cooperation among Participating Countries regarding [government procurement]" (ASEAN, 2017). While it does not include market access commitments, they could be added later.

At a November 2019 meeting, the leaders of 15 of the 16 countries participating in the RCEP negotiations concluded work on the text of the agreement and "essentially all their market access issues" and expressed the hope of signing it in 2020 (ASEAN, 2019). While India participated in the negotiations, it did not join in their conclusion, expressing significant issues with the results. The other participants will attempt to resolve India's concerns (ASEAN, 2019; Grier 2014b, 2019j).

Other Asian Regional Trade Agreements

According to the Asia Society Policy Institute, economies in the Asia-Pacific region are "actively pursuing plurilateral and bilateral trade deals within the region, and with major economies," such as the EU in response to the US withdrawal from the TPP and the development of a more "inward-looking US trade policy" (Asia Society Policy Institute, 2018). As illustrations, it cited the EU–Japan RTA, the RCEP negotiations, the 2017 conclusion of a Comprehensive Economic Partnership Agreement between Indonesia and Chile, an FTA and investment agreement signed in 2017 by ASEAN and Hong Kong China; and the 2017 conclusion of negotiations of an Australia–Peru FTA. It also pointed to ongoing bilateral RTA negotiations between Australia and Indonesia, Canada and China, Australia and Hong Kong China, New Zealand and China, and three-way talks among China, Japan and Korea. Also cited were bilateral negotiations launched separately by Australia, Canada, New Zealand and Singapore with the Pacific Alliance (Asia Society Policy Institute, 2018). While China is negotiating RTAs, it has not taken market access commitments relating to procurement in any agreement, pending its GPA accession (WTO, 2018a). An example is the commitment in the Australia–China RTA "to negotiate a reciprocal agreement on government procurement after the completion of China's negotiations to join the [GPA]" (Australian Government DFAT, 2014).

An RTA implemented by Korea offers an interesting expansion of coverage outside the GPA. In contrast to its coverage of only listed services in the GPA and other RTAs, Korea opened the procurement of all services by its listed central and sub-central entities, except financial services, in its 2016 RTA with Colombia. For coverage of services by its other entities, it covered only the "services listed in the revised GPA" (Colombia–Korea Free Trade Agreement, 2012).

Pacific Alliance

The Pacific Alliance, established in 2011 by Chile, Colombia, Mexico and Peru as a regional trading bloc, seeks the free movement of goods, services, capital and people. It is particularly interested in forging "stronger economic ties with the Asia-Pacific region" (Villarreal, 2016). In 2017, the Alliance invited Australia, Canada, New Zealand and Singapore to become Associate Members, a status that allows the Pacific Alliance coalition to negotiate trade deals as a bloc with them (ICTSD, 2017).

The economies of the current Pacific Alliance members "are among the most liberalized in the world" (Villarreal, 2016). Chile has 22 FTAs that link it to 60 countries; Colombia has 12 FTAs involving 30 countries; Mexico has 12 FTAs with 44 countries; and Peru has 15 FTAs with 50 countries. Together, the Alliance countries have 15 FTAs with countries in the Asia-Pacific region (Villarreal, 2016). All the Alliance members, except Colombia, are CPTPP signatories and Colombia is seeking entry into that RTA. None are GPA parties and only Chile and Colombia are observers to the GPA, both gained that status in the 1990s.

Conclusion

Since its implementation nearly 40 years ago, the GPA remains a plurilateral agreement that in 2019 applies to the procurement of 48 WTO members, slightly less than one-third of the organization's membership. All of the WTO members that are negotiating accession to the Agreement are fulfilling commitments made when they joined the WTO. Most long-term WTO members show little, if any, interest in joining it. Rather, they prefer to exchange procurement commitments in RTAs.

The US played a leading role in developing such agreements, from the early 1980s through 2016 and the signing of the TPP. However, with the Trump administration's withdrawal from the TPP, its eschewal of multi-party agreements and focus on bilateral agreements, it has yielded its leadership role. To date, the centerpiece of its negotiations has been the renegotiation of NAFTA, a 25-year-old agreement. The new USMCA excluded Canada from its procurement provisions and did not expand the coverage of Mexico or the US. The US has announced its intention to negotiate agreements with procurement commitments with the EU, Japan and the UK.

The EU is pursuing a much more ambitious trade agenda. In negotiating RTAs, it has obtained significant openings of procurement markets, and in the case of its GPA partners, commitments that go beyond their existing market opening. In a 2017 agreement, Canada provided unprecedented access to its MASH sector and Crown corporations. Similarly, Japan opened significantly more procurement than it covers under the GPA or the CPTPP. Singapore, too, expanded on its GPA commitments. The EU in each negotiation provided access to procurement that it withholds from its trading partner under the GPA. Vietnam undertook procurement-opening commitments in an RTA with the EU that are similar to those in the CPTPP. The EU is also negotiating RTAs in Latin America and Asia.

In both Latin America and Asia, trading partners have entered, or are negotiating, numerous RTAs. The CPTPP, with its 11 signatories, could become an even more significant agreement in the Asia-Pacific region with expansion to additional countries. In another Asia-based negotiation, the RCEP parties, which include China, added government procurement commitments related to transparency but could expand to market access commitments. The Pacific Alliance also warrants attention as it looks to broaden its reach with like-minded countries, both in Latin America and Asia.

Looking ahead, the prospects for expansion of the international procurement arena are likely to depend more on RTAs than the GPA, even though the GPA will continue to provide the template for those agreements.

Appendix: Architecture of international procurement agreements

The GATT Code established the basic architecture for government procurement commitments in international agreements. The GATT template, which has been refined in the GPA and RTAs, has two parts. One consists of the annexes or schedules that specify the procurement that each party commits to conduct in accordance with the agreement. The second part is comprised of principles and procedures that apply to the procurement that is covered by the agreement.

Countries do not open all of their procurement under international agreements. They specify the procurement that they cover under an agreement based on several elements: (i) thresholds, monetary values at or above which procurement is covered; (ii) entities listed or described in three categories: central government entities, sub-central government entities and other entities (utilities, state-owned enterprises, government enterprises); (iii) coverage of all goods except those excluded and defense items, for which covered goods are generally listed; (iv) services based on a negative list (all services are covered, except those listed) or a positive list (only listed services are covered); (v) construction services based on a negative list or positive list; and (vi) exclusions or derogations. Agreements vary in their treatment of these elements. For example, not all agreements cover sub-central government entities or other entities.

Under the GPA, market access commitments are specified in seven annexes: Annex 1 (central government entities); Annex 2 (sub-central government entities); Annex 3 (other covered entities); Annex 4 (goods); Annex 5 (services); Annex 6 (construction services); and Annex 7 (general notes). RTAs incorporate similar annexes depending on the scope of the agreement.

Non-discrimination is a cornerstone of procurement agreements, encompassing both national treatment and most-favored-nation (MFN) treatment. The national treatment obligation requires parties to treat the goods, services and suppliers of other parties no less favorably than domestic goods, services and suppliers. That means they may not apply domestic preferences or other discriminatory purchasing restrictions to procurement covered by the agreement. The MFN commitment does not allow one party to an agreement to be favored over another party, unless a party has taken a derogation in the agreement.

International agreements detail the transparency and procedural obligations that apply to the procurement process. They are intended to ensure that procurement covered by an agreement is conducted in a transparent, predictable, fair and non-discriminatory manner. They provide key procedural safeguards for each stage of the procurement process from development of procurement requirements through to contract award. They include: publication of procurement laws and regulations; types of tendering (open, selective and limited); conditions for participation; qualification of suppliers; development of specifications and tender documentation; publication of notices of intended procurement; minimum tendering periods; treatment of tenders and contract awards; and domestic review procedures for suppliers to challenge a procurement.

Notes

1 The procurement covered by GPA parties is detailed in WTO (2019c).
2 The European Union added 13 Member States: Cyprus, Czech Republic, Estonia, Hungary, Latvia, Lithuania, Malta, Poland, Slovakia and Slovenia in 2004, Bulgaria and Romania in 2006 and Croatia in 2013.
3 The accessions to the GPA were: Aruba in 1996; Hong Kong China, Korea, Liechtenstein and Singapore in 1997; Iceland in 2001; New Zealand in 2015; and Australia in 2019.
4 Armenia (2011), Chinese Taipei (2009), Moldova (2016), Montenegro (2015) and Ukraine (2016).
5 Of the nine, five joined the GPA through accession: Armenia (2011), Chinese Taipei (2009), Moldova (2016), Montenegro (2015) and Ukraine (2016); and four entered the GPA through enlargement of the EU (Croatia, Estonia, Latvia and Lithuania).
6 China applied for GPA accession in 2007 with an initial market access offer. Subsequently, it tabled six revised offers, with the latest in October 2019 (WTO, 2019f). For an examination of China's GPA initial offer and five revised offers, see Grier (2015a).
7 For an extensive discussion of the procurement issues in the TTIP negotiations, see Woolcock and Grier (2015).
8 In September 2018, the US and Korea finalized an agreement to amend the US–Korea FTA. Most amendments involved auto exports to Korea; none affected the FTA's government procurement provisions (USTR, 2018a; Grier, 2018f).
9 The side letter would have increased their NAFTA thresholds for the procurement of goods ($25,000) and of services ($77,533) to $191,000 for both, the thresholds Canada and the US apply under the GPA (Grier, 2016a).

References

ASEAN (Association of Southeast Asian Nations) (2017). Joint leaders' statement on the negotiations of the Regional Comprehensive Economic Partnership (RCEP), November 14. Available at: http://asean.org/joint-leaders-statement-negotiations-regional-comprehensive-economic-partnership-rcep/.
——— (2018). Regional Comprehensive Economic Partnership (RCEP). Available at: https://asean.org/?static_post=rcep-regional-comprehensive-economic-partnership.
——— (2019). Joint leaders' Statement on the Regional Comprehensive Economic Partnership (RCEP) November 14. Available at: https://asean.org/storage/2019/11/FINAL-RCEP-Joint-Leaders-Statement-for-3rd-RCEP-Summit.pdf.
Asia Society Policy Institute (2018). Shifting trade winds: U.S. bilateralism & Asia-Pacific economic integration, January 18. Available at: https://asiasociety.org/policy-institute/shifting-trade-winds-us-bilateralism-and-asia-pacific-economic-integration.
Australian Government Department of Foreign Affairs and Trade (DFAT) (2014). ChAFTA fact sheet: Electronic commerce, intellectual property, competition policy and government procurement, November 20. Available at: https://dfat.gov.au/trade/agreements/in-force/chafta/fact-sheets/Pages/chafta-fact-sheet-electronic-commerce-ip-competition-policy-and-government-procurement.aspx.
Blank, A. & Marceau, G. (1996). History of the government procurement negotiations since 1945. *Public Procurement Law Review* 5: 77–147.

Colombia–Korea Free Trade Agreement (2012). Organization of American States, Foreign Trade Information System. Available at: www.sice.oas.org/TPD/Col_kor/Draft_Text_06.2012_e/June_2012_Index_PDF_e.asp.

Council of the EU (2018). EU–Chile Modernised Association Agreement, directives for the negotiation of a modernised association agreement with Chile, January 22. Available at: www.consilium.europa.eu//media/32405/st13553-ad01dc01en17.pdf.

———— (2019). Trade with the United States: Council authorises negotiations on elimination of tariffs for industrial goods and on conformity assessment, April 15. Available at: www.consilium.europa.eu/en/press/press-releases/2019/04/15/trade-with-the-united-states-council-authorises-negotiations-on-elimination-of-tariffs-for-industrial-goods-and-on-conformity-assessment/.

CPTPP (Comprehensive and Progressive Agreement for Trans-Pacific Partnership) (2018). Available at: www.mfat.govt.nz/en/trade/free-trade-agreements/free-trade-agreements-in-force/cptpp/comprehensive-and-progressive-agreement-for-trans-pacific-partnership-text-and-resources/.

Dawar, K. (2017). The government procurement agreement, the most-favored nation principle, and regional trade agreements. In Georgopoulos, A., Hoekman, B. & Mavroidis, P., eds., *The Internationalization of Government Procurement Regulation.* Oxford: Oxford University Press, 111–139.

EU–Canada Comprehensive Economic and Trade Agreement (EU–Canada CETA) (2017a). Text of the Comprehensive Economic and Trade Agreement – Chapter 19: Government procurement. Available at: https://international.gc.ca/trade-commerce/trade-agreements-accords-commerciaux/agr-acc/ceta-aecg/text-texte/toc-tdm.aspx?lang=eng.

———— (2017b). Text of the Comprehensive Economic and Trade Agreement – Annex 19. Available at: https://international.gc.ca/trade-commerce/trade-agreements-accords-commerciaux/agr-acc/ceta-aecg/text-texte/19-A.aspx?lang=eng#a.

EU–Japan Economic Partnership Agreement (EU–Japan EPA) (2019). Available at: http://trade.ec.europa.eu/doclib/press/index.cfm?id=1684.

EU–Singapore Free Trade Agreement (EUSFTA) (2019a). Annexes 9-A through 9-I. Available at: http://ec.europa.eu/trade/policy/in-focus/eu-singapore-agreement/.

———— (2019b). EUSFTA text. Available at: http://trade.ec.europa.eu/doclib/press/index.cfm?id=961.

European Commission (2016). EU–Vietnam Free Trade Agreement: Agreed text as of January 2016. Available at: http://trade.ec.europa.eu/doclib/press/index.cfm?id=1437&title=EU-Vietnam-Free-Trade-Agreement-Agreed-text-as-of-January-2016.

———— (2018a). Fact sheet, key elements of the EU–Singapore Trade and Investment Agreements, April 18. Available at: http://europa.eu/rapid/press-release_MEMO-18-3327_en.htm.

———— (2018b). EU and Mexico reach new agreement on trade, April 21. Available at: http://europa.eu/rapid/press-release_IP-18-782_en.htm.

———— (2018c). Commission welcomes green light to start trade negotiations with Australia and New Zealand, May 22. Available at: http://trade.ec.europa.eu/doclib/press/index.cfm?id=1843.

———— (2018d). Joint U.S.–EU statement following President Juncker's visit to the White House, July 25. Available at: http://europa.eu/rapid/press-release_STATEMENT-18-4687_en.htm.

———— (2019a). EU–Japan trade agreement enters into force, January 31. Available at: http://trade.ec.europa.eu/doclib/press/index.cfm?id=1976.

———— (2019b). Report on the 4th round of negotiations between the EU and Chile for modernising the trade part of the EU–Chile Association Agreement, April 17, http://trade.ec.europa.eu/doclib/docs/2019/april/tradoc_157867.pdf.

———— (2019c). EU and Mercosur reach agreement on trade, June 28. Available at: http://trade.ec.europa.eu/doclib/press/index.cfm?id=2039.

———— (2020). EU and Mexico conclude negotiations for new trade agreement, April 28. Available at: https://trade.ec.europa.eu/doclib/press/index.cfm?id=2142.

Fergusson, I. & Davis, C. (2018). Trade Promotion Authority (TPA): Frequently asked questions. *Congressional Research Service*, Report No. R43491, September 4. Available at: https://fas.org/sgp/crs/misc/R43491.pdf.

G20 (2019). G20 members. Available at: http://g20.org.tr/about-g20/g20-members/.

Grier, J.H. (2013). U.S. agreements open foreign procurement (Perspectives on Trade, November 8). Available at: http://trade.djaghe.com/?p=121.

———— (2014a). Can U.S. offer comprehensive coverage of states in TTIP? (Perspectives on Trade, March 3). Available at: http://trade.djaghe.com/?p=473.

———— (2014b). Government procurement – key element in TPP: Missed opportunity in RCEP? *Asia Pathways*, March 3. Available at: www.asiapathways-adbi.org/2014/03/government-procurement-key-element-in-tpp-missed-opportunity-in-rcep/.

———— (2014c). EU–Canadian trade pact now public (Perspectives on Trade, October 6). Available at: http://trade.djaghe.com/?p=890.

———— (2015a). What are the prospects for concluding work on China's GPA accession in 2015? *Public Procurement Law Review* 24: 221–236.

———— (2015b). New Zealand implements GPA (Perspectives on Trade, August 12). Available at: http://trade.djaghe.com/?p=1835.

———— (2015c). TPP procurement: Malaysia's commitments (Perspectives on Trade, December 11). Available at: http://trade.djaghe.com/?p=2277.

———— (2015d). TPP procurement: Brunei's commitments (Perspectives on Trade, December 15). Available at: http://trade.djaghe.com/?p=2284.

———— (2016a). TPP procurement: Harmonizing FTAs (Perspectives on Trade, January 12). Available at: http://trade.djaghe.com/?p=2364.

———— (2016b). PPPs #4: TPP Parties (Perspectives on Trade, February 2). Available at: http://trade.djaghe.com/?p=2429.

———— (2016c). EU–Vietnam FTA: Procurement commitments (Perspectives on Trade, February 9). Available at: http://trade.djaghe.com/?p=2476.

———— (2016d). Government procurement in the Trans-Pacific Partnership (TPP). *The Government Contractor* 58, Issue No. 50 (February 17): 1–6.

———— (2016e). TPP procurement: Mexico's commitments (Perspectives on Trade, April 26). Available at: http://trade.djaghe.com/?p=2701.

———— (2016f). TPP procurement: Modest improvements in existing coverage (Perspectives on Trade, May 17). Available at: http://trade.djaghe.com/?p=2833.

———— (2016g). Government procurement in the WTO (Djaghe White Paper, DWP-1610, December 12). Available at: https://app.box.com/s/8byjo9re17zh1zx70fz70so cpwzrqr5j.

———— (2017a). Brexit: Not like TPP withdrawal (Perspectives on Trade, February 7). Available at: http://trade.djaghe.com/?p=3655.

———— (2017b). Brazil: Opening its government procurement (Perspectives on Trade, September 5). Available at: http://trade.djaghe.com/?p=4257.

———— (2017c). US & EU: Contrasting trade agendas (Perspectives on Trade, September 19). Available at: http://trade.djaghe.com/?p=4300.

———— (2017d). NAFTA procurement: Capping access? (Perspectives on Trade, October 4). Available at: http://trade.djaghe.com/?p=4351.

———— (2017e). Trade agreements open foreign procurement markets. *Thomas Reuter Briefing Papers*, Issue 17–10, September: 1–11.

———— (2018a). An assessment of WTO GPA membership: Current status and future prospects. *Public Procurement Law Review* 27: 33–48.

———— (2018b). EU–Japan FTA: Examining procurement commitments (Perspectives on Trade, January 17). Available at: https://trade.djaghe.com/?p=4578.

———— (2018c). New TPP: Procurement gains (Perspectives on Trade, March 9). Available at: https://trade.djaghe.com/?p=4690.

———— (2018d). EU–Mexico agreement in principle: Procurement (Perspectives on Trade, April 24). Available at: https://trade.djaghe.com/?p=4795.

———— (2018e). WTO GPA update #10: Accession negotiations (Perspectives on Trade, July 2). Available at: https://trade.djaghe.com/?p=4934.

———— (2018f). US–Korea FTA modifications examined (Perspectives on Trade, September 5). Available at: https://trade.djaghe.com/?p=5092.

———— (2018g). Reforming the WTO: EU proposals (Perspectives on Trade, September 19). Available at: https://trade.djaghe.com/?p=5123.

———— (2018h). USMCA – modernized NAFTA: Procurement (Perspectives on Trade, October 5). Available at: https://trade.djaghe.com/?p=5174.

———— (2018i). Australia: GPA membership approved (Perspectives on Trade, November 26). Available at: https://trade.djaghe.com/?p=5262.

———— (2018j). Britain's GPA market access offer approved (Perspectives on Trade, December 3). Available at: https://trade.djaghe.com/?p=5308.

———— (2019a). 2019 government procurement prospects (Perspectives on Trade, January 8). Available at: https://trade.djaghe.com/?p=5356.

———— (2019b). US–EU talks: Procurement prospects (Perspectives on Trade, January 23). Available at: https://trade.djaghe.com/?p=5395.

———— (2019c). EU–Singapore FTA: Procurement expanded (Perspectives on Trade, February 15). Available at: https://trade.djaghe.com/?p=5511.

———— (2019d). ITC: USMCA's moderate impact (Perspectives on Trade, April 24). Available at: https://trade.djaghe.com/?p=5695.

———— (2019e). Whither Trump's trade policy (Perspectives on Trade, May 16). Available at: https://trade.djaghe.com/?p=5753.

———— (2019f). GPA reciprocity: Providing leverage for bilateral agreements. Paper presented at Public Procurement: Global Revolution IX, University of Nottingham, Nottingham, England, June 17.

———— (2019g). EU–Mercosur Agreement in Principle: Procurement (Perspectives on Trade, July 2). Available at: https://trade.djaghe.com/?p=5852.

———— (2019h). US–Japan agreement: Examining the text (Perspectives on Trade, October 15). Available at: https://trade.djaghe.com/?p=6027.

———— (2019i). China's new GPA offer: Enhances accession prospects (Perspectives on Trade, November 7). Available at: https://trade.djaghe.com/?p=6073.

———— (2019j). RCEP advances: India out (Perspectives on Trade, December 4). Available at: https://trade.djaghe.com/?p=6120.

———— (2019k). Trump trade agreements: 2019 (Perspectives on Trade, December 18). Available at https://trade.djaghe.com/?p=6141.

———— (2020). EU–Mexico Agreement: Procurement results, May 15. Available at: https://trade.djaghe.com/?p=6438.

ICTSD (International Centre for Trade and Sustainable Development) (2017). Pacific Alliance, associate members kick off free trade negotiations. *Bridges* 21, November 2. Available at: www.ictsd.org/bridges-news/bridges/news/pacific-alliance-associate-members-kick-off-free-trade-negotiations.

OECD (Organisation for Economic Co-operation and Development) (2019). Member countries. Available at: www.oecd.org/about/.

Singapore Ministry of Trade and Industry (Singapore MTI) (2019). European Parliament approves EU–Singapore Free Trade Agreement and EU–Singapore Investment Procurement Agreement, February 13. Available at: www.mti.gov.sg/-/media/MTI/Microsites/EUSFTA/Press-Release-on-Approval-by-European-Parliament-of-EUSFTA-and-EUSIPA-final.pdf.

United Kingdom Department for International Trade (UK DIT) (2018). Public consultations on the UK potentially seeking accession to the Comprehensive and Progressive Agreement for Trans-Pacific Partnership (CPTPP), July 20. Available at: https://consultations.trade.gov.uk/policy/consultation-on-uk-accession-to-the-cptpp/.

U.S. International Trade Commission (USITC) (2019). USITC releases report concerning the likely impact of the United States–Mexico–Canada Agreement (USMCA), April 18. Available at: www.usitc.gov/press_room/news_release/2019/er0418ll1087.htm.

USTR (Office of the U.S. Trade Representative) (2010). U.S.–Canada Agreement on Government Procurement. Available at: https://ustr.gov/issue-areas/government-procurement/us-canada-agreement-government-procurement.

———— (2013). Final report of the U.S.–EU High Level Working Group on Jobs and Growth, February 11. Available at: https://ustr.gov/about-us/policy-offices/press-office/reports-and-publications/2013/final-report-us-eu-hlwg.

———— (2018a). USTR publishes agreed outcomes from US–Korea FTA amendment and modification negotiations, September 3. Available at: https://ustr.gov/about-us/policy-offices/press-office/press-releases/2018/september/ustr-publishes-agreed-outcomes-us.

———— (2018b). United States–Mexico–Canada Agreement, October 1. Available at: https://ustr.gov/trade-agreements/free-trade-agreements/united-states-mexico-canada-agreement.

———— (2018c). Trump administration announces intent to negotiate trade agreements with Japan, the European Union and the United Kingdom, October 16. Available at: https://ustr.gov/about-us/policy-offices/press-office/press-releases/2018/october/trump-administration-announces.

———— (2018d). United States–Japan Trade Agreement (USJTA) negotiations, summary of specific negotiating objectives, December 21. Available at: https://ustr.gov/sites/default/files/2018.12.21_Summary_of_U.S.-Japan_Negotiating_Objectives.pdf.

———— (2019a). U.S.–UK trade agreement negotiations. Available at: https://ustr.gov/countries-regions/europe-middle-east/europe/united-kingdom/us-uk-trade-agreement-negotiations.

——— (2019b). United States–European Union negotiations, summary of specific negotiating objectives, January 11. Available at: https://ustr.gov/sites/default/files/ 01.11.2019_Summary_of_U.S.-EU_Negotiating_Objectives.pdf.

——— (2019c). United States–United Kingdom negotiations, summary of specific negotiating objectives, February. Available at: https://ustr.gov/sites/default/files/ Summary_of_U.S.-UK_Negotiating_Objectives.pdf.

——— (2019d). Fact sheet on U.S.–Japan Trade Agreement, September. Available at: https://ustr.gov/about-us/policy-offices/press-office/fact-sheets/2019/september/ fact-sheet-us-japan-trade-agreement.

——— (2019e). United States–Mexico–Canada Agreement, Protocol of Amendment, December 10. Available at: https://ustr.gov/trade-agreements/free-trade-agreements/united-states-mexico-canada-agreement/protocol-amendments.

Villarreal, M.A. (2016). The Pacific Alliance: A trade integration initiative in Latin America. *Congressional Research Service*, Report No. R43748, March. Available at: https://fas.org/sgp/crs/row/R43748.pdf.

White House (2017). Presidential memorandum regarding withdrawal of the United States from the Trans-Pacific Partnership negotiations and agreement, January 23. Available at: www.whitehouse.gov/the-press-office/2017/01/23/ presidential-memorandum-regarding-withdrawal-united-states-trans-pacific.

Williams, B. (2018). Bilateral and regional trade agreements: Issues for congress. *Congressional Research Service*, Report No. R45198, May. Available at: https://fas. org/sgp/crs/row/R45198.pdf.

Woolcock, S. & Grier, J.H. (2015). TTIP and public procurement. In Hamilton, D. & Pelkmans, J., eds., *Rule-makers or rule-takers? Exploring the Transatlantic Trade and Investment Partnership*. London: Rowman and Littlefield International, 297–339.

WTO (World Trade Organization) (2005). Report of the Working Party on the accession of Tonga to the World Trade Organization. WT/ACC/TON/17; WT/ MIN(05)/4, December 2.

——— (2006). Report of the Working Party on the accession of Viet Nam. WT/ACC/ VNM/48, October 27.

——— (2012). Report of the Working Party on the accession of Lao PDR to the World Trade Organization. WT/ACC/LAO/45, October 1.

——— (2018a). Trade Policy Review Body, trade policy review. Report by the Secretariat, China. WT/TPR/S/375, June 6. Available at: www.wto.org/english/ tratop_e/tpr_e/tp475_e.htm.

——— (2018b). Report (2018) of the Committee on Government Procurement. GPA/ AR/1, November 29.

——— (2019a). Agreement on Government Procurement, parties, observers and accessions. Available at: www.wto.org/english/tratop_e/gproc_e/memobs_e.htm.

——— (2019b). Government procurement and Doha Development Agenda. Available at: www.wto.org/english/tratop_e/gproc_e/gp_dda_e.htm.

——— (2019c). Integrated government procurement market access information (e-GPA) portal. Available at: https://e-gpa.wto.org.

——— (2019d). Regional Trade Agreements and the WTO. Available at: www.wto. org/english/tratop_e/region_e/scope_rta_e.htm.

——— (2019e). UK set to become a party to the Government Procurement Agreement in its own right, February 27. Available at: www.wto.org/english/news_e/news19_e/ gpro_27feb19_e.htm.

————— (2019f). China submits revised offer for joining government procurement pact, October 23. Available at: www.wto.org/english/news_e/news19_e/gpro_23oct19_e.htm.

————— (2020). The United Kingdom's withdrawal from the European Union, communication from the United Kingdom, WT/GC/206, February 1.

12 Transatlantic trade and public procurement openness

Going beyond the tip of the iceberg

Lucian Cernat and Zornitsa Kutlina-Dimitrova

Introduction

Trade negotiations involving international public procurement rules are on the rise, stimulating a growing interest in having a clear picture of the economic stakes involved, including the current level of international openness. A recent paper published by the European Centre for International Political Economy (Messerlin, 2016) made an attempt to provide a range of estimates for the EU and the US and found relatively low rates of import penetration. This analytical approach, however, looked only at the 'tip of the procurement iceberg', as the data used covered primarily only one mode of international procurement (direct cross-border), which is not the main avenue for international government procurement. Other modes, such as procurement from foreign subsidiaries established in Europe, account for much more. Such an approach therefore ignores the main modes through which foreign firms win EU contracts. Once these other main procurement modes are taken into account, EU openness in procurement is much higher. Comparable data across all modes do not yet exist for the US, but we do have clear evidence that the US has introduced the largest number of protectionist procurement measures since 2009, affecting all modes for international procurement.

Against this background, this chapter makes four basic points:

i. Public procurement is a key area of trade negotiations, and future trade agreements will continue to include ambitious procurement chapters.
ii. The existing levels of openness in procurement markets need to be assessed across all three main procurement modes and not based only on direct cross-border procurement, which is not the main procurement avenue. According to this comprehensive metric, the EU market already has a high foreign participation rate, including by US companies.
iii. Unfortunately, similar data do not exist for the US market. But there is growing evidence of discriminatory measures introduced in recent years, which impede the ability of EU firms to compete on a level playing field in US procurement markets.
iv. The importance of procurement as a key negotiating area requires better data and greater analytical engagement.

Public procurement: A key policy area in international negotiations

Public procurement is a negotiating area that is gaining in importance at both the multilateral and bilateral levels, as evidenced by the growing number of procurement provisions in existing and future trade agreements. The importance of negotiations over public procurement stems from the size of procurement spending, which in most developed economies is in double-digit percentage points of GDP, and the fact that procurement has traditionally been subject to discriminatory policies in many jurisdictions. In all recent EU FTAs, public procurement was considered an important negotiating priority, given the considerable potential for economic gains and greater efficiency that can be achieved by further liberalising public procurement.

Despite the size and importance of international public procurement, however, the factual information available to trade negotiators remains scarce. Although public procurement patterns (e.g. size of procurement markets, composition of procurement spending and level of government procurement) can be derived from traditional national accounts statistics, these figures fall short of capturing the international dimension of public procurement (Kutlina-Dimitrova, 2018). Therefore, there is a clear need to provide further analytical evidence on the structure of international public procurement in the EU and the US.

A recent paper by Messerlin (2016) tried to shed light on some critical issues in the EU–US negotiations on public procurement. One important yardstick used in the paper is an indicator aimed at measuring the current level of openness in public procurement in the EU and the US, by comparing the share of imports in total demand for public goods and services in the EU and the US, based on WIOD input–output data. Starting from this proposed de facto openness metric, Messerlin (2016) argues that, the US and the EU (on average across its Member States) have similar levels of foreign penetration ratios in total public procurement markets, somewhere around 4 per cent. This indicator is then seen as clear evidence that there is little, if any, imbalance in the current level of openness.

While this assessment offers some interesting insights, it suffers from a number of serious shortcomings that could misguide current policy debates, if misinterpreted. Simply put, these import penetration rates overlook a number of important elements and as such represent only the 'tip of the procurement iceberg'.

What lies beyond the tip of the procurement iceberg?

One key element that needs to be borne in mind when looking at international procurement is that foreign firms can win public contracts in a variety of ways. Cernat and Kutlina-Dimitrova (2015) summarised these options into three modes of international procurement, a concept similar to the terminology employed in the General Agreement for Trade in Services (GATS):

- **Mode 1 – direct cross-border international procurement**: a foreign company submitting a bid and winning a public contract 'from abroad'.
- **Mode 2 – commercial presence procurement**: a domestic subsidiary of a foreign company wins 'locally' the public contract.
- **Mode 3 – Value-added indirect international procurement**: a foreign company participates indirectly with parts and components (goods and services) without necessarily being part of the winning bid. In this case the foreign company may supply goods and services to a domestic company winning the bid or to another foreign company that receives the public contract.

Out of these three modes of international public procurement, Messerlin (2016) captures only mode 1. However, previous empirical work (notably the Ramboll, 2011 study cited by Messerlin and Miroudot, 2012 as well) provides evidence that in fact the most important vehicle for international procurement is mode 2, followed by mode 3, while mode 1 is a distant third in terms of economic importance. The intuition behind this finding is clear: for a large number of products and services purchased by public authorities, proximity is key. Hence, the existing data seem to suggest that distance matters in public procurement and very often goods and services are procured from companies (foreign and domestic) that are located in the proximity of the procuring authorities.

Therefore, inferring overall procurement openness from mode 1 data alone puts a serious caveat on the main finding in Messerlin (2016) with regard to the level of 'de facto' openness in both the EU and the US. In addition, this indicator fails to capture the government investment[1] component of public procurement, which is a major element in public procurement spending. The reason for that lies in the structure of the underlying input–output tables. This framework, based on supply and use tables, reflects commodities demand for intermediate and final uses. The latter consist of private household consumption, government consumption and investment. The demand for investment goods, however, is not split into government and public investment, and hence the government investment dimension is missing in the input–output framework. National accounts statistics for the EU and the US, however, reveal that government investment in total procurement is quite important, standing at 20 per cent and 34 per cent in 2016, respectively (Kutlina-Dimitrova, 2018). Hence, one should also take into account international procurement related to government investment.

Another important drawback of the Messerlin (2016) indicator is the fact that public procurement as measured in the input–output tables framework based on national accounts includes the so-called *below-threshold procurement* (low value contracts that are not legally subject to international procurement rules). This is obviously of great significance as there is evidence that the value of a procurement contract has a positive influence on the probability of a foreign company winning a bid (Kutlina-Dimitrova and Lakatos, 2014). This finding is also linked to the fact that foreign companies are more likely to bid for large value contracts, as in general they are facing higher foreign market entry/penetration costs. Accordingly, an asymmetry bias is likely to be present with respect to foreign penetration shares below and above threshold procurement.

In light of this bias, the import penetration ratios used by Messerlin (2016) are not a good metric for assessing the openness of public procurement subject to international treaties. Last but not least, Messerlin's analysis does not capture import penetration ratios for public utility providers,[2] despite the fact that public procurement of utility services represents a sizeable share of public procurement in the EU. In fact, such services have higher import penetration shares for mode 1 compared to other procurement contracts (Kutlina-Dimitrova and Lakatos, 2014). To sum up, an analysis of procurement openness substantiated merely through input–output data as attempted by Messerlin is at best partial and at worst fails to provide a realistic picture of the actual situation.

Instead, more accurate evidence on the size of mode 1 (cross-border public procurement) in the EU and the US is provided by contract award data. The Ramboll (2011) study, for instance, finds mode 1 penetration rates for the EU at 3.5 per cent for the 2007–2009 period (with smaller EU Member States having higher import shares). These estimates are in line with the results of more recent analysis based on an extended dataset (2008–2012) by Kutlina-Dimitrova and Lakatos (2014), where it is found that the direct cross-border share for mode 1 in Europe stood at 3.7 per cent for that period. For the US procurement market, Fronk (2015) finds mode 1 import penetration ratios lower than 2 per cent prior to 2006 and between 3.6 and 4.1 per cent for subsequent years (2006–2010) (based on detailed US federal contract award data).

It should be pointed out, however, that these mode 1 import penetration rates of the EU and the US procurement are not directly comparable. The US estimates are based on a dataset that captures only US procurement at the federal level, whereas the EU figures cover both national and sub-national procurement. Knowing that US sub-federal procurement is less subject to international commitments, it is very likely that the overall (federal and subfederal) mode 1 import penetration ratio for the US is lower than the federal level estimated by Fronk (2015).

But as indicated, mode 1 is only the tip of the international procurement iceberg. When looking at mode 2 (procurement via foreign affiliates), we get a different picture in terms of levels of openness in EU Member States. The Ramboll (2011) study finds that 13.4 per cent of the EU public procurement market is awarded to foreign affiliates from non-EU countries. Strikingly, US foreign affiliates have obtained one-quarter of the extra EU foreign penetration rate, the largest share of any EU trading partner. Unfortunately, there are no available mode 2 estimates for the share of EU foreign affiliates in the US procurement market.

Under mode 3 (value-added procurement), foreign firms may obtain indirectly a share of public spending even when they are not part of the winning bid (as subcontractors or arms-length suppliers). The Ramboll (2011) study assessed the share of indirect procurement through such contractual relations to be at around 12 per cent of the total EU procurement market. Again, there are no estimates for mode 3 foreign penetration rates in the US procurement market, which hampers any comparison in this respect. It is important to note, however, that 'Buy American' provisions limit the possibility of firms winning public contracts to source certain inputs from abroad. Thus, whenever such 'buy-local' provisions induce a costly change in the production patterns of potential foreign bidders, they will not only impose restrictions on mode 3 international procurement but also indirectly on modes 1 and 2. Therefore, such restrictions may discourage entrance or reduce the ability to win public contracts for both foreign firms and US affiliates, if they have to source intermediate inputs in sub-optimal ways due to 'buy-local' provisions.

Since data on mode 2 and 3 do not exist for the US procurement market, we cannot at this stage make a proper comparison of the overall level of de facto openness of the EU and the US procurement markets. Without speculating about the likely magnitude of de facto US openness in these public procurement modes, one is left only with evidence on de jure openness, based on protectionist measures found in the US that may negatively affect such international procurement. The scope and discriminatory nature of local content requirements under 'buy-local' provisions is already well known and documented in Luckey (2012), for instance. Some of these measures have a clear negative impact on mode 3 procurement and one would expect such measures to negatively affect the ability of both US companies and foreign affiliates to source certain inputs from abroad. In fact a recent analysis of the impact of scrapping Liquidity Coverage Ratio (LCR) legislation in the United States by Dixon et al. (2017) shows that the effect of their elimination would be substantial: US GDP would augment by 0.12 per cent along with a job creation of 300,000. Overall, such discriminatory measures (with various degrees of domestic preferential treatment) tend to reduce the ability of foreign firms across all three procurement modes to win public contracts in the United States, notably at the sub-federal level.

Recent trends in public procurement policies and their discriminatory nature

Clear evidence of the impediments to international procurement in the US market can also be derived from the data provided by the Global Trade Alerts (GTA)[3] project that tracks newly introduced protectionist measures around the world, including in the field of public procurement.

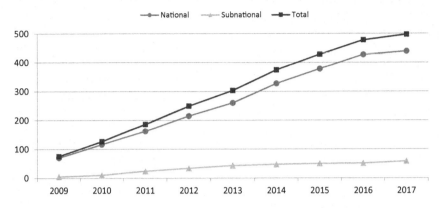

Figure 12.1 Newly introduced public procurement measures by government level, count of measures, 2009–2017.

Source: GTA database (2018). Total reflects the sum of 'red' measures at national and subnational level.

The GTA database contains detailed information about newly introduced policy measures affecting international procurement by a large number of implementing and affected jurisdictions, level of restrictiveness, government level, etc. Figure 12.1 provides an overview of the annual frequency of newly introduced state measures in the field of public procurement, which are assessed to be almost certainly discriminatory (red) in terms of affecting the ability of foreign companies to bid for government procurement contracts.

Since the database's creation, in the second half of 2008 until the end of 2017, the stock of protectionist measures has been steadily growing, reaching 508 measures by end 2017. In 2014 and 2012 governments made the most frequent use of harmful instruments amounting to 69 and 62 respectively. After 2014 there has been a flattening of the curve depicting total number of discriminatory measures, pointing to a decline in the pace of protectionist measures introduction in the aggregate (Figure 12.1). Looking at the government level split, Figure 12.1 makes clear that measures at the national level account for the majority of harmful instruments in international public procurement. In 2017 their share in the total discriminatory measures amounted to 88 per cent or 447 versus 61 newly introduced measures at the subnational level.

Most protectionist countries in the field of international public procurement

The trend described above refers to the whole sample of countries included in the GTA database and shows that protectionist measures in the field of international procurement have gained substantially in importance. The GTA trade measures repository also allows for identification of the countries that

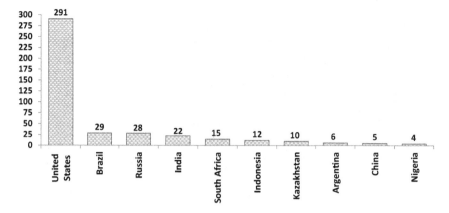

Figure 12.2 Top 10 most protectionist countries in public procurement, count of 'red' measures, 2009–2017.

Source: GTA database (2018).

have resorted to protectionist measures in international procurement more often than others as it contains information on the implementing jurisdiction. In this respect, Figure 12.2 provides an overview of the ten most protectionist countries (based on almost certainly discriminatory measures – 'red' measures) in the period 2009–2017.[4]

The United States is revealed to be among the countries that have introduced the largest number of new protectionist measures in the field of international procurement, according to the GTA database. Besides the US and Brazil, Russia, South Africa, Indonesia and Kazakhstan have also introduced a non-negligible number of measures so as to discriminate against foreign companies participating in government procurement tenders.

The most severely affected countries by discriminatory measures in the field of public procurement

After having identified the most protectionist countries in international public procurement it is important to know which are the most affected countries by these protectionist measures. In this respect Figure 12.3 presents the top 20 most affected countries by almost certainly discriminatory 'red' measures in the period 2009–2017. Looking at the data reveals that the country most frequently affected by protectionism measures in the world is Germany. German goods and services were subject to 403 discriminatory state measures in the field of government procurement followed by China affected in 397 cases. The third, fourth and fifth most affected countries by 'red' protectionist measures in the field of procurement are France, Italy and the United Kingdom which were subject to harmful measures in 387, 387 and 385 cases respectively.

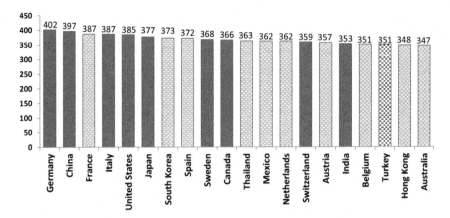

Figure 12.3 Top 20 most affected countries by measures that are almost certainly discriminatory ('red'), count of measures, 2009–2014.

Source: GTA database (2018).

In general, if the count of interventions impacting EU Member States in the top 20 regions is summed up, the EU would be subject to 3,371 discriminatory measures: nearly half of the 20 most frequently affected in the field of international procurement are EU Member States.

Public procurement: What role for new trade negotiations?

The various elements presented above point out three important facts. First, whether measured on a de facto or de jure basis, international openness in public procurement is a powerful element for economic gains, as part of a globalised economy. Second, there is clear evidence that the current level of EU openness is higher than the 'tip of the iceberg' when looking at all three procurement modes. While the overall US openness remains unknown, there is convincing evidence that major gains can be reaped from reciprocal openness in public procurement, across all modes of supply, and in particular in those areas where discriminatory measures have been identified. Third, it would be wrong to think that additional gains cannot be reaped by US firms in the EU market as a result of further opening of public procurement. As Messerlin (2016) pointed out, trade negotiations can go hand in hand with domestic regulatory reforms and can mutually reinforce future measures in the EU and the US, aimed at more open and efficient procurement markets. There is also clearly the need for better data on the international dimension of public procurement. The absence of a comprehensive, comparable global database on international procurement clearly presents a main challenge for the current and upcoming trade negotiations on procurement. There are encouraging developments from international organisations, however, that new data on international public procurement will soon become available.

Due to the COVID-19 global pandemic, world trade is set to suffer one of the worst declines in recent history. The global pandemic has put all national health systems under tremendous pressure, proving that no country can tackle the pandemic alone, notably in terms of procuring essential protective materials (masks, gloves, disinfectant, etc.), medicines and critical medical equipment (ventilators and other intensive care devices). Therefore, public procurement openness is more important than ever. Against the worrying trend towards protectionist measures, new trade agreements are poised to play a critical role in ensuring a more efficient global response in the post COVID-19 period.

Notes

1 The government investment component of public procurement, that is, the aggregate gross fixed capital formation, refers to infrastructure expenditures, for example, building new roads. See also OECD (2015).
2 Public utility companies provide electricity, natural gas, water or sewage services.
3 While the definition of 'harmful' trade measures in particular in respect to anti-dumping instruments by the GTA is subject to discussion this paper uses exclusively data on public procurement, which is considered representative by the author.
4 The Global Trade Alert database is a dynamic dataset that is updated regularly. There may be differences from the statistics provided in this chapter and the most recent version of the database, in case certain new measures have been introduced in the database, or if existing measures have expired or have been withdrawn.

References

Cernat, L. and Kutlina-Dimitrova, Z. (2015), 'International Public Procurement: From Scant Facts to Hard Data', RSCAS Policy Papers PP 2015/07, Robert Schuman Centre for Advanced Studies, European University Institute, Florence.

Dixon, P. B., Rimmer, M.T. and Waschik, P.G. (2017), 'Macro, Industry and Regional Effects of Buy America(n) Program: USAGE Simulations, Center of Policy Studies (CoPS)', Working Paper No. G-271 (April), Victoria University.

Fronk, J. V. (2015), 'International Agreements on Trade in Government Procurement: Formation and Effect?', Dissertation Thesis, Georgetown University, Washington, DC.

GTA (2018), Global Trade Alert Database, available at www. globaltradealert.org.

Kutlina-Dimitrova, Z. (2018), 'Government Procurement: Data, Trends and Protectionist Tendencies', DG TRADE Chief Economist Note 2018-3, DG TRADE, European Commission, Brussels.

Kutlina-Dimitrova, Z. and Lakatos, C. (2014), 'Determinants of Direct Cross-border Public Procurement in EU Member States', *Review of World Economics*, 152(3), pp. 501–528.

Luckey, J. R. (2012), 'Domestic Content Legislation: The Buy American Act and Complementary Little Buy American Provisions', U.S. Congressional Research Service, Report No. 7-5700, 25 April, Washington, DC.

Messerlin, P. (2016), 'The Beauty of Public Procurement in TTIP', ECIPE Bulletin No. 1/2016, European Centre for International Political Economy, Brussels.

Messerlin, P. and Miroudot, S. (2012), 'EU Public Procurement Markets: How Open Are They?', GEM Policy Brief, Groupe d'Économie Mondiale (GEM), Sciences Po, Paris. Available at (http://gem.sciences-po.fr/ content/publications/pdf/Messerlin-Miroudot_EU_public_procurement072012. pdf).

OECD (2015), *Government at a Glance 2015*. Paris: OECD Publishing.

Ramboll (2011), *Cross-border Procurement above EU Thresholds*. Final report for the European Commission, Ramboll Management Consulting, Copenhagen.

Index

Printed in the United States
By Bookmasters